SIX RENAISSANCE MEN AND WOMEN

This book is dedicated to the memory of Jesse Turnock (1909-2006)
who died peacefully on 19 May 2006

Six Renaissance Men and Women

Innovation, Biography and Cultural Creativity in Tudor England, c.1450–1560

ELISABETH SALTER
University of Wales, Aberystwyth, UK

ASHGATE

Published by
Ashgate Publishing Limited
Gower House
Croft Road
Aldershot
Hampshire GU11 3HR
England

Ashgate Publishing Company
Suite 420
101 Cherry Street
Burlington, VT 05401-4405
USA

Ashgate website: http://www.ashgate.com

British Library Cataloguing in Publication Data
Salter, Elisabeth, 1972-
   Six Renaissance men and women : innovation, biography and
   cultural creativity in Tudor England, c.1450-1560
   1. Banaster, Gilbert, ca. 1445-1487 2. England - Court and
   courtiers - Biography 3. England - Intellectual life - 16th
   century 4. Great Britain - History - Tudors, 1485-1603
   I. Title
   942'.05'0922

Library of Congress Cataloging-in-Publication Data
Salter, Elisabeth, 1972-
   Six Renaissance men and women : innovation, biography and cultural creativity in
Tudor England, c.1450-1560 / by Elisabeth Salter.
     p. cm.
   ISBN: 978-0-7546-5440-7
   1. Great Britain--History--Tudors, 1485-1603--Biography. 2. England--Civilization--
16th century. 3. Great Britain--Court and courtiers--Biography. 4. Great Britain--
Biography. I. Title.
   DA317.S25 2007
   942.05092'2--dc22
   [B]

2006032409

ISBN: 978-0-7546-5440-7

Printed and bound in Great Britain by MPG Books Ltd, Bodmin, Cornwall.

Contents

List of Figures		*vi*
Acknowledgements		*vii*
List of Abbreviations		*viii*

1	Introduction	1
2	Critical Introduction	5
3	Gilbert Banaster	30
4	Elizabeth Philip	62
5	The Anonymous Witness	78
6	William Cornysh	96
7	Katherine Styles	117
8	William Buckley	130
9	Conclusion	153

Index	160

List of Figures

2.1 *My Feerfull Dreme*, as transcribed in John Stevens,   48-9
Music and Poetry in the Early Tudor Court, Cambridge Studies in Music
(Cambridge, London, New York &c., CUP), pp. 373–4

4.1 Woodcut Image from *A Remembraunce for the Traduction &*   87
Mariage of the Princesse Kateryne Doughter to the Right High
and Right Myghty Prince the Kinge and Quene of Spayne as
Here in Articles it Dothe Ensure, STC 4814 (Published by Pynson,
London, c. 1500). By permission of the British Library and
Early English Books Online.

7.1 Arithmetic Diagram   140

7.2 Brass Quadrant, Attributed to Thomas Gemini, dated 1551,   149
British Museum, London [MLA 1858, 8-21.1] © Copyright the
Trustees of the British Museum

Acknowledgements

It has been a pleasure writing this book in Aberystwyth. I would like to thank all my colleagues in the Department of English, and beyond, and particularly the rest of the 'Med & Ren' teaching team (Jayne Archer, Mike Smith, and Diane Watt) for their support. I am grateful to the people at Ashgate – to commissioning editor Thomas Gray, to Pauline Beavers and the copyediting team for their assistance. For helpful and encouraging conversations about the book, I would like to thank Tiffany Atkinson, Bernard Salter, and Anne Worrall.

List of Abbreviations

BL	British Library
CUP	Cambridge University Press
DNB	Dictionary of National Biography
MS Add	Additional Manuscript
MS Eg	Egerton Manuscript
MS Harl	Harleian Manuscript
NA	The National Archive, London
NA C	The National Archive, Chancery
NA E	The National Archive, Exchequer
NA, PROB	The National Archive, Probate
ODNB	Oxford Dictionary of National Biography
OED	Oxford English Dictionary
OUP	Oxford University Press
STC	Short Title Catalogue

Chapter 1

Introduction

Six Renaissance Men and Women is an exploration of six lives. The six chosen individuals (three men, two women, and one anonymous) all have some kind of connection with the English royal households of the period c. 1480–1560. Gilbert Banaster and William Cornish were Masters of the Chapel in the reigns of Henry VII and VIII; the anonymous reader was a witness to the marriage ceremonies for Prince Arthur; Elizabeth Philip made costumes for the household and its pageants; Katherine Styles's last marriage was to a knight in the service of Henry VIII; William Buckley was a schoolmaster and a maker of scientific instruments in the household of Edward VI.

These six people were all significant figures of Tudor Renaissance England, not because of their high-profile activities at the centre of the international stage, but because of their important and influential roles just below that surface level of fame. I would like to suggest that the six people investigated here were all presented with particular possibilities for creativity during their lives.[1] There are two main specific reasons for this, which will be explored throughout the book. Firstly, because these men and women often come from the more minor social backgrounds not immediately conferred a place amongst the royal household by virtue of their own family connections with nobility, their potential for creativity may have been an important factor in enabling their rise to significance.[2] Secondly, and each in different ways, the six subjects occupy roles within and for the royal household that distinctly require creativity, such as the production of musical and literary compositions, the construction of fashionable costumes, the pursuit of new scientific knowledge, or involvement with education.

This book covers a wide range of themes including poetry, music, pageantry, religion and scientific instruments. Each chapter ranges over a selection of these themes, depending on the types of evidence surviving for each of the subjects. My aim is to introduce the reader to each particular piece of evidence and then to explore some of the issues it raises in relation to the life being reconstructed. For

---

[1] For an extended consideration of 'cultural creativity' see Elisabeth Salter, *Cultural Creativity in the Early English Renaissance: Popular Culture in Town and Country* (London, Palgrave Macmillan, 2006).

[2] See the apparent parallel here with the subjects chosen by Stephen Greenblatt in *Renaissance Self-Fashioning: From More To Shakespeare* (Chicago and London, University of Chicago Press, 1980, repr. 1984), pp. 7–8. Although, significantly, my subjects do not gravitate to canonical status.

some of the six individuals I have been able to find surprising new pieces of evidence for their lives by following a trail posed by one document which then leads to a number of discoveries.

In Gilbert Banaster's chapter, for example, one element I discuss is his translation of the tragic story of two lovers, Sismond and Guistard. Here, I begin by describing some elements of the context of these stories as well as its plot and its relationship to the style of writing adopted by Geoffrey Chaucer before engaging in a deeper consideration of specific themes which the story itself raises. In describing the context of 'Sismond and Guistard', I discuss the ways that this story might relate to the historical periods in which it was produced. Gilbert Banaster was writing and translating with the priorities of a fifteenth-century English writer whereas the template he used for this story was written in a late fourteenth-century Italian context, by Giovanni Boccaccio. I also describe what might be called the 'manuscript context' of the English version of this story because this helps with understanding why Banaster is considered to be the author in the first place. The two manuscripts containing 'Sismond and Guistard' also contain other stories and poems, which means it is possible to know what fifteenth-century people were reading alongside Banaster's story and this in turn helps with unravelling some fifteenth-century attitudes to the tragedy and the moral dilemmas it raises. In my deeper consideration of specific themes raised by 'Sismond and Guistard', I look at the ways that crying is represented differently by Banaster and Boccaccio. This comparison helps with understanding some of Gilbert Banaster's specific views on the themes of shame and dishonour which are raised by the story and enables us to move one small step closer to accessing what Gilbert Banaster himself may have thought about the problems of status, hierarchy and inappropriate marriages and how these views reflect the changing social world of fifteenth-century England in which he lived.

In Elizabeth Philip's chapter, I begin by introducing and discussing various issues associated with silk and silk work in England in this period, and follow this by addressing the culture of fashion, excess and revelry at the royal household of Henry VIII for which Elizabeth produced a lot of silk ware. For both the women discussed in this book there is relatively less evidence available that directly reflects their own lives in any detail and this is an important point more generally concerning the possibilities for reconstructing the lives of women from the past, especially those not of the higher status groups. However, Elizabeth Philip's name is mentioned in the revel and wardrobe accounts of this royal household a number of times. Each time she is mentioned there are details of the types of material she was supplying, the occasions for which this was required, and sometimes the particularities of the styles she created such as the specific national dress an outfit represents or the nature of costumes employed to represent specific mythical or historical characters. This means that it is possible, in this chapter, to investigate the ways that a woman such as Elizabeth Philip came into contact with the splendid richness of the culture of display at this royal household, as well as the access this gave her to the ways that important political concepts such as Tudor myths of identity were represented in drama and pageantry.

In William Buckley's chapter, one of the elements of his life I explore is his role as a maker of scientific instruments. Having found his previously unknown last will and testament, I am able to trace this schoolmaster's likely connection to a specific instrument, a brass quadrant, which survives in the British Museum. I provide a description of the way this quadrant is designed but this description also allows an insight into some of the excitement William Buckley may have felt at being on the verge of a new dawn of scientific discovery. The relationship between the will document and the material object also raises some questions about the number of instruments Buckley may have owned or helped to make. Buckley's chapter therefore uses the discovery of one piece of evidence, his will, in order to trace other elements of his creative productions as well as his network of influential friends and patrons.

In a number of the chapters, as with William Buckley, the exploration of one piece of surviving evidence leads to another. Where a range of types of evidence are brought together in one chapter, such as for Gilbert Banaster, William Cornysh, or William Buckley, the collection does not provide one consolidated picture of the life and attitudes of the particular individual. Instead, what happens is that the different themes raised by the various types of evidence indicate the many and multifaceted ways that Renaissance people such as these experienced the world. When brought together, therefore, the different forms of evidence such as music, poetry, science, that are connected to one individual across the period 1450–1560 also tend to show the ways that the changes in ideology and taste across these individuals' lifetimes were not rapid, easy, or smooth. For several of the six subjects the experience of the transitional period in which they lived seems to have been very turbulent. This is particularly the case for those individuals who were responsible for producing a range of cultural products such as music and literature.

The period of time covered by this book is now often seen to involve a transition from what we call 'Medieval' to what we call 'Early Modern'. The evidence for the lives of these people acts as a reminder that the division between these time periods should not be considered as abrupt and distinct. When the experiences of individuals living across this period is considered, there appears to be an altogether more fluid – even traumatic – boundary between the Medieval and Early Modern periods.

The following chapter is a 'critical introduction' which serves to give some background to the rationale for the book and to the critical approaches which have enabled this sort of investigation. In the first part of this chapter, I begin by discussing some elements of the historical context with particular reference to definitions of the Renaissance, followed by a consideration of the process of contextualising, and the ways that the reconstruction of these six lives impinges on attitudes to grand narratives of Renaissance. In the second part of the critical overview, I survey some issues concerning academic and popular approaches to the reconstruction of lives, including biography, life writing, and the historical novel.

In some ways this critical introduction stands alone as a separate element of the book which serves the specific purpose of positing the position of this kind of study within a historiography. So, the reader may wish to skip straight to the six life chapters in order to enjoy the various vivid details of these individuals' lives without wishing to be encumbered by the critical and historiographical background. However, I would urge readers who do not consider themselves to be academically interested in this period, as well as those who do, to engage with the issues presented in the critical introduction either before or after reading the life chapters.

The six life chapters in this book constitute self-contained episodes that provide specific personal and contextual details about 'Renaissance experiences'. My hope has been to make these chapters attractive to a wide audience, both popular and academic. I have attempted not to reiterate the issues of historiography and method surveyed in the critical introduction, although these issues form the basis of my approach.

Chapter 2

Critical Introduction

Defining the Renaissance of Tudor England

Implicit in this book is a consideration of what constitutes 'Renaissance' in Tudor England. It is traditional, in both teaching and research structures, to place the occurrence of English Renaissance in the second half of the sixteenth and the seventeenth centuries. This is particularly noticeable when considering the usual idea of a literary Renaissance in Britain in contrast with those other 'Renaissance' developments that have a European context, such as the impact of humanism or the cultural innovations of the Italian Renaissance courts which *are* generally firmly sited in the preceding century, c. 1400–1550.[1]

Some of those European aspects of Renaissance culture have, of course, traditionally been countenanced as a fifteenth-century phenomenon in England too: humanism, for example.[2] The impact of humanism on political thought, on educational ideals and the invigoration of classical learning and on perceptions of individuality are all generally considered to have infiltrated English thought and practices towards the later fifteenth century at the level of royalty, nobility, and university. Canonical English writers as early as Chaucer and his successor, Hoccleve, have also been identified with the humanistic interests of Italian writers both through their own modes of expression and in their translations of these European and classical greats.[3] The individual lives considered in this volume add some detailed evidence for understanding experiences of the impact of these 'new' modes of thought and how these ideas were understood and expressed by people just below those highest levels of the social and intellectual order.

Following from interest in the Italian Renaissance court as a site for the development of Renaissance ideas, a European context that excludes English society has also been significant in the exploration of royal courts as sites for

---

[1] This chronological disparity is exemplified by the recent Open University collection of readers and anthologies for the *Renaissance in Europe* course, see Peter Elmer, Nick Webb, and Roberta Wood eds, *The Renaissance in Europe: An Anthology* (New Haven, London, Yale University Press in association with Open University, 2000).

[2] See for example, Roberto Weiss, *Humanism in England During the Fifteenth Century* (Oxford, Basil Blackwell, 3rd edition 1967).

[3] S.H. Rigby, *Chaucer in Context: Society, Allegory, and Gender* (Manchester, Manchester University Press, 1996); and see H.S. Bennett, *Six Medieval Men and Women* (Cambridge, CUP, 1955), Chapter 3 'Hoccleve', p. 85.

cultural innovations, in thought as well as in the cultures of display associated with court ritual and pageantry. It is often proposed that the real impact of classical ideals in drama and display should be attributed to the English royal courts of the seventeenth century. Some writers have, however, tried to reassess the importance of the reigns of Henry VII and Henry VIII, but still tend to see these reigns as a prelude to the Elizabethan era.[4] The connections of the six men and women in this volume with the royal households of Henry VII and Henry VIII provide ample evidence for the cultural innovation and sophistication of these courts in terms of pageantry and music, fashions in luxury consumption, scientific discovery and literary invention. The reconstruction of these individual lives also shows some of the tensions and contradictions in the experience of this transitional cultural period of c. 1450–1560.

In a recent exploration of the archaeology of this transitional phase in English culture, Phillip Lindley has proposed that although 'Italian Renaissance came late to England even in the field of sculpture', there were distinct signs of an interest in Renaissance ideas about commemorative representations by the middle of the fifteenth century.[5] However, these instances of evidence for 'early' interest in Renaissance style apparently coincide more with the preoccupations of Britain's well-known humanists, such as Duke Humphrey of Gloucester, rather than any more comprehensive interest in 'Renaissance ideas'. So it is nevertheless the early sixteenth century that Lindley proposes as the beginnings of the 'penetration of Renaissance forms into Sculpture' in English society. Such 'new' ideas are often connected to changes of monument function in the mid-sixteenth century that accompanied the profound religious ideological shifts provoked by the Reformation in England. The chronology of changing tastes in English commemorative sculpture across this period is, however, much more complex than any wholesale transition on the basis of a single ideological shift.[6]

English interest in sculptured Renaissance styles is at least attributed to an earlier beginning than the English Renaissance of science, where there is still a tendency to focus on non–English 'European' scientists and writers for any developments occurring before the very late sixteenth or more usually the seventeenth century, when English figures like Leonard Digges and William

---

    [4]   Gordon Kipling, *The Triumph of Honour: Burgundian Origins of the Elizabethan Renaissance* (Leiden, Leiden University Press, 1977).

    [5]   Phillip Lindley, 'Innovation, Transition, Disruption in Tomb–Sculpture', in David Gaimster and Paul Stamper (eds), *The Age of Transition: the Archaeology of English Culture 1400–1600* (Oxford: Oxbow Books in association with the Society for Medieval Archaeology and the Society for Post-Medieval Archaeology, 1997), 77–92, p. 78 ff discusses 'periodisation, stylistic change and the Renaissance'.

    [6]   See Elisabeth Salter, *Cultural Creativity in the Early English Renaissance: Popular Culture in Town and Country* (London, Palgrave Macmillan, 2006), Chapter 6.

Gilbert emerge.[7] Gerard L'E. Turner does, however, consider one of the subjects of this volume, William Buckley (d. 1552), at the earliest point of his chronological catalogue of scientific instruments and inventions. This is probably largely because his death date has generally been considered to fall in the Elizabethan era.[8]

Renaissance Self–Fashioning

There is one book focusing on lives which has to a significant degree defined English Renaissance for recent generations of scholars. This is Stephen Greenblatt's *Renaissance Self–Fashioning: From More to Shakespeare*, which remains a flagship for the approach to criticism known as New Historicism. It is noticeable that the starting date of this study is c. 1534;[9] complying with the traditional view of the dates for English Renaissance, which is planted firmly on the Early Modern side of the Medieval to Renaissance divide. Since its first publication back in 1980, this book has had an influence on countless studies of individuality, literature and culture in the English Renaissance, as well as beyond this chronological period. In six chapters, Greenblatt considers six Renaissance men: More, Tyndale, Wyatt, Spenser, Marlowe, and Shakespeare. The book explores (Renaissance) 'culture' through the 'literary texts' written by and associated with these six people.[10] And specifically it explores the process by which these six greats (all of whom, Greenblatt suggests, were particularly sensitive to the construction of identity by virtue of their 'profound mobility') engaged in the fashioning of identity. Whether it is their own identity or something more representative of the sixteenth and seventeenth centuries that is uncovered is a point for discussion.

There are obvious parallels between *Renaissance Self–Fashioning* and this book. In part, these similarities signal the influence of Greenblatt's work, and its significant role in legitimating this kind of inquiry. However, despite similarities of structure and perhaps apparently of ethos, the distance that exists between *Six Renaissance Men and Women* and Greenblatt's seminal text is both 'critical distance', and also a distance produced by the difference in the kinds of people that are considered. There is no denying that Greenblatt's *Renaissance Self-Fashioning* is an important book and the excitement, positive and negative, generated amongst reviewers during the 1980s is testimony to this. While most reviewers compliment Greenblatt on his intelligence, the three main areas of criticism concerning *Self-Fashioning* of relevance to this discussion are: firstly, issues of historical contex;

---

[7]   Peter Dear, *Revolutionizing the Sciences, European Knowledge and Its Ambitions, 1500–1700* (Basingstoke, Palgrave, 2001).

[8]   Gerard L'E. Turner, *Elizabethan Instrument Makers: the Origins of the London Trade in Precision Instrument Making* (Oxford, Clarendon, 2000).

[9]   Stephen Greenblatt, *Renaissance Self-Fashioning: From More To Shakespeare* (Chicago and London, University of Chicago Press, 1980, repr. 1984), p. 11.

[10]   Greenblatt, *Self-Fashioning*, pp. 4–5.

secondly, the absolutist approach; and thirdly, related to these, the apparent lack of reflexivity in this method.[11]

Contextualising Lives

The six lives I am exploring in this book are considered as entirely expressive of the cultural context in which they lived. They are seen, then, as culturally embedded figures central to particular networks of thematic and biographical connection. The importance of cultural context for the assessment of individuals and their literature has also recently been voiced by Diane Watt in her study of women prophets, *Secretaries of God*. Watt focuses on the lives and surviving literary evidences of a set of four women. They lived between the fourteenth century (Margery Kempe, c. 1373 to later than 1439) and the seventeenth century (Lady Eleanor Davies, c. 1588–1652).[12] The several centuries covered in *Secretaries* marks one difference from the relatively tight chronological focus I am taking in this book. Watt's attention to the need to contextualise the role and expression of these prophets, however, places a similar emphasis on the importance of considering historical specificity as I seek to do in this book: no '*single* tradition of female prophecy' is imposed in *Secretaries* and there is no suggestion that it is a consistent, transhistorical phenomenon.[13]

Contextualisation and Presentism

Greenblatt's subjects (More to Shakespeare) are all very well–known figures whose lives generated large quantities of text (in the form of their own works as well as contemporary and subsequent writings). The material selected for use in each chapter is therefore a 'small group of texts' from the surviving mass. Greenblatt describes the process of choosing such groups of texts as 'our invention and the similar cumulative inventions of others'.[14] This somewhat blatant attitude to the right of the present-day interpreter to decide which texts to choose has brought charges concerning a disregard for historical context. These include Alastair Fowler's suggestion that Greenblatt imposed his own contemporary concerns with power onto his own consideration of individual motives for Renaissance 'self fashioning', and J.E. Howard's suggestion that despite his use of 'cultural poetics' to investigate the 'cultural construction of identity', Greenblatt

---

[11]   See Anne Barton, 'Perils of Historicism', *New York Review of Books*, March 28th (1991): 53–55.

[12]   Diane Watt, *Secretaries of God: Women Prophets in Late Medieval and Early Modern England* (Cambridge, D.S. Brewer, 2001), p. 2.

[13]   Watt, *Secretaries*, pp. 8-10.

[14]   Greenblatt, *Self-Fashioning*, p. 6.

cannot 'disentangle himself from notions of individual autonomy'.[15] Others comment on his disregard for the chronological distance between the six writers he discusses.[16] These problems with Greenblatt's use of contextual details are the antithesis of my aim to understand the contextualised subtleties of the individual lives in this book and their cultural products.

Marguerite Waller's criticisms of Greenblatt's absolutism are trenchant, describing his 'essentialising rhetoric' as 'imperial', and suggestive of the supremacy of the twentieth-century reader, adding that this reader is also 'stereotypically male'.[17] Summing up much of her detailed criticism, Waller suggests that the problems lie in Greenblatt's 'disinclination to contextualize and relativize – to consider as an ideological construct – the critical ground from which he is operating'.[18] This is what I would describe as a lack of reflexivity. The methods by which evidence is chosen and juxtaposed in the context–carefree mode of analysing with which New Historicism is often associated is sometimes described as 'arbitrary connectedness'.[19]

I do not seek to deny that choice is an important element in my construction of this book. Indeed, I have strategically selected these particular six people and have therefore chosen a particular narrative.[20] However, the process of choice advocated by Greenblatt and other New Historicists tends to prioritise the present concerns of the choice–maker. Lisa Jardine suggested of New Historicism that its 'criticism has brilliantly excavated the way in which a kind of issue–grounded *explication de texte* or close reading can elucidate our own cultural assumptions'.[21] It is expressly my intention to attempt to overcome the natural tendency to privilege present–day contemporary issues in my consideration of evidence. This is not to deny, foolishly, my personal involvement with the choices I make about interpreting the evidence, but rather to see my own presence as a starting point in the elucidation of

---

[15] Alastair Fowler, 'Power to the Self', *Times Literary Supplement*, September 4th (1981): 10–12; J.E. Howard, 'The Cultural Construction of the Self in the Renaissance', *Shakespeare Quarterly*, 34 (1983): 378–81, p. 380. Also see Janet Coleman, *Ancient and Medieval Memories: Studies in the Reconstruction of the Past* (Cambridge, New York, CUP, 1992), p. 463, for a similar critique to Fowler, and a suggestion that differences between history writing in Medieval and Renaissance times are generic and linguistic.

[16] P. Edwards, Review Article, *Renaissance Quarterly*, (1982): 317–321, p. 321; Richard Strier, 'Identity and Power in Tudor England: Stephen Greenblatt, *Renaissance Self-Fashioning from More to Shakespeare*', *Boundary, 2: A Journal of Post Modern Literature* (1982): 383–94, p. 384.

[17] Marguerite Waller, 'Academic Tootsie: the Denial of Difference and the Difference it Makes', in *Diacritics*, 17, 1 (1987): 2–20, p. 4.

[18] Waller, 'Academic Tootsie', p. 5.

[19] Catherine Gallagher and Stephen Greenblatt, *Practising New Historicism* (Chicago, London, University of Chicago Press, 2000), p. 81.

[20] See also Watt, *Secretaries*, p. 11, for the apparent admission: 'This is still a narrative, albeit an often discontinous one'.

[21] Lisa Jardine, *Reading Shakespeare Historically* (London, Routledge, 1996), p. 6.

cultural process. The six individuals I have chosen, then, enable an exploration of the broader cultural issues associated with this exciting period of transition. Traditional themes from the Renaissance in Europe are addressed through the lives of these six men and women, providing specific perspectives on these key themes in the historiography of 'Renaissance' through: poetic style, including epitaph and Italian humanist poetry; new dramatic forms; clothing fashions; pageantry; scientific re–birth; changes in secular and religious musical composition; changing religiosity and transitional piety, to name a few. However, at no point should these six lives be considered to provide a model for Renaissance experience which may be simply generalised and imposed onto the lives of others.

I have chosen to comment largely on the Introduction to *Renaissance Self–Fashioning* rather than provide exhaustive criticisms of the whole book, although the critical views I have cited here relate to the whole book. Interestingly, Marguerite Waller commented on the problematic relationship between the introduction and the 'repressive' attitude of the remainder of this book. The introduction, she suggests, presents a 'clearly articulated, highly nuanced account of the conditions of self–fashioning'.[22] The implication of this statement is that it is in the chapters and their close readings of texts that Greenblatt's desire to impose his ideological position becomes most strained and most visible. However, I would suggest that it is only in the revocation of the grand statements which are made, not in the making of them, that the Introduction indicates subtleties of method.

The Grand Narrative

Because the chronological range of the six lives in this book is c. 1450–1560, the consideration of 'Renaissance' themes constitutes a re–consideration of the nature and timing of English Renaissance. For the sake of clarity and to signal this re–assessment of chronologies, the period covered in this volume should be thought of as 'the early English Renaissance' or perhaps the Renaissance of Tudor England.[23] The focus on individual experience also takes this volume into the arena of the longstanding debate between 'Medievalists' and 'Early Modernists' about the emergence of individualism, or 'interiority' in literature and other cultural spheres.[24] The still remarkable prevalence of Jacob Burkhardt's thesis on Renaissance individualism partly accounts for this, particularly in the context of

---

[22]   Waller, 'Academic Tootsie', p. 19.

[23]   See Colin Burrow, 'The Experience of Exclusion: Literature and Politics in the Reigns of Henry VII and Henry VIII', in David Wallace (ed.), *The Cambridge History of Medieval English Literature* (Cambridge, CUP, 1999), pp. 793–820.

[24]   See, for example, Brian Cummings, 'Reformed Literature and Literature Reformed', in *The Cambridge History of English Literature*, pp. 821–51.

the traditional dating of English Renaissance in the 'Early Modern' period.[25] This volume therefore adds a comment to David Aers' recent polemical essay on this subject, in which as the title suggests, he takes to task Early Modernists who seem to deny the existence of the immediate Medieval past (rather like the scholars of the Renaissance period themselves sought to).[26]

By focusing on the chronological breadth of women's lives which covers the fourteenth to the seventeenth centuries, Diane Watt also demonstrates the critique of the traditional view that there was a 'great divide' lodged somewhere in these three hundred years.[27] Denying the homogeneity of expression for the female prophets c. 1350–1650 is consistent with Watt's resistance to that grand narrative of English Renaissance which tells the story of a definitive break between the Middle Ages and the Early Modern; a narrative which tends to exclude women in its 'master narrative'.[28] In my examination of the lives of both men and women, I hope to avoid a distinction of experience which is based solely on gender (although this is not to deny that there are some significant differences especially in the period covered here). Similarly, Watt is not seeking to assert a separate narrative of female experience because such a construction is liable to the same accusations of essentialism as any grand narrative.[29]

Grand Narratives and Fragments of Evidence

The men and women studied in this book do not leave sufficient evidence to enable any claims to the vast significance or general applicability of a study of their lives. However, I would suggest that even the lives of the famous or canonical should not be seen as essentially and simply representative of any single identifiable trait in the history of a society. Simple models for cultural phenomena, in other words, should not be built around reconstructions of individual lives. The key word here is 'simple', because I *do* wish to advocate a method that employs the individual life as a valuable resource for understanding the past. This involves considering the reconstruction of individual lives as a route through to understanding the vagaries and complexities of perception and experience in a specific cultural context.

There are a couple of important points to make about the fragmentary nature of the evidence surviving for the six lives explored in this book. Recently, various cultural historians have stressed the importance of examining what are often

---

[25]   Jacob Burckhardt, *The Civilisation of the Renaissance in Italy*, edited by Peter Burke (Harmondsworth, Penguin, 1990).

[26]   David Aers, 'A Whisper in the Ear of Early Modernists; or, Reflections on Literary Critics Writing the "History of the Subject"', in David Aers (ed.), *Culture and History 1350–1600: Essays on English Communities, Identities and Writing* (New York, London, Harvester Wheatsheaf, 1992).

[27]   Watt, *Secretaries*, p. 7.

[28]   Watt, *Secretaries*, pp. 8–9.

[29]   Watt, *Secretaries*, pp. 9–11.

'fragmentary' evidences of popular culture, yet the word 'fragmentary' is sometimes used, negatively, to suggest 'implausible'. However, it is important to stress that the detailed consideration of individual fragments of evidence actually provides access to six lives which would not otherwise be possible.[30] The narrative produced in each of the chapters is dependant on the pieces of evidence which survive for each individual. These fragments may therefore be described as 'anecdotes'. But the anecdote has been claimed as a New Historicist tool, which is 'irritatingly antithetical to historical discourse'.[31] I would like to make it clear, here, that in my method of working with evidence, and with the evidence for these six lives specifically, the way to define the appropriate boundaries of the patchwork of 'historical discourse', and therefore the way to use these 'anecdotes' of individual representation, is by adherence to the categories of contemporary perception made manifest by the evidence itself. This definition of appropriate boundaries is in contradistinction to the 'arbitrary connectedness' often associated with New Historicism.[32]

The fact that the evidence which survives often does not provide a consistent pattern or fall neatly into a set of categories necessitates that the narrative I have written for each of the six lives is not seamless. Any relatively abrupt transitions between sections or themes in each chapter are actually expressive of the method adopted here. Discontinuities in the narrative help to exemplify the inconsistencies of thought and attitude experienced during a life; such inconsistencies reflect the multifaceted nature of the reservoir of resources for making meaning known as 'culture' and the ambiguities involved in the process of using that reservoir to negotiate identity.[33]

Stephen Greenblatt proposed the 'impossibility of fully reconstructing and reentering the culture of the sixteenth century'. On the subject of the necessity that any inquiry into the sixteenth century must be indeterminate and incomplete, he suggested that he compensates for this by 'constantly returning to particular lives and particular situations'.[34] I am engaged in a similar activity in this book by

---

[30]   See, Robert Darnton, *The Kiss of Lamourette: Reflections in Cultural History* (London, Faber, 1990), pp. 195, 213. Roger Chartier, *Cultural History: Between Practices and Representations* (trans. L.G. Cochrane, Oxford, Polity, 1988), pp. 5, 35, for the suggestion that 'the ways in which an individual or a group appropriates an intellectual theme or a cultural form are more important than the statistical distribution of that theme or form'; see also Carlo Ginzburg, *The Cheese and The Worms: The Cosmos of a Sixteenth Century Miller*, trans. J. and A. Tredeschi (London, Routledge, 1981), p. xxii.

[31]   Gallagher and Greenblatt, *Practising*, p. 50.

[32]   Gallagher and Greenblatt, *Practising*, p. 81; David Aers, 'New Historicism and the Eucharist', *Journal of Medieval and Early Modern Studies*, 33, 3 (2003): 241–59, pp. 255–6, for a critique of Gallagher and Greenblatt's use of inappropriate 'binaries' for analysis.

[33]   For a longer discussion of culture and meaning see Salter, *Cultural Creativity*, pp. 45–6.

[34]   Greenblatt, *Self-Fashioning*, p. 5.

focusing on six individual lives and the cultural products they have left. But Greenblatt implies that the 'small number of resonant texts' which form that focus on particular lives and situations also somehow enable a focus on 'the material necessities and social pressures that men and women daily confronted'.[35] Given his choice of great figures, and his avowedly selective choice of resonant texts, I would suggest that this is too big a claim. When do the texts chosen, from More to Shakespeare, actually come anywhere near to providing evidence for the daily experiences of sixteenth-century men and women? The inappropriateness of Greenblatt's claim to be moving beyond rhetorical structures to anything akin to actual experience is magnified in the following sentences of the same paragraph. Here he seems to imply that by interpreting the ways that the 'symbolic structures' of these texts 'interplay' with (the symbolic structures in) the careers of their authors and (the symbolic structures in) the real world we might gain access to a 'single complex process of self-fashioning'. Once identified, this single complex process would enable us to 'come closer to understanding how literary and social identities were formed in this culture'. I am strongly inclined to say that there is no such thing. But maybe *Self-Fashioning* does elucidate a 'single complex process of self-fashioning'. If it does, this is presumably indicative of those choices made at the point of interpretation (and which the author posits as a virtue of his approach), rather than any cultural reality. In fact, that is precisely the conclusion with which the author opens the following paragraph, '[I]nevitably, the resonance and centrality we find in our small group of texts and their authors is our invention and the similar, cumulative inventions of others.' Despite this timely denial that a 'single complex process of self–fashioning' is recoverable, the previously posed certainty lingers. Such certainties seem to be seductive, they offer the possibility of answering a very big question through the use of a programmatic model. This may help to account for the popularity of *Renaissance Self–Fashioning*. I hope to offer no such easily applicable model.

Lives

Biography

This book has connections with the form of writing which is often called biography so it makes sense to address some issues concerning this genre, and also the form known more recently as 'life–writing'. There are countless biographies in print and out of print, of countless people, past and present. I do not intend to survey this field of literature here. The subject of biography itself, as a literary form, has also recently received a surge of interest. A book published in 2002 to mark the centenary of the British Academy, for example, took the uses of biography as its focus. This is certainly a signal of the current scholarly interest in what is described

---

[35]   Greenblatt, *Self-Fashioning*, p. 5.

there as a 'vitally important cultural phenomenon'.[36] The book, called *Mapping Lives* (perhaps to reflect the recent critical vocabulary of 'life–writing') is packed with eminent critics and practitioners covering all manner of issues relating to its central concern which is to evaluate the issues and problems inherent in writing biography as well as 'the functions which it can serve and has served in different societies, its *uses*'.[37] But even this authoritative book shies away from producing a 'full–scale history of biography'.[38]

Popular and Academic Biographies

One of the reasons that the history of biography is such a huge subject is that it is also a popular form; in other words it is a form which extends way beyond the relatively narrow confines of academic discourse, to the freelance and professional writers of biography and also even beyond that to the realms of biographical novels.[39] The opening chapter of *Mapping Lives* interrogates the validity of biography by questioning whether or not it is a 'proper subject' for academic courses.[40] Richard Holmes playfully suggests that the essential spirit of English biography has always been a 'maverick and unacademic one'.[41] And perhaps as a consequence of this, academics have often criticised the form as 'trivial, revisionist, exploitative, fictive, a corrupter of pure texts and probably also of scholarly models' and worst of all as 'irredeemably subjective'.[42] With a view to the possibility of formalising the academic study of Biography, Holmes goes on to define a 'possible canon of twenty–five English works written between 1670 and 1970'.[43]

Despite the 'town and gown' division on the subject of biography (which itself has a long history), the 'cultural significance of biography's growing popularity' was recognised from the nineteenth century.[44] Richard Holmes points out that, now, over 3500 new titles are published in Britain every year, and that all high street bookshops have a 'Biography' section which is next in size to the 'Fiction' and quite distinct from 'History'. And he makes the very interesting observation that both bookshop organisational systems and popular reviews of biographies

---

[36]   Peter France and William St Clair, 'Introduction', in Peter France and William St Clair (eds), *Mapping Lives: The Uses of Biography* (Oxford, New York, published for the British Academy by OUP, 2002), p. 4.

[37]   France and St Clair, 'Introduction', *Mapping*, p. 4.

[38]   France and St Clair, 'Introduction', *Mapping*, p. 5.

[39]   On the development of biographical novels and specifically 'The New Biography', see Laura Marcus, 'The Newness of the "New Biography": Biographical Theory and Practice in the Early Twentieth Century', in *Mapping*, p. 201ff.

[40]   Richard Holmes, 'The Proper Study', in *Mapping*, p. 7.

[41]   Holmes, 'Proper Study', p. 7.

[42]   Holmes, 'Proper Study', pp. 7–8.

[43]   Holmes, 'Proper Study', p. 13.

[44]   Holmes, 'Proper Study', p. 11.

focus on content (Boswell's *Life of Johnson* for example being filed under J). As a consequence, the processes of writing involved in the production of these texts tend to be ignored, and that means that the influence of the writer on the life story which is narrated is also not considered to be significant. Holmes writes: 'Essentially biographies are understood to write themselves, self–generated (like methane clouds) by their dead subjects'.[45] It is to be hoped that current academic interests in the process of writing will begin and continue to infiltrate the 'Biography' shelves of popular bookshops and perhaps cause some reordering of existing stock – making more space for Boswell under 'B' perhaps; just as it is to be hoped that the elitist attitude of academics to this form of literature will continue to be eroded.

Life-Writing

More recently, from about the 1980s, interest has developed in 'life–writing', a subject area which includes biography. The publication of the *Encyclopaedia of Life-Writing* in 2001 attests to this interest.[46] In the 'Editor's Note' Margaretta Jolly points out that the new conventional term (which has been in use since the eighteenth century) is intended to signal a more inclusive approach which includes 'autobiography' as well as other forms of recording a life, in art, music, and even oral history.[47] In two volumes, this encyclopaedia covers five 'flexible working categories' of: genres, common themes in life–writing, contexts and criticism, regional surveys, and writers and works.[48]

Biographies, the editor suggests, have been produced since the start of recorded literature, and autobiography, diaries and personal letters have been widespread since the eighteenth century. But Jolly's sense of the effect of the particular circumstances produced by the postmodern era on attitudes to 'lives' seems to indicate a very present–orientated attitude. She writes: 'As the individualism unleashed by Capitalism cracks and reshapes in the fire of globalization and the communications revolution, a literature that foregrounds the shape of a single life and its span seems to focus the anxieties of the age'. This elegant sentence seems to hint at a tendency towards viewing changes in the construction of a self, a life, the writing about it, in terms of that traditional grand narrative which denies the existence of individuals before 'capitalism'.[49] Any criticism about tendencies towards presentism or an overarching approach should be tempered, however, by an acknowledgement of the huge project involved with bringing this wide-ranging material together. As Jolly deprecates, 'while the conception of any encyclopaedia

---

[45]   Holmes, 'Proper Study', p. 12.

[46]   *Encyclopaedia of Life Writing: Biographical and Autobiographical Forms*, ed. Margarette Jolly, 2 vols (London, Fitzroy Dearborn, 2001).

[47]   *Encyclopaedia of Life Writing*, vol. 1, p. ix.

[48]   *Encyclopaedia of Life Writing*, vol. 1, p. x.

[49]   *Encyclopaedia of Life Writing*, vol. 1, p. ix.

involves a measure of foolhardy ambition, the hope of describing fully a subject of such celebrated ambiguity and disciplinary iconoclasm is certainly vain'. And indeed, the entries in the two volume work do not deny these earlier lives a voice, with a whole chronological category devoted to the 'Ancient, Classical and Medieval' and another to 'Renaissance and Early Modern to c. 1700'. It is interesting, though, that Medieval and Early Modern are divided.

Biographies of Canonical Figures

The *Encyclopaedia of Life Writing* is at pains to produce an inclusive survey which is not dominated by the writings of canonical figures or by the attention often accorded to writing about them.[50] Both academic and popular reconstructions of lives have, however, often been drawn towards the famous and the canonical. Resistance to grand narratives is signalled in this book by my focus on literary figures which do not fit into the very compressed 'canon' of authors for this period. The canonical status ascribed to certain writers still tends to go hand in hand with the view that these writers were 'geniuses'.[51] The (fallacious) concept of a genius places the gifted individual outside of his or her (usually his) own time thereby enabling the said genius to adopt forms of literature (or art, music and so on) which those living at the same time who do not possess this elevated status can not hope to understand. Chaucer is an obvious candidate for this status in the Medieval period; Shakespeare in the Early Modern. Something of this effect exists when humanist interests are identified in the writings of a late fourteenth century English writer such as Chaucer when at the same time the English literary Renaissance is maintained as occurring wholesale only from the traditional sixteenth century. As a result, the interests of the lesser-known poets and transcribers of the fourteenth and fifteenth centuries in these ideals are overlooked or denied. More recently there has been a move away from this cult of the genius to make way for a more broadly conceived understanding of the changes and transitions occurring in English literature across the period c. 1300–1600, including the transmission of European and specifically humanist ideas into England.[52] The interest of someone such as Gilbert Banaster in those classical traditions of writing provides fertile ground for exploring further the impact and transmission of 'Renaissance' ideas in English literature, before that traditional epoch of c. 1575–1700.

---

[50]   *Encyclopaedia of Life Writing*, vol. 1, p. x.

[51]   On the development of this concept in relation to biographically orientated literary criticism of Charles-Augustin Sainte-Beuve (1804–69), see Ann Jefferson, 'Sainte-Bauve: Biography, Criticism, and the Literary' in *Mapping*, pp. 140–143, 154–5.

[52]   See, for example, James Simpson, *Reform and Cultural Revolution*, The Oxford English Literary History, vol. 2, '1530–1547' (Oxford, OUP, 2002). Here Simpson provides a survey of the complications involved with the transitions in literary practice and style across this period.

The literatures of the four women prophets discussed by Diane Watt in *Secretaries* are non–canonical with the exception of *The Book of Margery Kempe* which Watt suggests is semi–canonical.[53] As a result, these women's works have often mistakenly been considered 'marginal and "sub–literary" '.[54] I would suggest it is now probably more appropriate to think of Margery as a fully canonical figure which is perhaps testament to the surge of scholarship on women such as Kempe in the 1990s. The *Six Medieval Men and Women* that H.S. Bennett chose to write about were, with the exception of one, either the more famous figures of their day or those who have become famous representatives of Medieval times in retrospect.[55] The people who form the focus of each of the six chapters in *Renaissance Self–Fashioning* are also canonical figures – that is, four from the traditional canon of Renaissance literature, and two (More and Tyndale) from the canon of historical events (Thomas More has also more recently been assigned a place in the literary canon). The six subjects (from Banaster to Buckley) in this book are not canonical figures (although neither are they and their works entirely unknown).

Greenblatt's canon–orientated mode of thinking is indicated by his opening sentences in which he carefully distances himself from the claim that there were no selves before the Renaissance. He states:

> there are always selves – a sense of personal order, a characteristic mode of address to the world, a structure of bounded desires – and always some elements of deliberate shaping in the formation and expression of identity. One need only think of Chaucer's extraordinarily subtle and wry manipulations of *persona* to grasp that what I propose to examine does not suddenly spring up from nowhere when 1499 becomes 1500.[56]

I agree that there have always been selves, but in my opinion one need think of more than only Chaucer in order to examine selves in the fourteenth century (and one need think of more than 'More to Shakespeare' to examine selves in the sixteenth century). Greenblatt, of course, does not deny this need, although he sets it aside for the purposes of his book. The tendency to jump from one canonical author to another (thereby leap–frogging much of the very stuff of the cultural processes I imagine to be central to the formation of identity) is also found in Greenblatt's summary of his six chapters when there is a digest of the different manifestations of the 'Renaissance self–fashioning' of the six authors.[57] Of course,

---

[53]   Watt, *Secretaries*, p. 6.
[54]   Watt, *Secretaries*, p. 6.
[55]   H.S. Bennett, *Six Medieval Men and Women*. The six individuals are: Humphrey Duke of Gloucester, Sir John Fastolf, Thomas Hoccleve, Margaret Paston, Margery Kempe, Richard Bradwater.
[56]   Greenblatt, *Self-Fashioning*, p. 1.
[57]   Greenblatt, *Self-Fashioning*, p. 9.

the purpose here is to indicate the unity of the book; the connections are present because of the interpretive choices that have been made.

There is nothing wrong with working on canonical figures, although it is expressly not what I am doing in this book. Indeed the exploration of a literary life which has generated great interest over a number of years reaps certain rewards. And there is plenty of potential for considering, and in so doing seeking to extend, the scope of popular conceptions of such lives. One recent example of such a study is Steve Ellis's *Chaucer at Large* which examines the 'varied and diffuse' impact of Chaucer on the twentieth century, by examining a range of popular responses to and interpretations of Chaucer's life and works in modern translations, poetry, children's versions, adaptations in television, radio, film and theatre and the marketing of this life as 'heritage'.[58] Through his focus on the popular uses of this canonical author, Ellis uncovers some important questions concerning whether or not it is possible to extend the 'non-academic' appreciation of this author without 'perpetuating simplifications and trivializations of his work'.[59]

There may be something about the chronological distance between Chaucer's life and the twentieth century which makes satisfactory popularisations problematic.[60] Issues such as the problems of understanding Middle English and the very different mentality of the Medieval age all make it difficult to achieve popularisations of this life that are any more adequate than the rather worrying sounding wider existence of Chaucer as 'the mouthpiece of an uncomplicated bawdy affability'.[61] The six lives I deal with in this book will not be subject to the dangers of over–exposure through their canonical status. Even with the current popular interest in all things Tudor (especially where royal households are concerned), these six will not fall victim to the sort of 'general "heritage" hullabaloo' surrounding a figure such as Chaucer which is capable of telling a story so alien to that writer that he might seem to have 'slipped out unnoticed'.[62] Nevertheless, one of my hopes for this book is that by bringing together these six lives and the evidences surviving for them it may be possible to bring the intricacies and complexities of the experiences of these individuals, and people like them, to a wider consciousness.

The difference between exploring the lives of canonical authors and the lives of the non-canonical does also lead to a significant critical issue. This arises when there is a tendency to treat the lives of the extraordinary few and the 'great art' they produced as in some way representative of an identifiable 'cultural voice' which is

---

[58]   Steve Ellis, *Chaucer at Large: the Poet in the Modern Imagination* (Minneapolis, London, University of Minnesota Press, 2000), p. xiii.

[59]   Ellis, *Chaucer at Large*, p. 162.

[60]   Ellis, *Chaucer at Large*, p. 163. Ellis also raises the question of whether or not other canonical writers who are from the more recent past, such as Milton and Wordsworth, are better recognised and understood 'at large'.

[61]   Ellis, *Chaucer at Large*, p. 163.

[62]   Ellis, *Chaucer at Large*, p. 159.

expressive of something greater than a minority view.[63] It seems to me that Stephen Greenblatt tends to do this whilst at the same time he is careful to show that he is not attempting to assess the 'formation of identity' for the countless thousands of people living in the English Renaissance. (Although actually, his suggestion that this is a hopelessly large task reliant on statistical analysis is somewhat reductive; and his suggestion, alternatively, that 'we are not patient enough to tell over a thousand stories' might be a clue to his motivation for choosing canonical subjects.)[64]

Writing Lives and Approaches to Popular Culture

This book constitutes an exploration of men and women who lived below the levels of royalty, aristocracy, gentry or those with a position in the canon of English literatures. 'Popular culture', the reconstruction of culture and society below the élite, and what is sometimes known as 'history from below', have become increasingly explored scholarly subjects in recent years. These developments have seen a move towards the analysis of 'marginal and deviant people', instead of the 'élites and those in power'.[65] With the invigorated interest in the majority of the population and their everyday lives, there has also come a tendency to treat those masses as a mass or, in other words, as a statistical sample. A French school of thought, known as the Annales School, for example, which developed the analysis of *mentalité* (which approximates to our word 'mentality' and refers to the modes of thought and representation of a specific age) has tended to conduct large–scale studies covering several centuries in its assessment of the historical subject.[66] In recent studies of the English peasantry there has also been a tendency to focus on a more statistical and empirically based investigation of everyday life, which seems to have shied away from the actual details of individual person and experience.[67] While my approach to the individual lives in this book is influenced by these developments in the study of *mentalité* and 'history from below', the very detailed focus on six subjects is clearly not engaged in a large–scale, chronologically extensive, or statistical study.

---

[63]   Greenblatt, *Self-Fashioning*, pp. 6–7.

[64]   Greenblatt, *Self-Fashioning*, p. 6.

[65]   See, for example, Aron Gurevich, *Medieval Popular Culture: Problems of Belief and Perception*, trans. János M. Bak and Paul A. Hollingsworth (Cambridge, CUP, 1988); also Michel Vovelle, *Ideologies and Mentalities*, trans E. O'Flaherty, first published in French in 1982 (Cambridge: Polity Press with Basil Blackwell, 1990), p. 6; see also Chartier, *Cultural History*, pp. 5, 27–8; Darnton, *Kiss of Lamourette*, p. 213. See also Keith Thomas, 'History and Anthropology', *Past and Present*, 24 (1963): 3–24.

[66]   Vovelle, *Ideologies and Mentalities*, p. 2, for a discussion of the difficulty of defining mentality; also Ludmilla Jordanova, *History in Practice* (London, Arnold, 2000), p. 214.

[67]   See, for example, Christopher Dyer, *Standards of Living in the Later Middle Ages. Social Change in England, c. 1200–1520*, 2nd edn (Cambridge, New York, CUP, 1989).

The desire to listen to the otherwise unheard voices of Late Medieval men and women has driven my investigation of these six lives. This might on the surface seem similar to the agenda proposed by Catherine Gallagher and Stephen Greenblatt as a 'commitment to the value of the single voice'.[68] It is not. Rather my approach is related to a more ethnographically orientated analysis. Following the 'linguistic turn' in anthropological work, which has sought to prioritise the spoken or written discourses of the subjects, there has been a move towards enabling the language of the historical subject to 'speak for itself'.[69] In other words, my method treats the ways that individuals choose to express their perceptions (in language, music, image) as indicative of their attitudes and experiences. My approach to the subjects in this book is aligned with that ethnographic endeavour because I am attempting to gain access to the cultural experiences of the six subjects by exploring the various textual evidences that remain.

Having suggested that my way of working relates to relatively recent developments in approach to the historical subject, however, it is also necessary to mention that in some ways, the focus on lives of the ordinary was considered in a more personable and 'experiential' way by scholars working in the early part of the twentieth century: witness Eileen Power's *Medieval People*, first published in 1924. She prefaced her book with a claim to the importance of the 'personal treatment' of the 'ordinary people' of social history, in order that the 'past may be made to live again'. And she warns:

> It is the idea that history is about the dead, or, worse still, about movements and conditions which seem but vaguely related to the labours and passions of flesh and blood, which has driven history from the bookshelves where the historical novel still finds a welcome place.[70]

There is also H.S. Bennett's collection of *Six Medieval Men and Women* first published in 1955, which as I mentioned earlier, is mainly concerned with canonical subjects, yet one individual, called Richard Bradwater, was a husbandman and trouble-maker on a feudal estate.[71] Bennett's aim is described on the dust cover with the exclamation that '...the reader entertained by his personages finds that he has been absorbing social history in the easiest and pleasantest way...'. My intentions for this book have some similarities with this, which is striking as Bennett wrote his collection of lives over fifty years ago, and given the changes that have occurred in attitudes to historical fact and historical reconstruction between 1955 and 2005. My method therefore takes influence from very recent approaches to writing ethnography and cultural history as well as

---

[68]   Gallagher and Greenblatt, *Practising*, p. 16.

[69]   Darnton, *Kiss of Lamourette*, pp. 195, 213.

[70]   Eileen Power, *Medieval People* (Harmondsworth, Penguin Books, 1951, first published 1924), p. 7.

[71]   H.S. Bennett, *Six Medieval Men and Women*, pp. 151–65.

looking back to earlier methods in historical reconstruction which pre–date the surge of interest in the quasi–scientific quantitative analyses of society and economy which occurred in the second half of the twentieth century.

And, having indicated the influence of the recent trend to look at the marginal, unknown, non–élite subject, I should also make it clear from the outset that none of my six Renaissance individuals are truly representatives of the difficult end of 'popular culture': they are not the poorest members of society, nor are they even the lowest of the 'humble servants' of the royal household. Nor are they entirely unknown, indeed three of them, Gilbert Banaster, William Buckley, and William Cornysh all have entries in the old and new versions of the *Dictionary of National Biography*; the musical works of Banaster and Cornysh are also detailed in compendia such as *The New Grove Dictionary of Music and Musicians* (2001), and Buckley's scientific achievements feature in catalogues of scientific practitioners and instruments such as L'E Turner's *Elizabethan Instrument Makers* (2000), and Taylor's *Mathematical Practitioners* (1954).[72] Significant in the strategic choice of my six men and women, therefore, has been their particularly pivotal positions as interlocutors between the highest élite and the more popular cultures of this period.

Fictional Biographies

Apart from attempts to reconstruct actual lives, biography is also a seductive genre for the writing of fiction. One example of an early twentieth-century writer's interest in the intersection between the 'granite and rainbow' of pretending to biographical facts in a fictional narrative is Virginia Woolf's biography of Elizabeth Barrett Browning's dog, *Flush* (1933). Richard Holmes suggests that interest in writing biographical fictions stretches as far back as the eighteenth century.[73] And actually (as long as carefully contextualised definitions are used for what is meant by 'fact' and the 'fictions' of storytelling), I would venture to suggest that Medieval life–writers such as the producers of hagiography (or their readers) were not oblivious to the interplays between storytelling and certifiable 'facts' in the construction of quasi–mythical narratives.

The Historical Novel

One field of fictively biographical writing which has recently experienced a surge of production and popularity is the historical novel; Philippa Gregory and Tracey

---

[72]   *The New Grove Dictionary of Music and Musicians*, ed. Stanley Sadie, 20 vols (London, Macmillan, 1977–2001); Turner, *Elizabethan Instrument Makers*; E.G.R. Taylor, *The Mathematical Practitioners of Tudor and Stewart England* (Cambridge, CUP for the Institute of Navigation, 1954).

[73]   Holmes, 'Proper Study', p. 17.

Chevalier are just two of the many recent authors.[74] Historical fictions which base their narrative around one well–known individual, or one particularly popular situation or period in history, are not in any sense a new phenomenon; the popular works of writers such as Anya Seton, writing in the 1950s, attest to this.[75] These are books which should be and have been enjoyed, they are often a 'quick read' providing sufficient measure of intriguing historical information and titillation; but they are also now entering into the ambit of literary criticism. There is very much to analyse in this historical fiction – its uses of evidence, styles of narration, vocabularies, attitude to 'fact' (and to 'fiction') and so on. Just one example from Anya Seton's works, *Katherine*, and one example from Philippa Gregory's works, *The Other Boleyn Girl* (both fairly appropriate to the chronological period I am investigating) will suffice here to examine the relationship of such historical fiction to my writing of this book, and also to suggest some possibilities for future critical analysis of this literature.

Katherine is about Katherine de Roet 'who came to the court of Edward III at the age of fifteen, [and] found that her fate was inexorably entwined with that of John of Gaunt, the King's younger son'.[76] It is a story, really, of a passionate affair between a beautiful woman (Katherine) and a powerful man (John of Gaunt) who is of much greater status and wealth than Katherine – a man who is publicly feared for his brutish and violent nature but whose inward tenderness is revealed in the presence of Katherine. It is also a story of war – the fourteenth century was a turbulent time – and a story of the death of loved ones, both as a consequence of war and because of the apocalyptic force of plague which kills whole villages and also John of Gaunt's first wife, the sublimely beautiful Duchess Blanche. There is room for heroism, too, when Katherine risks her own life to administer to the dying Duchess in the plague infested castle of Bolingbroke. And through his connections with this household as a scrivener, because of his poem addressed to Blanche, and perhaps because of his eternal appeal, there is a character called Geoffrey Chaucer who is about twenty six although already rather stout, soberly dressed with unfashionable hair, ink–stained fingers and hazel eyes which 'twinkled as at some private joke'.[77] Katherine first meets him at court as the fiancée of her older sister, Philippa.[78] He observes events with his 'alert gaze' and supplies information to

---

[74]   See, for example, Philippa Gregory, *The Other Boleyn Girl* (London, Harper Collins, 2002); and Tracey Chevalier, *Girl with a Pearl Earring* (London, Harper Collins, 2000).

[75]   See, for example, Anya Seton, *Katherine* (London, Coronet Books, Hodder and Stoughton, 1981, first published 1954); see also Eileen Power's comment above (1924).

[76]   Seton, *Katherine*, Preface.

[77]   Seton, *Katherine*, p. 35. Chaucer is discussed in Ellis, *Chaucer at Large*, pp. 141–5.

[78]   Seton, *Katherine*, pp. 35–6.

Katherine about the important historical characters at court in a voice which is 'tinged with light irony'.[79]

The Other Boleyn Girl is Mary Boleyn who 'catches the eye of Henry VIII when she comes to court as a girl of fourteen'.[80] It begins with various flirtations such as the early event when, at a court masque, Mary (already married at this young age) faints into the King's arms, feigning surprise that she had been conversing with the disguised Henry. The fall is carefully assisted by another of the ambitious Boleyns, Anne, so that Mary's hair 'tumbled down like a stream over the king's arms'.[81] This is a story of several short-lived and extremely dangerous passionate affairs, beginning with Mary, whose 'joy is cut short when she discovers that she is a pawn in the dynastic plots of her family'.[82] It also tells of the rivalry between the Boleyn sisters, the fair-haired Mary and the dark-haired elder Anne, and the transfer of the king's attention from Mary at the beginning of the book (Spring 1522), to the determined Anne by about a third of the way through the book (Autumn 1525), and Anne's fall from favour beginning from about the Spring of 1535.[83] Of course this is also the story of the disappointing marriage to Katherine of Aragon which yields no son, the break from Rome (with an emphasis on the issue of divorce from Katherine, rather than on any broader cultural matters of religious change), various well–known names of Henry VIII's court such as Thomas More, Cardinal Wolsey, and the poet Thomas Wyatt, the miscarriages of Anne, the increasingly morose mood of Henry, the executions of the various major players at Henry's court. There is also space in this plot for some lurid details concerning the witchcraft accusations levelled at Anne Boleyn after her third miscarriage when she gives birth to 'a monster', which is (allegedly) the child of George Boleyn (brother of Anne and Mary).[84] Eventually Anne is executed as Jane Seymour takes her place, but 'the other Boleyn girl' withdraws from this dangerous court to a life with her husband William Stafford, in Rochford.

In the 'Author's Note', both Seton and Gregory mention the influence of biographical studies for their novels. Seton's rehearsal of sources and debts of thanks is lengthier than Gregory's, and here she mentions two biographies: *Geoffrey Chaucer of England*, by Marchette Chute, which is credited with providing the initial inspiration for the novel; the other, a favourable biography of John of Gaunt by Sydney Armitage–Smith, seems to have legitimated her positive portrayal of the Duke.[85] Gregory's shorter note mentions specifically Retha M. Warnicke's *The Rise and Fall of Anne Boleyn* whose thesis she follows, and

---

[79]   Seton, *Katherine*, 37.

[80]   Gregory, *Other Boleyn Girl*, Back Cover.

[81]   Gregory, *Other Boleyn Girl*, p. 14.

[82]   Gregory, *Other Boleyn Girl*, Back Cover.

[83]   Gregory, *Other Boleyn Girl*, p. 146 ff.

[84]   Gregory, *Other Boleyn Girl*, p. 472. Many of these accusations were actually made in retrospect.

[85]   Seton, *Katherine*, p. 10.

includes several biographical works alongside some other academic studies in a short bibliography.

There are many elements of these novels and others in this genre which could be discussed for their connections with my reconstruction of lives. I will mention just two aspects here, briefly, in order to comment on the style of 'life–writing' pursued here by Anya Seton and Philippa Gregory. Each of these is actually of interest because it seems to emphasise elements of storytelling which are relatively inappropriate for the project I am engaged with here. The first pertains to what might be described as 'Mills and Boon' techniques and subject matter to engage and hold the reader's attention; and the second concerns an issue of language use and vocabulary. It is perhaps with a sense of envy that I highlight these differences in technique between the historical novel and the reconstructions in this book. This is envy formed from the knowledge that one of these two elements of style in particular – the 'Mills and Boon' technique – helps to change a book from being an interesting read to a real page turner. And yet, I think it is the case that such elements could not find a place in the sorts of biographical reconstruction with which this book is engaged in its six life chapters.

Despite being inappropriate for this book, I will nevertheless explore these two elements of technique in the historical novel below, briefly, because the phenomenon of this sort of fiction is, in general, worthy of much further scholarly consideration. The continued and increasing popularity of this form in the twentieth and twenty-first centuries raises a range of questions such as: What do the demands for literature which involves historical reconstruction indicate about the popular interest in the past? How might this genre of literature be employed to encourage readers to develop their own greater knowledge of the historical past? What do the changes in style used in the historical novel between c. 1950 and the present indicate about academic attitudes to historical evidence or about the changing attitudes of readers across this period? How might the audiences for historical novels be encouraged to develop an interest in the past which involves reading slightly more detailed accounts of individual lives? All these are serious subjects for critical engagement.

'He Crushed Her Furiously'

Katherine is a steamy novel. Given that the plot is centred on a passionate affair, this is not surprising. Apart from the underlying eroticism in the descriptions of the young Katherine de Roet who arrives at court from a nunnery in Kent – immediately transfixing the household knights with her beautiful grey eyes, burnished masses of auburn hair, and beautiful pale skin – the earliest sexual encounter is one of violence. On her introduction to the royal household (of Edward II) at which her sister, Philippa, is a servant, the shy, humble, and naïve Katherine who is enchanted by the splendour and beauty of the royals does not realise the effect of her own presence. The taciturn 'Battling Saxon Ram' Hugh Swinford, a knight (Katherine's future husband), is particularly affected much to the amusement of others at court.[86] Katherine's honour is protected by her slightly envious sister, but one dusk, at the sound of singing (a 'gay lilting air newly come from France'), Katherine leaves the company of the other women and wanders into the walled garden 'pleasaunce' of the palace. On stooping to pick a daffodil (pressing the blossom to her nose to inhale the sweet scent), she hears the 'clanking of a sword' and in her naïve innocence assumes that she is trespassing. Of course it was Hugh who 'strode' into the scene still wearing his hauberk and chain–mail, sword and spurs, from jousting. He blocks her way breathing 'like a winded stag' his 'thick set chunky body' visibly trembling. He is bewitched by her, and before she can move he lunges for her:

> He grabbed her around the waist with one arm while his other hand tore down the shoulder of her dress. The worn velvet ripped the gauze, exposing her arm and one breast. He crushed her furiously against him and the sharp links of his chain–mail ground into her flesh. He bent her backward and her spine cracked. She struggled for breath, then fought him with frantic terror. She beat him in the face with her fists and clawed with her nails until one of her frenzied blows hit his left eye. He tossed his head and loosed her just enough so that she could let out one long agonised scream.

> 'Don't, Katherine, don't–' he panted, his grip on her tightened again. 'I want you, I must have you–'. He forced her against a hedge, bearing down towards the ground.

She is rescued just in time, of course, by the great Duke of Lancaster, she sitting in a dishevelled state panting and shivering on the path with her hair braids unbound so that 'the cascade of hair half hid the naked shoulder and white breast that was imprinted with bloody flecks from the chain–mail'.[87]

As the story progresses, and the attraction between John of Gaunt and Katherine is ever clearer, the reader is promised passion only to have its consummation withdrawn on several occasions. Very soon after the Duchess's funeral, for example, Katherine is summoned to attend an audience with the Duke alone in the 'Avalon Chamber' of the privy apartments of his residence in London, the Savoy; she is taken there by a secret route so that no one sees her enter. The Duke is stricken with grief. Nevertheless, alone together, Katherine manages to comfort him, and he reads her the opening of Chaucer's as yet unfinished *Book of the Duchess*, before they are drawn together still closer:

---

[86]   Seton, *Katherine*, p. 45.

[87]   Seton, *Katherine*, p. 47.

'Jesu–' he whispered. 'Jesu–'. He pulled her slowly towards him and she came as one who walks through water, each step impeded, until she leaned against him and yielded him her mouth with a low sobbing moan.[88]

They stay in this pose for some time it seems, while it goes dark, until he presses her to the bed and she feels the 'sharp pressure of her betrothal ring' against her at which point she 'twisted from him wildly and flung herself off the bed exclaiming, 'My dearest lord I cannot!'. It is not until some time later, and after the death and funeral of Katherine's husband, Hugh, in Bordeaux where she visits him, that John and Katherine actually get to the point of consummation. He carries her off on horseback to a castle in Les Landes where they spend three days in ecstatic rapture.[89]

It is obvious that these 'Mills and Boon' elements represent some of the more fanciful interpretations and embellishments of the historical evidence sought out by Anya Seton. Interestingly, such elements seem to be toned down in *The Other Boleyn Girl*, despite the fact that the whole story revolves around the inconstant passions of Henry VIII. Elements of the suspense elicited by frustrated attempts at conquest before first consummation are present in Gregory's novel, using similar techniques to Seton. The first possible act of adultery between the young Mary and Henry, for example, is narrated on page 29: there is a brief conversation between the two; he demands 'I must see you alone', she replies, 'I dare not'; and there are some deep breaths and 'locked' gazes, a kissed hand, a revelation by Mary that she had wondered what being kissed by the King might feel like, whereupon she runs off, but not before she promises Henry to send her 'favour' in the form of her scarf.[90] Soon after, her family decide to send her to Hever Castle for several months 'exile' on account that she upset the King by complaining at the discovery of her scarf hidden in his breastplate after he fell at the joust.[91] It is not until page 59, on her return to court and when she is sent for by the King, that Mary finally yields to Henry:

> His head came down and he kissed me gently at first and then harder, the touch of his lips very warm. Then he led me by the hand towards the canopied bed and lay me down on it and buried his face in the swell of my breasts where they showed above the stomacher that Anne had helpfully loosened for him.[92]

At this point there is a section break, and the text re–opens with the two lovers waking at dawn, only to become pressed closely together once again, whereupon the reader learns of Henry's strong thighs and the rest is left to the imagination; by

---

[88]   Seton, *Katherine*, p. 209.

[89]   Seton, *Katherine*, pp. 260–263.

[90]   Gregory, *Other Boleyn Girl*, p. 29.

[91]   Gregory, *Other Boleyn Girl*, pp. 39–41.

[92]   Gregory, *Other Boleyn Girl*, p. 59.

the next sentence the sun is fully up and there is a flurry of dressing (with a brief mention of laces that need tying) in order that Mary can attempt to return to her room before the servants are about.[93] Perhaps in the permissive twenty-first century the attraction to the reader is increased by not hinting so hard at lurid details which may have turned pages in the 1950s.

'But a Block Away'

The use of language in historical novels in general deserves a full-length study. Both Seton and Gregory use dialogue to great effect, and this of course marks a key difference between the style of narration appropriate for this reconstruction of six Tudor lives, and the requirements of a page-turning historical novel. There are actually some marked differences between the modes of narration used by Seton and Gregory which are connected to the voices in operation in these novels. Whereas Seton's *Katherine* is told by a narrator who is not experiencing the plot as it unfolds (the story is told in the third person), Gregory's *Other Boleyn Girl* is told in the first person from the perspective of that girl, Mary. Such differences in narrative tone and technique may perhaps reflect these two novels' different dates of production. Indeed, Gregory's use of the first person may reflect trends in the telling of historical narratives more generally with the increasing acknowledgement of the reflexive involvement of the teller (be they academic, biographer and so on) in the outcome of the tale over the last twenty years or so.

There is also a marked difference in the extent to which these two writers attempt to make their dialogue 'authentic' to the Medieval or Tudor period. Gregory appears to have made a conscious decision to put modern words into the mouths of her Tudor characters. This does not diminish the 'Tudoresque' atmosphere which is maintained through the use of detailed descriptions of the various scenes in this Tudor court (buildings or landscape as well as clothing and fabrics are particularly emphasised) and an attempt to explore the psychologies of the Tudor characters. Seton's dialogue, by comparison, is littered with what sometimes seem like excessive usages of 'ye olde' language and her narrative descriptions of the psychological states of the characters seem, also, consciously less subtle than Gregory's.

Just one episode in the story of *Katherine*, Chapter XIV, serves to demonstrate a number of the elements of Seton's language–use both in relation to the words spoken by the Medieval characters and also the words used to reflect their thoughts. The scene is Hugh Swinford's lodgings at Bordeaux where he has been at war and is currently injured. He is visited by Katherine who is guided by the Gascon servant of the Duke called Nirac. On seeing the dingy conditions of the 'stuffy sour room' and Hugh lying on a bed with 'hempen sheets' Katherine greets him with: 'Ah my dear, 'tis well I've come to nurse you'. This use of ''tis' is frequent for all the speakers throughout the book, and it sometimes sits uneasily

---

[93] Gregory, *Other Boleyn Girl*, pp. 59–60.

with modern commonplaces in abbreviated forms such as 'I've'. Hugh responds to
the entry of the two visitors with a retort to the the Gascon servant Nirac of 'Oh,
it's you, you meaching cockscomb. I'd forgot all about you', using the rustic
grammar and colloquial curses typical of this 'Medievalised' language. On hearing
that Hugh's wound has 'near done festering', she replies with 'Alack!', followed
by ''tis the flux again? But 'twill pass – you've got over it before'.[94] Again, this
sentence exhibits a typical exclamation and use of the 'tis and 'twill forms. Nirac
also provides an example of Seton's uses of language. He speaks in a mixture of
easily understood French phrases such as the *'Comme vous voulez ma belle dame'*
reply to Katherine when she asks him to guide her to Hugh's lodgings, and
dialectically written phrases such as this report on Hugh's health when they first
arrive at his bedside: ' 'Is Grace's own leech 'as cared for 'im, an' now 'e 'as the
best medicine in the world!'[95]

The next day in the same episode, Katherine leaves the bedside of her husband
in order to attend early mass at Bordeaux Cathedral. The reader is told that she
'yearned for the blissful comfort of the act of communion, when the sweet body of
Jesu should enter into her own body and strengthen her'.[96] Here is an example of
the way Seton attempts to convey elements of a Medieval mentality using a
narrative technique which explicitly includes a 'Medievalised' vocabulary.
Katherine, dressed in a green and gold gown and a fine silk–hooded mantle 'to do
honour to the festival', slips into the cobbled street on her way to the service at
which point there is a sentence which indicates the potential for delicious linguistic
infelicities: It was hotter than it would ever be in England, but she gave thanks for
the morning freshness and hurried to the cathedral, which was but a block away'.[97]

Fiction and the Archives

Anya Seton's 'Author's Note' at the beginning of *Katherine* makes some
interesting comments regarding the book's connections with 'History'. Seton
begins by stressing that it has been her 'anxious endeavour to use nothing but
historical fact', and that the story is based on 'actual history'.[98] The extent of her
historical research for this project was considerable, and included visits by this
American writer to England and 'each of the counties' relevant to the story, on
which occasions she informs the reader that she 'searched ever' in 'the British
Museum, town libraries and archives, in rectory studies, in local legend – for more
data on Katherine's life'.[99] Seton makes an admission, however, that 'it has
sometimes of course been necessary to bring my own interpretations' into the

94   Seton, *Katherine*, p. 239.
95   Seton, *Katherine*, p. 239.
96   Seton, *Katherine*, p. 243.
97   Seton, *Katherine*, p. 243.
98   Seton, *Katherine*, p. 9.
99   Seton, *Katherine*, p. 9.

story. This statement is indicative of those attitudes to History, at the time she was writing in the mid-twentieth century, as something which is engaged in the search for a provable truth. Twenty-first century attitudes to interpretation (including historical reconstruction) tend much more towards considering the impossibilities of distinguishing between fact and fiction. This may account for the shorter Author's Note produced by Gregory. As Richard Holmes points out in relation to biographical writing, it has now become more necessary and more acceptable to examine the 'subtle question' of the relationships between the ' "significant facts" ' of a life and the ' "revealing" stories' needed to make sense of the otherwise 'apparently random circumstances of a life'.[100] I have attempted to explore revealing stories about the lives of the six subjects in this book but, perhaps unfortunately, the evidence available has not enabled a consideration of the intimacies of personal emotion addressed in the historical novels discussed above, and nor has the surviving evidence provided access to the modes of speech used by my subjects on a daily basis.

The Six Lives in this Book

For this book, I have tried to take an honest and postmodern attitude towards the archival evidence for the six lives. By this I mean that I have sought to examine the various types of source pertaining to each individual in a way which maintains a sense of the significance of context; and also with an acknowledgement of my own involvement in the construction of the written narrative, so far as there is one, in each chapter. The sense of context I am using here is not the fact that all the evidence is all 'Tudor', but much more importantly the specific contexts of the production and reception of the different pieces of evidence. This means attempting to understand the motivations behind the particular cultural products which survive. And I have sought to use these modes of interpretation to recover the experiences, for these six men and women, of living at the Tudor court and in the early English Renaissance.

Each chapter explores various fragments of evidence for the six Renaissance men and women.

---

[100]   Holmes, 'Proper Study', pp. 16–17.

Chapter 3

Gilbert Banaster

Introduction

Gilbert Banaster's lifespan is, chronologically, the earliest covered by this book. He died in 1488, before William Buckley – the latest person in the book – was born. The surviving evidence for Banaster's life and cultural interests consists of several literary works; several musical compositions (mainly formal and popular religious settings, and an antiphon celebrating his patrons); some administrative details concerning his property ownership; and a last will and testament concerned again with substantial property holdings and also the bequest of various luxury goods to his family and social network.

By examining the range of creative outputs with which Banaster is connected, this chapter explores what can be discovered about this man's commitments to the traditional values of a Medieval social and religious order alongside his experiments with cultural innovation. The mixed uses of tradition and innovation by Gilbert Banaster provide a fruitful way of accessing this individual's experiences of early English Renaissance; experiences which, perhaps, suggest a tension between the excitement of the new and of the fresh opportunities for such a man in the changing world of the second half of the fifteenth century, alongside a strong personal and scholarly commitment to the maintenance of traditional ideals.

First Encounter

The first time I encountered Gilbert Banaster was through his last will and testament, whilst trawling through all those that survive for the period c. 1450–1560 in Greenwich, and writing about the ways that these documents give access to creative constructions of identity.[1] Banaster's last will and testament, produced in 1487, is quite an interesting document, although it is fairly short and does not give many immediate clues to this man's involvement with the royal household which is known from other sources: he was a 'Gentleman of the Chapel' then 'Master of the

---

[1]   NA PROB 11/8/11/90. See Elisabeth Salter, *Cultural Creativity in the Early English Renaissance: Popular Culture in Town and Country* (London, Palgrave Macmillan, 2006) on the uses of wills as evidence, and also for a brief consideration of this, see Chapter 6 on Katherine Styles in this volume.

Choristers' between the dates of c. 1475–1486.[2] But, at the beginning of Banaster's will, where there is traditionally a description of the testator in terms of occupation and status, he is simply described as 'gentilman'. It is significant and intriguing that the will document makes no mention of all his various creative productions which are addressed in this Chapter.

I am not going to talk about Banaster's will in detail, here, as there are many other interesting issues to consider from the evidence not mentioned in that document. However, it is worth mentioning his substantial property holdings in Greenwich and the vicinity, and also the property and gifts he leaves to his wife, his mother ('if she then be living'), and four daughters. All of these details have been briefly noted in other biographical summaries because they enable some calculations of his likely age, as well as his wealth, at death. The fact that his mother was still alive at the time he made his will (although the caveat regarding her suggests she was quite elderly) attracts particular attention in this regard.[3]

Most of the property bequeathed in Banaster's will is in Greenwich and it includes a number of tenements. The way these property holdings are described is particularly detailed, listing the individuals who rent the various waterside units and quays by identifying them according to their occupations, and the specific position of this set of neighbouring properties on the banks of the Thames.[4] This tends to suggest that Banaster had what might be called 'local knowledge' concerning these properties – his knowledge of the waterfront includes the scale and position of the specific properties to which he refers, as well as the particular tenants who rented them. His wife who is alive at the time of writing the testament (Joanne) and three of his daughters (Agnes, Margaret, and Elizabeth) are the main beneficiaries of this property. It includes a number of tenements and wharves by the waterside, a brewhouse called 'The Vine' with more than fifteen acres of land attached to it in various parcels, crofts, gardens, a barn, and some pieces of marshland which was a highly prized type of land in this area.

Banaster's wealth as well as his appreciation of material goods is indicated by the descriptions of the gifts of silverware and furnishings he left to his four daughters. His gifts of silverware to the three daughters who inherit property (Agnes, Margaret, and Elizabeth) are listed first including, 'a chased cupp of sylv*er* p*ar*cel gilt Koveryd weying xxx unces and a maser with a brode band Koverid', 'a pece of sylv*er* p*ar*cel gilt chased w*ith* a sterre in the bottom w*ith* a knopp w*ith*out a kovering', and 'a litil maser w*ith* a print in the botom'. Banaster's fourth daughter,

---

[2]   Fiona Kisby, 'Officers and Office-Holding', in *Royal Musical Association Research Chronicle*, 34 (2001).

[3]   See, for example, Jonathan Hall and Magnus Williamson, 'Banastre , Gilbert (*d.* 1487)', *ODNB*, http://www.oxforddnb.com/view/article/1266.

[4]   These are mentioned in Elisabeth Salter, 'Some Differences in the Cultural Production of Household Consumption in Three North Kent Communities', in Sarah Rees Jones *et al.* (eds), *Managing Power, Wealth and the Body: The Christian Household in Medieval Europe, c. 850–1550*, pp. 391–400.

Alice, is given a slightly different bequest which includes 'my sylver spones the knoppis called diamond poynte and a maser that I hadd with hyr moder with a rounde bonde and a bossell weyng xiii unces'.[5] This daughter, Alice, is mentioned slightly separately from the other three throughout the will which might indicate that she is the single child of one marriage whereas the other three are the children of another marriage. Alice certainly appears to have a special connection with her mother as the description of the silverware indicates; she also has a specific connection with both her parents, as indicated by Banaster's bequest to her of 'my wedding gowne that I was last weddid in'.

The will document also provides a nice detail that hints at Banaster's interest in books. He bequeaths:

> to the forseid Agnes my daughter my prim*er* koveryd w*ith* purple Chamlett and a payre of clapsis upon the same of sylver and gilt. Item I bequeath to John Combe my prymer now of late bownden

It was not unusual for a man of Banaster's wealth and status to own a primer or two (a type of devotional book similar to a Book of Hours) in the fifteenth century. Such books were widely available in this period, especially in the London area. The descriptions of these particular two primers, however, provide some clues to the quality of these books and also to Banaster's attitude towards them. The first one, given to his daughter, may be an ordinary enough volume but its binding is rather ornate and precious; the description seems to indicate that Banaster enjoyed the aesthetic quality of the purple cover and silver gilt clasps. The second book, given to John Combe (a citizen of London and a tailor by trade who was to act as an executor), also appears to have been cared for by Banaster. The fact that it is identified by its new binding may have made it clear which of his books Banaster wanted to give to his executor; but it may also signal that he had taken special care to provide Combe with a particularly handsome gift, singling out this particular book from what must have been a fairly substantial library. Unfortunately, no other books from the library I imagine Banister to have owned, and none of the literary or musical compositions which he produced, are mentioned in his will.

Banaster's Literary Works

A Translation of a Tragic Love Story

It is fairly certain that Gilbert Banaster produced a verse translation of a story from the Italian collection of moral tales known as the *Decameron,* which was written

---

[5]   NA PROB 11/8/11/90. A 'bossell' is a kind of pattern pressed into the silver. A 'maser' is a wooden cup often decorated with silver. 'Knoppis' are the knobs on the end of a spoon handle. I use italics here, and throughout, to signal letters missing in the original text.

by Giovanni Boccaccio. According to the last two lines of the closing envoy of the version attributed to Banaster, he made this translation for someone called 'John Rayner';[6] an emissary to the Italian Embassy.[7] The *Decameron* is a collection of interconnected popular stories, spread over ten days, each day having ten stories.[8] The stories attend to a number of different moral scenarios. They are explicitly or distantly expressive of the social context of their writer who was living in Italy in the fourteenth century. This was an Italy composed of communes which were, in this period, proud of their civility. These were also communes immersed in factional squabbles which encouraged those in power to search for a 'Good Society' which could be ruled well and peacefully. In the fourteenth century in Italy (as in England) there was a conjunction of factors which brought about radical social and economic changes, including the ravages of the Black Death. These changes encouraged the emphatic emergence of bourgeois cultures, and the concomitant interest in matters of conduct and morality as these groups sought to define their identities. Such emergent groups therefore had a keen interest in the 'classical and feudal past and in their own mercantile present'.[9] Similar to Geoffrey Chaucer's *Canterbury Tales*, the stories of the *Decameron* are expressive of the moral and social issues raised by the clash between old and new cultures and also the 'culture shock' of the Black Death.[10]

Banaster translated the story of 'Ghismonda and Ghiscondo' which is the first story of the fourth day in the *Decameron*. The ten stories for this day are introduced by Boccaccio as concerning people whose love ended unhappily. The first story narrates the consequences for a high-born woman, called 'Sismond' in the English translation, of loving a man of lower status, called 'Guistard'. It is a tragic story and, in keeping with others in the *Decameron*, it considers the moral problems and consequences of a changing world (in fourteenth-century Italy) and all the implications change has for the interactions and power relations between different status groups.[11] One main route for such examination, used also by Geoffrey Chaucer, is the social and political units which form and perpetuate society, such as love and marriage.[12] The tragic tale of noble Sismond's love for her father's servant, Guistard, results in Guistard's death on the orders of her

---

[6]   *Early English Versions of the Tales of Guiscardo and Ghismonda and Titus and Gisippus from the Decameron*, ed. Herbert G. Wright, Early English Text Society (London, OUP, 1937), p. 36, l. 625.

[7]   M.C. Seymour, *A Catalogue of Chaucer Manuscripts*, vol. 1, 'Works Before the Canterbury Tales' (Aldershot, Scolar Press, 1995), pp. 89–90.

[8]   N.S. Thompson, *Chaucer, Boccaccio and the Debate of Love: A Comparative Study of The Decameron and The Canterbury Tales* (OUP, 1996), pp. 1–2.

[9]   Thompson, *Chaucer, Boccaccio*, p. 316.

[10]   Thompson, *Chaucer, Boccaccio*, p. 314–6.

[11]   Thompson, *Chaucer, Boccaccio*, p. 316.

[12]   Thompson, *Chaucer, Boccaccio*, pp. 229–241.

father, Prince Tancred. In his anger, Tancred sends Sismond a cup containing Guistard's heart:

> The whiche hert forth brought to the prince it ys
> In a ryche cope off golde he kan it dresse
> And by a secrete messenger off hys
> He send it hys doghter in grete fersnesse
> Sending hyr worde that a present off noblesse
> He hath hyr sent, to make hyr mery and glade
> Thyng off the world wheroff moste ioye she hadde[13]

This version of the story exists in two manuscripts both compiled in the fifteenth century, one now housed in the British Library and one in the Bodleian Library, both of which contain more than one text.[14] Both of these books provide a context for the Sismond story. This 'context' provides evidence for some aspects of how this story was understood in the fifteenth century and tends to suggest that the role of Fortune in deciding the fate of people, in the context of a changing world, was seen as a key element in the Sismond story.

The other text in the British Library manuscript is an extract from Geoffrey Chaucer's *Legend of Good Women,* which occupies the first part of the book. This is a set of stories which uses the tragic lives of women from classical legend to comment on various ways in which Fortune deals treacherous blows. Because of its modern binding, the British Library manuscript looks like a complete book, but it is in fact incomplete. It begins abruptly with what Herbert Wright identified as line 273 of the tale of 'Hypsipyle and Medea' in the *Legend.*[15] The book as it survives also finishes earlier than the compiler originally intended at the end of the tale of Sismond, which is described in the following way: 'heyr endyth the legend of ladyse and begyneth the compleynte of Mars and Venus'. There is no tale of Mars and Venus. The Bodleian manuscript also contains other works, and these are also concerned with women and the vagaries of Fortune. A poem which focuses on the effects of the 'transmutacion' of the world uses, for its examples, some of the same classical women as Chaucer does in the *Legend.* And a second poem ends by warning the reader to beware of Fortune which 'turneth sodenly'.[16] The Sismond story follows these poems in the Bodleian manuscript and begins with an introduction not found in the British Library version. The tone of this introduction (which is probably incomplete for an unknown reason) is that Fortune is responsible for the tragedy befalling these lovers, both causing them to fall in love and causing their love to be made public, with tragic consequences.

13　　Wright, *Tales from the Decameron,* p. 24, ll. 407–413.
14　　These are BL MS Add 12524, and Oxford Bodleian Rawlinson C 86.
15　　Wright, *Tales from the Decameron,* p. xi.
16　　Wright, *Tales from the Decameron,* p. xiii.

I will use the British Library manuscript for the purposes of quoting the Sismond tale in this chapter as it is the version most strongly associated with Banaster. One significant reason for the attribution of this translation to Banaster is that the final few stanzas which are only present in the British Library manuscript provide an envoy. This 'envoy' takes a traditional form – of the 'go little book' type – which sends the work forth into the world:

> Go Forth, lytill tayle, full bare off elloquens,
> With humble sprete make thi supplicacioune;
> Prey all tho, theras thou comyst in audiens,
> To have piete on thy simple translacione,
> Oute off prose by myne unkonnyng directioune
> Made in balade; wherof myne innocence
> Submytting lowly unto coreccioune
> And supportacion of youre benevolence,
>
> Besekyng all the maisters of this science
> Me holde excused, for goode ys myne entencion,
> Thogh I florysh nat with metyr and cadence;
> Off rethoryk and poetry making mencioune;
> Such clerkly werkys passith my discrecion;
> Natwithstonding, if here be fawte or offens,
> Speke to Gilbert banester, which at the mocioune
> Off Iohn Raynere this made aftir the sentence
>   Explicit legenda
>   Sismond[17]

Other traditional aspects of this envoy are the author's deprecation concerning his skills; in this case the poet ('banester') apologises for his poetic technique (Stanza 2, quoted above, ll. 3–4). Despite the fact that it conforms to a traditional rhetoric of authorial apology, critics have seemed determined to take the envoy at face value.[18] Perhaps there is something seductive about the presence of a name – a claim to authorship – which finds us dropping our critical guard. Charles Wallace, for example, appears to have used the naming of Banaster in the envoy as a basis for the proposition that this manuscript version of Sismond is actually in Banaster's hand.[19] Ultimately we cannot know whether or not this is the work of Gilbert

---

[17]   Wright, *Tales from the Decameron*, p. 36, ll. 610–625.

[18]   Magnus Williamson, 'Royal Image-Making and Textual Interplay in Gilbert Banaster's *O Maria et Elizabeth*', *Early Music History* (2000), 19, 237–77, p. 255 which suggests that Banaster 'declared his authorship unambiguously'.

[19]   See Charles William Wallace, *The Evolution of the English Drama up to Shakespeare, with a History of the First Blackfriars Theatre* (Berlin, Georg Reimer, 1912), p. 24; also Thomas Warton, *History of English Poetry from the Twelfth to the Close of the Sixteenth Century*, ed. W. Carew Hazlitt, 4 vols, vol. 3 (London, Reeves and Turner, 1871), p. 132.

Banaster; however, the fact that it is attributed to him in the fifteenth century shows that, at that time, this versification and translation was thought to be the kind of work which Banaster may have produced. I shall take this as an assurance of thinking about the work in relation to this man's life and interests; and I will refer to the work as Banaster's translation.

The envoy plays upon the fact that Banaster's translation of the Ghismonda story is in verse. Herbert Wright examined some of the possibilities for its immediate source, and suggested that Banaster's use of the name 'Sismond' indicates that he may have worked from a French prose version of a Latin version translated by Leonardi Bruni in about 1436 – Wright points out that Banaster makes the word 'Sismond' rhyme with the word 'fownde' which he suggests is French in sound; and also that 'Sismond' is more closely related to Bruni's Latin form of the name which is 'Sigismunda' than to Boccaccio's form of the name which is 'Ghismonda'.

Herbert Wright provided a useful analysis of the differences and similarities between Banaster's translation and Boccaccio's story. In general, the prevailing view in Wright's analysis is that Banaster's translation 'idealizes the story', making the relationship between the lovers 'less sensual' than Boccaccio's version.[20] For example, Wright points out a number of instances in which the Sismond character appears to be less cunning or scheming and more honourable; she is also less defiant as Banaster's Sismond than she is as Boccaccio's Ghismonda, who makes a challenge to her father when she is confronted by him about her actions. Both heroines do, however, use marriage as a vehicle for casting blame on Tancred for the illicit affaire. Sismond, for whom 'it was her will inwardly / To have lyffid in the law of matrimony', casts blame on Tancred for not allowing her ever to remarry after the sudden death of her first husband which caused her so much grief.[21] Ghismonda, on the other hand, claims that it was only since she developed a taste for the delights of marriage, after this was condoned by her father for her first marriage, that she could no longer deny herself these pleasures.[22] Ghismonda's reason certainly appears to be more physically motivated, and more selfish, than Sismond's. Wright also indicates that Banaster's Guistard is more innocent than the rather experienced and knowing Ghiscondo of Boccaccio's tale. There are also certain instances where the mode of the lovers' meeting is altered by Banaster: whereas Ghismonda gives a hollow reed to Ghiscondo to invite him to their first tryst and cunningly arranges for Ghiscondo to use a secret passage through the caves to her chamber, Sismond does not do this and simply declares her intentions to the young innocent squire who is 'abashed sore'.[23]

---

20   Wright, *Tales from the Decameron*, p. xxx.

21   Wright, *Tales from the Decameron*, p. 14, ll. 237–8.

22   Giovanni Boccaccio, *The Decameron*, Translated with an Introduction by G.H. McWilliam (Aylesbury, Penguin, 1972, repr. 1987), p. 338.

23   Wright, *Tales from the Decameron*, p. 14, l. 225.

It is very likely that one reason why Wright suggested that Banaster was deliberately removing the erotic charge of the Italian poet's work, making a determined effort to idealise the characters and the story, concerns some prevailing critical assumptions at the time Wright was conducting his analysis (in 1937). There was a tendency, prevalent in the early twentieth century, to take a view that in the fifteenth century Italian sensibilities were more 'Renaissance' in orientation (and therefore advanced) compared to English sensibilities which were more Medieval (and therefore lagging behind). This being the case, and not with the intention of discarding Wright's astute comparisons, it becomes possible to detect a certain pressure on his analysis of Banaster's attitude which would find the English translator uncomfortable with the 'Renaissance' style of Boccaccio's stories and morals. In fact, Banaster's musical compositions, which I discuss below, show that he was interested in the use of both old and new forms, and sometimes in the mixing of these for specific purposes. So it is likely that he should be considered fairly self-conscious about his uses of Medieval and Renaissance styles in literature too.

Also on the subject of critical assumptions in the period c. 1937, there was probably pressure on Wright to see Banaster as an imitator of Chaucer. Chaucer, of course, had to be viewed as the great forerunner in the Anglicisation of continental Renaissance themes.[24] To view Banaster as an imitator of Chaucer is a seductive idea. The manuscript context of the British Library version lends some credence to this because the fifteenth-century compiler of that manuscript thought that the works of Chaucer and Banaster fitted in the same book; although this might equally indicate that the compiler considered these two writers to have an equality of skill, rather than that Banaster was an imitator of Chaucer. It is possible that Banaster was an admirer of Chaucer's work and that he may have sought to emulate this in his versification of Boccaccio's prose. But, perhaps it is more fruitful to think of the emphases in Banaster's translation as representative of a specific moralising purpose, rather than as imitative or resistant to the style of one or other great writers.

Further Consideration of Banaster's Story

In Banaster's version, Sismond's pitiful but noble reaction to the murder of her lover, Guistard, is described in detail. Although she had 'sorow inestimable' on seeing the gift, she responds to the messenger 'withoute changing off faconde or

---

[24]   Wallace, *Evolution of the English Drama*, p. 24. Also, see *The Decameron of Giovanni Boccaccio Translated by Richard Aldington with Aquatints by Buckland-Wright*, 2 vols (Westminster, Folio Society, 1954, repr. 1960), vol. 1, p. 15 for the idea that Boccaccio 'wrote the first psychological novel of Europe' and that '[H]e is one of the three authors [...] who mark the tradition which made humanism of the Renaissance'. I am grateful to Joe Higgins, for the posthumous donation of this book.

countenance', returning thanks to her father for the noble gift which encases 'so noble an hart'.[25] Subsequently and presumably after the messenger has left (although it is fairly immediate in the narrative), Sismond bewails the gift from her 'cruell fader' speaking to the heart of her lover in the cup and promising that she will follow him in 'dethis traunce'.[26] She poisons herself, drinking the poison from the cup with the heart in it, 'water and blode withal / [...] as if it were hony suete'.[27] Tancred comes to his daughter and his shock seeing her poisoned body, when 'deth was at hande / Crampyshing her lymes' causes him to fall to the ground and weep until he thought his heart would burst.[28] She has enough energy for one final speech in which she suggests that through her death this event which 'was secret and now ys rumoure' will become known over all the world.[29] Tancred, 'seyng his moste ioye off the worlde agone' falls dead.[30]

The final section of the story, before the envoy, provides a moral for the reader and also a prayer for the salvation of the two lovers. The narrator moralises that the tragedy comes about through the overhasty violent judgement of Tancred which lacked prudence; that he should have known that love cannot be prevented and indeed that love will be increased by a hundred-fold when there is 'trouble and vexacioune'.[31] And this is particularly the case, the narrator suggests, for these two lovers who were 'yong and in fluryshyng age'.[32] The narrator then specifically indicates that it was the prevention of their marriage which 'was cause of this myscheve, withouten faile'.[33] He ends with a prayer for the souls of the two lovers, and for the unreserved forgiveness of Guistard; and of Sismond on account of the fact that she would have married Guistard if she were allowed. He proposes her as a 'miroure to women all / Ensample of treue and stedfast lowe gyffyng'.[34] This makes an obvious connection with those stories in this manuscript which are taken from Chaucer's *Legend of Good Women*.

Crying: A Case Study

There are many aspects of Banaster's translation of Boccaccio's work that merit detailed consideration, and there is not space to do this here; it deserves a separate study taking into account the manuscript contexts of each version and adding some further perspective on Banaster's motives by examining how his work relates to the

---

[25]   Wright, *Tales from the Decameron*, p. 26, ll. 421, 424 and 428 respectively.

[26]   Wright, *Tales from the Decameron*, p. 28, ll. 453 and 460 respectively.

[27]   Wright, *Tales from the Decameron*, p. 30, ll. 507–8.

[28]   Wright, *Tales from the Decameron*, p. 32, ll. 530–531.

[29]   Wright, *Tales from the Decameron*, p. 32, l. 544.

[30]   Wright, *Tales from the Decameron*, p. 34, l.555.

[31]   Wright, *Tales from the Decameron*, p. 34, l. 576.

[32]   Wright, *Tales from the Decameron*, p. 34, l 583.

[33]   Wright, *Tales from the Decameron*, p. 34, l. 587.

[34]   Wright, *Tales from the Decameron*, p. 36, ll. 605–6.

later translations. I will take just one short case study here as a means of opening up some issues concerning Banaster's attitude to this story and what he was seeking to convey: this concerns the representation of crying.

This type of story is very sensitive to the moral problems inherent in issues of status, honour, identity, as well as the moral dilemmas of the relation between inward virtue and outward status. This is especially the case as these stories were written in the context of a society experiencing radical changes in relations of hierarchy and power (this applies to both fourteenth-century Italy and fifteenth-century England). In such stories, intense feelings of shame and dishonour, as well as frustration, may be elicited through liaisons of love which are inappropriate in terms of social hierarchy. One traditional way for this to be represented is through the very physical reaction of crying.[35] In seeking to stamp his own moral position onto his translation, an author using one of these stories as a source for his own may, therefore, be inclined to change the extent to which a certain character cries. In 'The Franklin's Tale', for example, Chaucer changed the crying character in a most significant moment of tears: rather than having Dorigen the heroine of the story in tears when she confesses to her lower born husband (Arveragus) that she has rashly promised herself to another man, Chaucer makes Arveragus the crier as he insists that his wife must honour her promise. This heightens the frustration and pain experienced by Arveragus as he desperately seeks to be noble whilst also being acutely aware of being low born by comparison to his wife, the noble Dorigen. In one of Chaucer's main sources for this story, Boccaccio's *Filocolo*, it is the lady who weeps, not the husband.[36]

In Banaster's 'Sismond', there are also some changes to the crying order. Tancred seems to cry less in the English version than he does in the Italian. As Wright pointed out, Tancred is represented as more evil by Banaster than by Boccaccio. In Boccaccio's telling, Tancred appears to take his violent actions because he is caught in an impossible situation – the kind of impossible moral and psychological bind that crying represents in these types of scenarios with their sensitivity to the fraught issues of social constraint. In Banaster's version, Tancred is more irrational and perhaps more malevolent.

Banaster also appears to make a specific emphasis in the way the female heroine cries at the point when this character holds the cup containing her lover's heart, which is different from Boccaccio's emphasis. Both weep a huge quantity of tears; they are likened to a welling spring, a fountain, or a flood issuing from the women's heads into the cup. Ghismonda's active determination to cry is made despite a warrior-like resolve she has to 'die with tearless eyes and features unclouded by fear...'; she decides to cry to provide the customary funeral rites

[35] See Peter Brown and Andrew Butcher, *The Age of Saturn: Literature and History in The Canterbury Tales* (Oxford, Blackwell, 1991), pp. 106–113 'Why Did Arveragus Cry'.

[36] N.R. Havely, *Chaucer's Boccaccio: Sources for Troilus and the Knight's and Franklin's Tales* (Woodbridge, D.S. Brewer, 1992), pp. 11, 158.

which required the 'tears of the woman you loved so dearly'.[37] And she plans to regulate this interlude of crying before she begins, saying: 'And the instant my tears are finished I shall see that my soul is united with that other soul that you kept in your loving care'.[38] Sismond also makes a decision to cry, but in a subtly different way, reversing the cause of the crying from his love for her to her love for him: her tears are on account of the custom that someone so worthy as he should receive this rite of 'the terys off hyr that loffyt the unfeynid'.[39] Defiant Ghismonda cries 'suppressing all sound of womanly grief';[40] more gentle Sismond cries '[w]ithout crye making'.[41] Ghismonda appears to be speaking whilst she is crying (her ladies in waiting are unable to make any sense of her words);[42] Sismond's thoughts as she cries hurt her heart so greatly that she has no power to 'make noyse'.[43] Banaster describes this episode for Sismond as follows:

> And so depely she wept, that it semyd
> Lyke two spring wellys, rynnyng as a flode
> In hyr hede, the which withoute sesyng stremyd
> In to the cop off golde, and also bloode
> Mengyd with them about the hert stoode
> The sprentying of the salt teres to the bone
> Feting the Chekys; so woo she was bygone
>
> Kyssyng the hert tymis mo then I kan nombre
> Withoute crye makyng, but with esy voyce
> Thought dyd her hert perse and so encombre
> That she no pouste had to make noyse [...] [44]

The way that the crying (described by Boccaccio as being 'in a fashion so wondrous'[45]) finishes is also described in each version with a different emphasis. Boccaccio's Ghismonda once again appears to be more in control of her responses:

> But when she had cried as much as she deemed sufficient, she raised
> her head from the chalice, and after drying her eyes, she said: 'Oh,
> heart that I love so dearly, now that I have fully discharged my duties
> towards you, all that remains to be done is to bring my soul and unite it
> with yours.[46]

---

37   Boccaccio, *Decameron*, Penguin Translation, p. 340.
38   Boccaccio, *Decameron*, Penguin Translation, p. 340.
39   Wright, *Tales from the Decameron*, p. 46, ll. 441–48.
40   Boccaccio, *Decameron*, Penguin Translation, p. 340.
41   Wright, *Tales from the Decameron*, p. 28, l. 417.
42   Boccaccio, *Decameron*, Penguin Translation, p. 341.
43   Wright, *Tales from the Decameron*, p. 28, l. 473.
44   Wright, *Tales from the Decameron*, p. 28, ll. 464–73.
45   Boccaccio, *Decameron*, Penguin Translation, p. 340.
46   Boccaccio, *Decameron*, Penguin Translation, p. 341.

Sismond appears to make no such active decision either to stop crying or in the calculation of the appropriate discharging of her duties. The corresponding passage in Banaster's poem is:

> And ever she sayde, withoute speche cessaunte:
> 'O right dereworthy, beloved, suete hert
> Honoure the I shall, whyl I am vivaunte,
> And when the soule from the body doth stert,
> To the felyship off thyne it shall awertt;
> Where ever it become, in wo or welle,
> I gyf no fors, so it may the sequele'[47]

In fact, if anyone is making decisions in Banaster's story it appears to be the narrator; Sismond's actions seem to be unavoidable imperatives brought about by her anguish and the impossible situation in which Fortune has placed her. There is something about the intensity with which Banaster represents the crying moment for Sismond through which he perhaps seeks to absolve her of the guilt, and also emphasise her plight as being a product of the impossible situation in which she found herself. I am tempted to suggest that, for Banaster, representing Sismond's tears in this way was expressive of his emphasis, in this translation, on the very innocence of those casualties of moral dilemmas which involve relations of status, power and inappropriate liaisons in the changing world of fifteenth-century England. And Sismond's crying does seem much more like Arveragus's tears of frustration and helpless social anxiety than Ghismonda's more active intervention. Perhaps Banaster's experiences at the royal household, where the very élite mixed with the humble servant, may have found him sensitised to some of these problems.

Miracle Poem and Interlude

One of the very fascinating issues concerning the evidence for these Renaissance lives, and Gilbert Banaster is no exception, is the way that different biographical accounts produced over the last century or so vary in the extent of the certainty with which they attribute certain works to the individual concerned. In the case of Banaster there is an interesting trail of citations concerning two of his works, firstly some uncertainty surrounds his authorship of a poem on the subject of St Thomas Becket (*Miraculum Sancti Thome Matiris*); secondly, and rather more elusive, is his 'interlude' of 1482. Charles W. Wallace suggested of *Miraculum* that it is a 'mediocre saint-worshipping English poem under this Latin title, consisting of five seven-line stanzas, each ending with the Latin theme'. His footnote adds that it is due to the attribution in Thomas Warton's *History of English Poetry*, that it is

---

[47]   Wright, *Tales from the Decameron*, p. 30, ll. 491–7.

presumed to be Banaster's, 'but few seem to know it first hand'.[48] The interlude is more problematic and Wallace simply writes of Banaster that, '[h]e is also credited with an interlude'.[49] Herbert Wright, in his introduction to the printed edition of 'Guiscardo and Ghismonda' (1937), furnishes this issue with a little more detail, recording the fact that the name 'Gylbartus Banystre' is written 'over the top of the third line in the first stanza'.[50] Wright takes the trail back into the eighteenth century and Thomas Tanner's Latin survey of the literature of Britain published in 1748. Unfortunately Tanner simply states that the poem of St Thomas was written by Gilbert Banaster, whom he describes as 'poeta et musicus' (poet and musician), and that it is found in a Corpus Christi Manuscript; without any further information about the source for this attribution. So Wright remains unconvinced, stating 'as will be perceived without difficulty, the attribution rests on an insecure foundation'.[51]

In many ways it is subsequent and specifically biographical accounts which provide the most interesting variety of emphases in their attributions. The *Dictionary of National Biography* implies no doubt about Banaster's authorship of the 'Miracle of St Thomas', but is more cautious about the interlude.[52] The much more recent *Oxford Dictionary of National Biography*, however, is very tentative about the poem, recording that: 'the chronicle of John Stone, a monk of Christ Church Priory, preserves a poem attributed (if uncertainly) to Banastre ...'.[53] Another very recent account, *The Biographical Dictionary of English Court Musicians 1485–1714* appears to have no doubts that Banaster was the author of the poem, but is more uncertain of the interlude.[54] And finally the *New Grove Dictionary* (revised 1981) seems certain about the poem but does not mention even the possibility of an interlude.[55]

The poem itself, which has the repeated refrain of 'Novis fulget Thomas miraculis' (which roughly translates as 'Thomas shines through new miracles'), has a rather apocalyptic air to it. It appears to tell the story of a storm on 7 July which was caused by the fiend, and which almost destroyed the ships of pilgrims sailing to the shrine of St Thomas in Canterbury.

---

[48]　　Wallace, *Evolution of the English Drama*, p. 24; Warton, *History of English Poetry*, p. 132.

[49]　　Wallace, *Evolution of the English Drama*, p. 25.

[50]　　Wright, *Tales from the Decameron*, p. xx.

[51]　　Wright, *Tales from the Decameron*, p. xx.

[52]　　*DNB*, vol. 2, p. 1025.

[53]　　*ODNB*, at www. oxforddnb. com/ view/ printable/1266.

[54]　　*The Biographical Dictionary of English Court Musicians 1485–1714*, compiled by Andrew Ashbee and David Lascocki assisted by Peter Holman and Fiona Kisby, 2 vols, vol. 1 (Aldershot, Ashgate, 1998), pp. 61–2.

[55]　　*The New Grove Dictionary of Music and Musicians*, ed. by Stanley Sadie, 20 vols (London, Macmillan, 1977–2001), vol. 2, p. 619.

Upon the see suche tempest ther felle
Ther with Sathan apperyd in figure
As a dragon with fyry flamys of helle
On the watyr brennyng a long leysur
The shippys to wracke, unnethe might endur
Withoutyn fayle, trew it was and is
Novis fulget Thomas miraculis.[56]

According to the poem it was the pilgrims' shouts – 'With dredefull noyse on Seynt Thomas thei cride' – which summoned St Thomas who was 'seyne be the shippis side / As a bisshop …'.[57] After which the storm abated, 'Sathan he fled', and, after resting for the night, all the pilgrims, unharmed, were able to finish their journey to Canterbury.[58]

The context in which this poem survives is interesting. Inserted into John Stone's chronicle of Christ Church Priory, Canterbury, amongst records of the year 1467–68, it sits between several entries which report various masses being held at the Chapel of St Thomas. Also worth mentioning is that in the record for subsequent days, there is a report of a flood in the crypt which surrounded the tomb of St Thomas.[59] One piece of circumstantial evidence which seems to add weight to the idea that Banaster was the author of the St Thomas poem concerns the date of the festival of the translation of St Thomas. When seen in conjunction with one of Banaster's musical compositions *O Maria et Elizabeth*, which I discuss below, there appears to be an interesting coincidence. *O Maria* marks the biblical festival of the Visitation (of Mary mother of Jesus to Elizabeth mother of John the Baptist). The Visitation was a newly formalised feast day in the second half of the fifteenth century, celebrated on 2 July. It therefore interfered with the octave for the celebration of the Translation of St Thomas, 7 July. There was some concern surrounding this, which involved letters being written by members of the English royalty to the pope.[60] Of course it may be purely coincidental that two of the surviving pieces of evidence connected with Gilbert Banaster celebrate a festival which falls in the five days between 2 and 7 July, but perhaps he actually had a specific interest in this time of year, and its holy festivals. As a resident in Kent, albeit the northern part, perhaps he felt a special allegiance to that most famous of Kentish saints' shrines at Canterbury Cathedral.

---

[56]   Wright, *Tales from the Decameron*, p. xx, Stanza 2. I am grateful to Bjorn Weiler for his suggestions about the Latin text in this and subsequent extracts.

[57]   Wright, *Tales from the Decameron*, p. xx, Stanza 3, line 4, and Stanza 3, ll. 5–6 respectively.

[58]   Wright, *Tales from the Decameron*, p. xx, Stanza 4, l. 2.

[59]   *Christ Church, Canterbury: The Chronicle of John Stone, Monk of Christ Church 1415–1471*, ed. by William George Searle, Cambridge Antiquarian Society (Deighton, Bell & Co., 1902), pp. 78–81.

[60]   R.W. Pfaff, *New Liturgical Feasts in Later Medieval England* (Oxford, Clarendon Press, 1970), pp. 47–8.

Banaster's Musical Compositions

Four of Gilbert Banaster's musical compositions survive in three different manuscripts each of which is now housed in a different library: British Library Additional Manuscript 5465; Cambridge, Magdalene College Pepys Manuscript 1236; and Eton College Manuscript 178. These are three of the most famous surviving English music books from the Tudor period. Not many English music books survive from this date, one reason for this may be that there were never very many large music books, known as 'choirbooks', made, perhaps because of the cost of producing them.[61] Banaster's compositions in these three books show that he composed across a range of different styles and types of music, from the devotional to the secular and political; from the traditional carol form to what was at the time a very modern polyphonic.

Magdalene Pepys 1236

Two pieces by Banaster survive in this manuscript. They are a setting of the hymn *Exsultet Caelum Laudibus* and a two-voice Mass respond *Alleluia: Laudate Pueri*. The manuscript has been described as a 'commonplace book', it is in its original binding and was probably written in England, very possibly at Canterbury Cathedral Priory.[62] Its contents are primarily devotional and it appears to constitute a 'handbook' of music for the mass and the office of the particular liturgical form known as the Salisbury Use. It contains various antiphons, litanies, lamentations, canticles versicles and so on. Its 130 folios are made from both parchment and paper and it is apparently written in a single hand throughout (apart from some marginal annotations and additions which I discuss below). This is thought to be a unique book amongst English music collections of the pre-reformation period because it is a personal collection of music, perhaps 'compiled by an enthusiast'.[63] Its rather small format (it measures 181mm by 127mm with the written area being 152mm by 108mm), and the inclusion of various non musical material tends to corroborate this.

Pepys 1236 was probably compiled over the decade c.1465–75. Most of the compositions are anonymous, but sixteen pieces are attributed to eight named composers: six to John Tuder, two each to Gilbert Banaster, William Corbrond and Sir William Hawte; and one each to John Nesbet, [John] Garnesey, Walter Frye and [?] Fowler.[64] The music itself includes pieces from around forty years before

---

[61]   John Stevens, *Music and Poetry in the Early Tudor Court*, Cambridge Studies in Music (Cambridge, London, New York &c., CUP), p. 8.

[62]   This description is primarily taken from Iain Fenlon (ed.), *Cambridge Music Manuscripts 900–1700* (Cambridge, CUP 1982), pp. 111–114.

[63]   Fenlon, *Cambridge Music Manuscripts*, p. 111.

[64]   Fenlon, *Cambridge Music Manuscripts*, p. 112.

this, with some pieces employing what would have been a modern continental style with the contra-tenor going below the tenor to create authentic cadences, and generally smoother part-writing, while others employed a more traditional 'parallel sixth-chord' style of widely varying quality.[65] It has been suggested that the manuscript's music covers a range of styles which represent the 'transitions taking place in fifteenth-century music'.[66] It may have been compiled by a clerk who had connections with Canterbury Cathedral Priory, 'most particularly to the Chapel of the Almonry of Christ Church Canterbury'. As well as the chapel the almonry buildings housed a boarding school for a team of eight boys whose principal service was as the singing boys of the Lady Chapel choir of the Cathedral. Some of the contents of this book, such as the inclusion of a number of settings for the feast of St Nicholas, appear to reflect use by this choir.[67]

The Fayrfax Manuscript: My Feerfull Dreme

Gilbert Banaster's carol *My Feerfull Dreme* survives in one version in a manuscript compilation of music containing the works of ten late Medieval composers including William Cornysh, John Tuder and Robert Fayrfax.[68] *My Feerfull Dreme* is Banaster's only composition extant in the Fayrfax Manuscript. The date of this book is uncertain although it was almost certainly produced after the death of Banaster, probably around 1500. This collection is known as 'The Fayrfax Manuscript' because it was owned by the Fayrfax family in the early seventeenth century.[69] It is a large book measuring 29cm by 7cm and its pages are vellum, apart from the missing folios which have been substituted with paper leaves.

Eton Choirbook: O Maria et Elizabeth

Frank Harrison's description of the Eton Choirbook in *Musica Britannica* indicates that this book, which measures 60cm by 44cm, is described in the chapel inventory of 1531 as a 'grete ledger of prick song'. The staves are about 1.75 cm high and each note about 0.5cm high so that it is quite possible for a choir of twenty or so to sing from the book together. Among the expenses of the chapel in the Audit Roll for 1497–98 is an item recording the payment of 11s 6d for two iron braces to support a book given by Hugh France, a fellow of the college. It is possible that this was the new choirbook for which no payment is recorded in the surviving

---

[65]   Fenlon, *Cambridge Music Manuscripts*, p. 114; Sydney Robinson Charles, 'The Provenance and Date of the Pepys MS1236', *Musica Disciplina* (1962): 57–71, p. 63.

[66]   Charles, 'Pepys MS1236', 57, 63.

[67]   Fenlon, *Cambridge Music Manuscripts*, p. 114.

[68]   BL Add MS 5465, fols 77v–82r.

[69]   Stevens, *Music and Poetry*, p. 351.

accounts.[70] It has recently been shown that the likely date of production of Banaster's song is 1486.[71]

The Material Nature and Layout of the Manuscripts

The layout of the settings of music and words in these three different manuscripts indicates something of how they were used. For the two large books, Fayrfax and Eton, it is probably fairly safe to assume they were intended for use as single copies around which the several part-singers might gather, each to read his own line. The form of these books contrasts with that of the Magdalene manuscript, the size of which points to its use as a personal collection. This is considered in more detail, below, in relation to thinking about how music by composers such as Gilbert Banaster became available to the wider community.

The traditional layout for what is known as the 'choirbook' form ensures that each of the parts is visible simultaneously. Each part is represented separately, rather than in separate 'part books' as later became the fashion, but all on a single 'opening'.[72] This is otherwise called *cantus collateralis*.[73] If the song is longer than one 'opening', therefore, as is *My Feerfull Dreme*, all the singers are ready to turn the page together, and should there be more than one book containing this song at the same time, it would probably be designed such that all the books turned the page at the same time. This would add a rather nice visual effect in a performance. It is generally thought that the large church manuscripts of this period and of this design were intended each to meet the needs of a group of singers standing together at a lectern, hence the name choirbook. The Fayrfax manuscript copies this prevailing mode of music-book production but is not on the scale of the church choirbooks and therefore probably 'only large enough for a small group of singers'.[74] The Eton Choirbook, by comparison, is altogether larger, and designed to be used by up to fifteen or sixteen singers. To help this veritable crowd of performers to see their lines, the scribe has employed red and black scripts to assist with the definition of the various parts. Evidence for the choirbook method of using the Fayrfax book is provided, in *My Feerfull Dreme*, by the fact that the

---

[70]   This description is largely taken from Frank Ll. Harrison, 'Preface', in *Musica Britannica* vol. 10 (revised reprint 1967), p. xvi; see also W. Barclay Squire, 'On an Early Sixteenth Century Manuscript of English Music in the Library of Eton College', *Archaeologia*, (1898): 1–14.

[71]   Magnus Williamson, 'Royal Image-Making', 267–8. See below.

[72]   Stevens, *Music and Poetry*, p. 6; see also W. Barclay Squire, 'An Early Sixteenth Century Manuscript', p. 1.

[73]   Dom Anselm Hughes, 'An Introduction to Fayrfax', in *Musica Disciplina*, vol. 6 (1952): 83–104, p. 90; also, John Milsom, 'Music', in Lotte Hellinga and J.B. Trapp (eds), *The Cambridge History of the Book in Britain*, vol. 3, '1400–1557'(Cambridge, CUP, 1999), p. 544.

[74]   Stevens, *Music and Poetry*, p. 6; Hughes, 'Introduction', p. 90.

scribe appears to have made an active effort to squeeze the three parts for each verse onto each of the four double page spreads that the verses of this song occupy.

Despite all the opportunities that modern technology provides for reproducing these precious books in other formats, nothing can replace looking at the actual book when trying to imagine how the object was used, and how, therefore, the music within it was sung and performed. Nothing, also, can replace looking at the actual book for invoking an appropriate amount of uncertainty concerning the past use of the object.[75] Although it is possible to deduce those issues of use which relate to layout from a microfilm, the black and white reproduction loses the rubrications, as for example on the '*ut supra*' phrases in Fayrfax which indicate a return to the refrain. And although the page size can be seen on the microfilm, seeing the actual book is much more evocative of imagining the impressive appearance of these large tomes (and also their weight), as they are held open before the assembled musicians.

My Feerfull Dreme [see FIG. 2.1]

This carol is centred on the events of the Passion. Like many other Medieval devotional poems, the words focus on the suffering of Mary, 'maydyn' and mother of Christ. The poem's four verses tell a story which begins with Christ carrying his cross to Calvary and ends with the moment that he calls out 'Eloi, Eloi ...' on the point of death ('Hely Hely' in the Medieval poem). It is a heart-rending story, as many others of this type are. The suffering of Mary watching the painful crucifixion of her son is described in detail; as is the torturous strain of the ordeal on the 'inmortall' body of Christ himself. The details of their anguish are made vivid by relating the violence of the occasion, the physicality of their reactions to it, and the emotional turmoil of anger and 'motherly pity' (moderly pete) it causes for Mary. The subject matter and tone of this poem place it as expressive of the Medieval tradition known as 'affective piety – a form of religious expression which involved the worshipper in a deep emotional engagement with the religious subject.

The story is told by an observer who is in fact the dreamer experiencing the 'fearful dream'. It is tempting to think of this dreamer as Gilbert Banaster himself, despite him probably not being the original writer of these words – although the fact that he spent the time setting the words to music does give some license to equate the dreamer with him, at least in respect of this particular version of the poem. The observer's telling of this horrible story provides a commentary on the reactions of the dreamer to what he has seen, or is seeing. The observer also recounts the feelings of Mary, as well as retelling words spoken by Mary, John, and Christ. In the first verse, for example, it is the dreamer's emotions that we are

---

[75] On this subject, see John Stevens' rather poetic opening paragraph in *Music and Poetry* (p. 1). A facsimile book edition may, however, go some way towards providing the same effect.

told about; the dreamer is the 'I' of 'Myn hart can yern and mylt'. The dreamer is feeling anguish particularly in relation to his observation of Mary's sufferings. In the second verse, the dreamer describes to us Mary's pale and trembling physical condition in the face of the horror of watching her child die, and he also reports on Mary's accusation that it was 'for myne offence' that her son was 'betraide'. Also in this second verse the dreamer directly reports something that Mary said to him ('yet thou are unkynd, which sleith myn hert') which can only enhance the feelings of guilt for both dreamer and reader. In the fourth verse, our dreamer reports a dialogue between John and Mary. John asks her why she is so afraid of her son's death when she knows that he is 'inmortall'. The fifth verse returns to the dreamer's narration of the events of the Crucifixion, particularly the physical violence of the nailing of Christ's hands and feet, the rough way in which the cross was placed in the mortars and, in effect, the breaking of this human body – sinews and veins. This verse ends with the dreamer reporting Christ's 'lamentable' cry, the weeping of Mary, and finally his awakening from the dream 'sore aghast'.

So far I have been discussing the *words* of *My Feerfull Dreme*. This, of course, is only half the story especially as the music is the aspect of this carol which is more definitely attributable to Banaster. The term 'carol' is used here to describe a particular form of music. A carol is a song which has a refrain (called the 'burden') which is repeated between each of a number of verses. The carol form was used, popularly, in Medieval music for songs relating to a number of different kinds of themes such as various devotional festivals (including the Passion, Christmas) and also more secular approaches to the theme of love.[76] Such carols are thought to have been characterised by their vigour and direct simple language. The carols of the Fayrfax manuscript, including Banaster's, focus on the Passion to the exclusion of other themes. These carols are what have been described as 'clerical carols' and are different from those carols described as 'popular' and characterised as having a 'rough and direct' manner combining a 'warmth of human feeling with a matter-of-factness and a sense of wonder'.[77] Rather, the ascription of 'clerical', relates to their ornate musical form and the ways that they 'dwell with dramatic intensity on the spiritual and physical anguish of the Passion'.[78] With reference to the transmission and reception of these musical forms, I would suggest that the distinctions are probably not entirely clear-cut.

> My feerfull dreme nevyr forgete can I:
> Methought a maydynys childe causless shulde dye.
>
> To Calvery he bare his cross with doulfull payne,
> And theruppon straynyd he was in every vayne;
> A crowne of thorne as nedill sharpe shyfft in his brayne;

---

[76] Stevens, *Music and Poetry*, p. 8.
[77] Stevens, *Music and Poetry*, p. 10.
[78] Stevens, *Music and Poetry*, p. 10.

His modir dere tendirly wept and cowde not refrayne.
>Myn hart can yerne and mylt
>When I sawe hym so spilt,
>Alas, all for my gilt,

Tho I wept and sore did complayne
To se the sharpe swerde of sorow smert,
Hough it thirlyd her thoroughoute the hart,
So ripe and endles was her payne.

His grevious deth and her morenyng grevid me sore;
With pale visage tremlyng she stode her child before,
Beholdyng ther his lymmys she stode her child before,
Beholdyng ther his lymmys all to-rent and tore,
That with dispaire for feer and dred I was nere forlore.
>For myne offence, she said,
>Her Son was so betraide,
>With wondis sore araid,

Me unto grace for to restore:
'Yet thou are unkynd, which slieth myn hert,'
Wherewith she fell downe with paynys so smert;
Unneth on worde cowde she speke more.

Saynt Jhon than said, 'Feere not, Mary; his paynys all
He willfully doth suffir for love speciall
He hath to man, to make hym fre that now is thrall.'
'O frend', she said, 'I am sure he is inmortall.'
>'Why than so depe morne ye?'
>'Of moderly pete
>I must nedis wofull be,

As a woman terrestriall
Is by nature constraynyd to smert,
And yet verely I know in myn hart
From deth to lyff he aryse shall.'

Unto the fross, handes and feete, nailid he was;
Full boistusly in the mortess he was downe cast;
His vaynys all and synowis to-raff and brast;
The erth quakyd, the son was dark, whos lyght was past,
>When he lamentable
>Cried, 'Hely, hely, hely!'
>His moder rufully

Wepyng and wrang her handes fast.
Uppon her he cast his dedly loke,
Wherwith sodenly anon I awoke,
And of my dreme was sore aghast.

Figure 2.1 *My Ferefull Dreme*

Song or Poem?

There are some important differences between the appearance of the Medieval version of *My Feerfull Dreme* on a page (or more correctly a double page) of the music manuscript and the way that the poem from that music is reproduced in modern print, as given here. The song has repeated phrases from the poem, whilst each line appears only once in the poem text. The printed poem text prioritises the poem as a piece of writing with particular and fairly regular rhythmic shape. The effect of the three-part song, however, is such that there are repetitions of these lines. A comparison of these two formats emphasises some important factors which must be addressed if we are to become closer to imagining the late Medieval experience of hearing this song.

Although it is possible to get a general impression of the way a setting works, reading the Medieval notation is a challenge for anyone but the musicologist who is also a specialist in Medieval music. Transcription into modern notation therefore provides essential access to the experience of this music.[79] Seeing it in modern score format provides two striking impressions immediately. These are: the significance of the repetitions occurring over certain key phrases caused by the different moments that the three parts reach the poem's phrases (polyphonic elements), and the emphasis which the opening refrain and chorus (the burden) gives to the word 'die'. A recording of this song, now out of print, also enables the modern listener to imagine the powerful effect of this carol.[80]

'Die' is the last word of the opening refrain. The sustained 'melisma' by all three parts on this word has a significant effect which emphatically sets up the carol's focus on the Passion of Christ. In the verses, the three voice parts are also used to emphasise themes which have particular affective power. This is done by resting one of the parts and then reintroducing it to create emphasis. For example, in the third line of each verse the mid-pitched alto, which controls much of the 'tune' elsewhere, rests and the highest part, treble, and the lowest part, bass, take the words. So in the first verse, the line 'A crown of thorn as needle sharp' is sung by treble and bass, and alto rejoins at 'shift in his brain'. In the second verse, the treble and bass line 'Beholding there his limmes all' is rejoined by alto at 'to rent and tore'. Similarly in the third verse the two parts singing 'He hath to man, to make him free' are rejoined by the alto at 'that now is thrall'; and in the fourth verse 'His veines all and sinews' is rejoined by the alto at 'to raff and brast'.[81] All of these alterations between two and three parts occur, significantly, across a single line in the poem. In verses one, two and four, this third line is concerned with describing the painful physical experience for Jesus of the crucifixion. The reintroduction of the alto part at the second half of this line intensifies this

---

79   'Early Tudor Songs and Carols', *Musica Britannica*, 36, ed. by John Stevens (1975): 110–113.

80   Track 6, 'My Fearfull Dream', version by Bruno Turner, in *Tears and Lamentations*, Pro Cantione Antiqua (Quicksilva, repr. 1995).

81   Stevens, 'Early Tudor Songs and Carols', pp. 110 and 112.

description of the physical pain. The 'Pro Cantione Antiqua' recording makes much of this at verse four. The burden also uses this device. In the repeat of the 'Me thought a maiden's child' phrase, the alto rests as treble and bass sing the first of the two 'causeless should die' phrases, the alto rejoins with the repeat of 'causeless should die', the 'die' of which phrase being the final word of the burden with its extended melismatic emphasis on this word.

Another significant musical effect appears to be the transition to a more 'minor' sound at the eighth line of the verse. This is perhaps intended to herald the four lines which form the closure of the eleven-line verses, rather than to emphasise the specific theme of line eight. It does form a marked transition, especially to modern ears, and it also leaves scope for the final word of the verse to revert to a more 'major' sound, although this does not provide an easy transition back to the refrain, which also sounds like a marked change of key.

The poem itself, being in the tradition of affective piety which seeks to call the reader into painful reflections on the Passion of Christ, is intense. But it is important to stress that in this setting produced by Gilbert Banaster this is considerably intensified. He almost certainly did not write the poem, but in setting it to music he did fully engage in the Medieval tradition of affectivity, skilfully setting the words to maximise the painful effect of reflection on Christ's Passion.

O Maria et Elizabeth

This motet is in the form of an antiphon, in honour of the Virgin Mary. It is written in the traditional language of late Medieval worship, Latin, and is in five parts. *O Maria et Elizabeth* follows the format of many fifteenth-century antiphon texts where the first half is addressed to a saint (often the Virgin Mary) identifying him or her and praising his or her miraculous powers, and the second half is an invocation of that saint asking for his or her help in the search for salvation.[82] Banaster's antiphon is actually slightly different from this simple generic model. Rather than being addressed to one saint, this piece is addressed to both Elizabeth and Mary; and the first half vigorously celebrates the pregnancies of these two most important childbearing female saints. The second half departs more obviously from the religious agenda of many such antiphons because rather than continuing with the praise of, and invocation to, the saints, the praise appears instead to be for more secular authorities. So, while Mary the Virgin is invoked at the beginning of this second section of the antiphon, the Elizabeth of the earlier section is dropped. The petition to Mary specifically mentions the rightfulness of her position next to her Son. And this mention of the Son appears to make the necessary connection to the following request which is 'Protect, we beseech you, the devout champion our king N. Give copious grace whereby he might reign for a long time with clemency and justice'.

---

[82]   See Williamson, 'Royal Image-Making', pp. 244–5.

The remainder of the antiphon is a rather stirring incitement of the potential power of   this unnamed king, 'N'. This is a king who will have 'triumphant valour', 'subdue his raging enemies under a just yoke', and 'increase our prosperity'. The remainder of the antiphon then confirms the potency and legitimacy of the lineage which the king N is born into by looking forward to its continuation, beyond what has now become the 'long-lived father's' reign to the descendents of this line. It also cements its message by referring to this lineage's incumbents of the throne before N, his 'father', their 'ancestors', their 'famous forbears'.

As Magnus Williamson has shown, it is likely that Banaster wrote this piece to celebrate the pregnancy of Queen Elizabeth of York, in 1486, with the Prince Arthur. The feast of the visitation, a feast day only established in the last quarter of the fifteenth century, is celebrated on 2 July which would have been the mid-term of Elizabeth's pregnancy.[83] It seems likely that Banaster carefully interwove the themes of visitation with the political, even propagandist, concerns with the royal lineage of the Tudors. Williamson's analysis, for example, of the musical sources for the *cantus firmus* (in effect, the part which takes the tune) has shown the self conscious ways that Banaster created a 'multitextual synthesis' of words and music.[84] Banaster used music from a response known as *Regnum mundi* (Ruler of the world), which was traditionally used on festivals such as the Consecration of Virgins. This respond uses words from Psalm 45 which contains a number of themes relevant to the propagandising tendencies of *Maria et Elizabeth*. This includes, for example, themes of regal divinity, victory over the king's enemies, a royal wedding, the prospect of sons, and the promise of future glory.[85]

Banaster's skills in the production of subtle intertextual references that combine religious moments with political propaganda may not have been equalled by his skills in the production of the musical setting – it has been suggested that the polyphony of his motet was only a partial success in extended five-part writing. One reason for this may be that Banaster was working with an early example of a form which was only perfected by the next generation of composers.[86] He was perhaps, in other words, working at the cutting edge of a new musical style. By contrast, Banaster's earlier piece, *My Feerful Dreme*, uses a less ambitious musical style in terms of its technical complexity.

There is probably a connection between the different musical forms Banaster used for each setting and the forms of the texts. *My Feerfull Dreme* is a poem text of relatively short lines with a strongly present metre and rhythm of their own. This text therefore has a regular shape which lends itself to the carol form and to syllabic stresses. *O Maria et Elizabeth*, on the other hand, is in prose and lacks the same regularity of structure. There are, nevertheless, some stylistic similarities

---

83   Williamson, 'Royal Image-Making', p. 267–8.
84   Williamson, 'Royal Image-Making', p. 249.
85   Williamson, 'Royal Image-Making', p. 251.
86   Williamson, 'Royal Image-Making', p. 256–7.

between the two (he uses 'cellular imitation', 'syncopation', 'occasional homophonic writing' in both).[87] The *New Grove Dictionary* suggests that the syllabic element is notable in *O Maria* and was probably used because the text is rather long and unfamiliar.[88] This tends to suggest that even when writing in these different musical styles of differing difficulty and using different types of written text, Banaster was also in possession of a certain, personal, sense of compositional style.

Why Did Gilbert Banaster Write This Motet?
There may be specific reasons why Banaster produced the motet *O Maria et Elizabeth* at this time. The work was probably commissioned by one of the members of the royal dynasty that this song 'praises', possibly Elizabeth of York herself, her mother Margaret Beaufort, or Elizabeth's grandmother Elizabeth Woodville.[89] As a servant of the royal household, Banaster was perhaps under the pressure of patronage to produce a celebration of the legitimacy of this royal dynasty and in order for this piece of music to be used at the court, and perhaps more publicly, he may have thought it wise to add what is essentially a secular celebration of royalty onto a piece suitable for use in a devotional context. Or it may be that Banaster did not particularly wish to compose a piece with a non-religious focus and so he might actually have felt better about producing the propaganda desired by his patrons if he wrapped it in a devotional parcel.[90]

Issues of Style and Taste

The two very different musical compositions of Banaster that I have discussed here evoke some interesting questions about his attitudes to style, and his taste. Whether or not Banaster wrote the words for these musical compositions, it seems fairly safe to say that he considered, carefully, the relation of particular words and textual phrases to his musical settings.

The relation of old and new forms in these settings is worthy of comment. It is interesting to ask how self conscious Gilbert Banaster was being about his uses of old and new forms. The carol form of *My Feerfull Dreme* is essentially a traditional (old) form of music – even if Banaster's particular ('clerical'), use of it differs from the simpler, perhaps more vulgar, popular carol. It is interesting to note in this context, then, that the *New Grove Dictionary* of Music proposes that 'the carol is perhaps the most interesting piece because it displays a more modern

---

87   Williamson, 'Royal Image-Making', p. 257.
88   *New Grove*, vol. 2, p. 619.
89   Williamson, 'Royal Image-Making', pp. 270–271.
90   See Williamson, 'Royal Image-Making', p. 255 for a speculation on the possibility that Banaster 'disclaimed' any authorship of the words to this composition.

syllabic style with much use of imitation'.[91] *O Maria et Elizabeth* adds another dimension to this issue. The fact that Banaster uses the theme of the Visitation for this antiphon strongly indicates that he was not afraid of newness because the feast only became an official festival day around the years 1475–80.[92] Alongside a technically modern form of polyphony, he also used what may be thought of as either a clumsy or archaic compositional technique for *O Maria*, which is indicated by 'the prevalence of direct or scarcely avoided consecutive fifths and octaves'.[93] As Williamson points out, he does not use this technique in *My Feerfull Dreme*. Perhaps it was because of technical difficulties that Banaster resorted to a clumsy or archaic form for the more complicated *O Maria* and used a modern syllabic form for the simpler *My Feerfull Dreme*.[94]

But, on further examination it seems interesting to posit that Banaster was actually being very self aware in his uses of form in these compositions because in each he appears to mix an old form with a new technique. In the carol, the poetic form and structure is old but the music has modern elements, whereas in the antiphonal motet, the music uses archaic forms for the celebration of a feast day which is relatively new, whilst also using some modern syllabic techniques. Such self-consciousness by Banaster in his usages of old and new style might add to the impression of his mode of adapting the 'Sismond' story from the *Decameron*. As discussed above, he appears to have intentionally altered the emphasis in his poetic version by subtle changes to key symbolic aspects like the crying episode. In doing this, he may have been deliberately adapting the style for an English version, which reflected specific tensions and moral dilemmas in the changes and turmoils of fifteenth-century England. And indeed, perhaps Banaster did copy a Chaucerian style, not only because he admired the great English writer so much, but perhaps in the face of the many changes of the fifteenth century, he wished to write in a quintessentially Medieval style.

But why would Banaster have wished to produce this motet with archaic forms? Is there something about the grandness of its secular mood and claims which was requiring of a grand style? Perhaps political legitimisation required the grandeur of an older style. It is perhaps essential to the activity of legitimating a new dynasty that the cultural form used to purvey this is not itself overtly symbolic of newness. This might make such a dynasty appear newfangled and therefore lacking in strength and the weight of power which rests on tradition. I would suggest that a mixture of old and new forms is very important for the process of legitimisation and naturalisation. Old cultural forms in text or music may therefore be appropriated in order to promulgate something new. So, the 'audaciously conceived' uses of intertextual references in the text of *O Maria* are transmitted

---

[91] *New Grove*, vol. 2, p. 619.

[92] Pfaff, *New Liturgical Feasts*, pp. 47–8; Williamson, 'Royal Image-Making', p. 245–6.

[93] Williamson, 'Royal Image-Making', p. 257.

[94] Williamson, 'Royal Image-Making', pp. 257–8.

through an archaic musical sound.[95] In the case of *O Maria*, this necessary mixing of the old with the new is perhaps especially resonant given that the celebration of the Visitation may have been fairly new at this time. So if the new things are considered together (royal lineage, Visitation festival, impending birth of a child), something old and stable might be needed to counteract all this newness and give an impression of the established strength (and therefore importance, sturdiness, reliability, continuity, power, and trustworthy-ness of the Tudor royal lineage).

Inferring from the Musical Evidence

The evidence provided by the various pieces of music composed by Banaster prompt some questions about other people's experiences and perceptions of his music during his life as well as soon after his death. What does the inclusion of Banaster's music by the personal collector of the Magdalene manuscript indicate about late fifteenth-century attitudes to such music? What does the very late fifteenth or early sixteenth-century copying of Banaster's antiphon into the Eton Book indicate about early attitudes to his music at this date? These questions and any answers to them do not directly retell the events of Gilbert Banaster's life. However, investigating these wider issues of perception and experience has implications for understanding some of the feelings that Banaster may have held concerning his own work, as well as helping to evince what he experienced of other people's attitudes to him. In asking these types of questions about the broader contexts of the reception of an individual's work, this exploration of Gilbert Banaster enters into one of those areas of reconstruction where there is a process of extrapolation back from material evidence relevant to the context of that person's life in order to enhance our sense of that individual's experiences, perceptions and attitudes. This may in turn help with the search for that person's intentions in the production of these creative outputs.

The provenances and contexts of production for two of the music books seem to offer some particular possibilities for this sort of reconstruction. For the Eton Choirbook there is an interesting trail to follow associated with the likely date of its production, some fifteen years after Banaster's death and probably therefore sixteen or seventeen years after *O Maria et Elizabeth* was first produced. For the Magdalene manuscript, its likely identity as a personal collection poses a number of questions, concerning the relationships between Banaster's compositions and the other works copied into this book, which may be used to furnish a sense of how at least one individual thought of Banaster's works.

The Eton Choirbook was almost certainly designed for performances of music by Eton choristers in the public space of the nave of the Chapel.[96] It was probably produced between about 1498 and 1502, all the entries being copied in at the same

---

95   Williamson, 'Royal Image-Making', p. 256.
96   Williamson, 'Royal Image-Making', pp. 271–2.

time. Some of the earliest compositions in the book, such as those of Banaster, were therefore over a decade old when it was compiled, whereas the compositions of the later composers, such as William Cornysh, were very new. There are two issues concerning Gilbert Banaster's composition in that book which seem particularly interesting in this context: the first concerns the style of his music; the second concerns the political content of the words. If, as has been suggested, the musical style of Banaster's motet was becoming outmoded by the date it was copied into the Eton Choirbook, then this tends to suggest that these choristers at least were not overly bothered by the thought of performing old-fashioned music. I proposed earlier that Banaster may have been very self-conscious about the mixtures of old and new style for this composition, especially given its politically propagandising tone in the legitimisation of the Tudor dynasty. I suggested that Banaster may have used the archaic form in the music of *O Maria* in order to provide an overall effect which balanced a sense of old established tradition with an attempt to legitimate a new dynasty. The continued use of *O Maria*, and what after another fifteen years must have sounded like an even more outmoded form of musical style, tends to suggest either that the issue of legitimisation was still sufficiently new that Banaster's old style was still in operation as a counterbalance to this propaganda, or that the motet had lost its immediate propagandising message when it was transcribed into the Eton Choirbook. In fact the older tunes in the Eton Choirbook may have been copied with a similar 'spirit of respect and nostalgia' which found Elizabethans copying 'obsolete' catholic music into their books.[97]

The issue of the words adds further to this conundrum about attitudes to Banaster's composition, and its meaning. The only version we have of *O Maria* is from the Eton Choirbook, and it is in this version that the king is given the name 'N'. If the Eton book was produced before the death of Prince Arthur in April 1502, and the composition was seen in propagandising terms, it seems strange that the scribe did not put the name of Arthur into the text, as this would make a rather more potent piece of propaganda than simply 'N'. If, on the other hand, Banaster's song was copied into the Eton book after 1502, even an indirect reference to Prince Arthur would have been insensitive. It also seems strange to think of the Eton choristers celebrating the impending birth of a prince, in the early sixteenth century, when the future Henry VIII was already flourishing. Assuming the antiphon did have this propagandising intention and meaning when it was written and performed, in 1486, there is a question mark over the longevity of that meaning. In other words, did *O Maria et Elizabeth* have a different meaning which was less precisely tied to one royal pregnancy by the time it reached the Eton Choirbook, and the Eton choir?

All of which morass of possibilities tends to suggest that when Banaster's composition of *O Maria et Elizabeth* was copied into the Eton Choirbook some time in the very early sixteenth century, it was not for the detailed meaning of its

---

97   Milsom, 'Music', p. 545.

propagandising words that it was included. And this seems to imply that it was something about Banaster's musical setting which was the reason for its inclusion in the book, and we can infer from this that Banaster's style of music was still very much appreciated over a decade after his death. This may be because it sounded archaic (inspiring nostalgic appreciation), because it sounded good, was a useful training exercise for choristers, or perhaps a combination of these factors.

The Magdalene manuscript raises a different set of issues which nevertheless add to our understanding of the relationships between Banaster's intentions for his music and the reception of that music near or soon after the time when he was alive. In any discussion which extrapolates from the contents of a 'commonplace book' it is important to remember that fifteenth-century attitudes to books were a little different from twenty-first-century attitudes – and in this case it is important to consider that just because particular literary or musical compositions have been written into one book does not mean that the copyist considered these entries to be intrinsically connected. The contents of Magdalene Pepys 1236, for example, have been described as a 'haphazardly' compiled private collection without any attempt at rational ordering or organization.[98] Perhaps it is preferable to think of the rationale for organisation as being different from a twenty-first-century one. So we can imagine the individual entries of a personally compiled commonplace book as indicative of one collector's sense of what constitutes a compendium of cultural artefacts; and indeed perhaps this collection may have been produced with specific occasions of use in mind.

Alongside the identification of this as a personal collection, it has also been suggested that the 'plain utilitarian format' indicates that it was intended for practical use.[99] The immediate site of its use in the late fifteenth century may well have been for singing service in the Almonry Chapel at the Priory and Convent of Canterbury Cathedral. On festivals when there was no school, the schoolboys attended services in the Almonry Chapel along with the two clerks and six secular priests who were maintained there on the revenues of Bredgar College and the chantry of King Edward I (established in the chapel since 1319–20). Together these people constituted a 'liturgical choir' obliged by the statutes of the chantry to observe the form of service known as 'Salisbury Use' not the 'Benedictine Use' of the monks. The book is very likely to have belonged to one of the clerks who had charge of the upbringing of the boys and who therefore used it as both a commonplace book and a repository of choice items of polyphonic and monophonic music; most of it being suitable, and some perhaps intended, for use at services in the chapel. The book may even have been specifically written with the choir of boys in mind. Evidence for this is found in the care taken by the scribe in forming his musical notation, 'adding Arabic numbers when alteration occurs in perfect time, and accidentals'; a simplification of the script for young singers which would have been unnecessary under the usual contemporary rules for

---

[98]   Fenlon, *Cambridge Music Manuscripts*, p. 114.
[99]   Charles, 'Pepys MS 1236', p. 70

writing notation. There is also further evidence provided by the fact that one of the settings appears in the Magdalene manuscript in a much simpler form than in the other contemporaneous version of this piece.[100] One further piece of evidence for this likely intended use of the Magdalene manuscript is its unusual preponderance (seven in all) of settings proper to the feast of St Nicholas, the patron saint of schoolboys, along with five monophonic blessings sung by a Boy Bishop who presided over church services on the feasts of St Nicholas or Holy Innocents.[101] Cathedral accounts show boy-bishop ceremonies annually celebrated by these boys, and it is likely therefore that they used the Magdalene manuscript for their music.[102]

Going beyond positing a likely intended use for this manuscript it has even been suggested that the identity of the compiler of this collection may be established as John Tuder, one of the composers whose works are represented in this volume.[103] John Tuder (together with another of the book's named composers John Hawte), was a Kentish gentleman. Tuder was a fairly influential figure in the borough of New Romney to the south of Canterbury. Whether or not he wrote this book – and it is an attractive idea given the provenance of this manuscript's use – John Tuder's compositions within the book establish him as a skilled amateur composer.[104] The inclusion of compositions by Gilbert Banaster in this book indicate that his works were very probably considered to be appropriate to the choir of boys described above. The presence of the two other Kentish gentlemen's works in the same book implies also that Banaster's music may well have been experienced by other people in this locality, perhaps in the local communities of Kent, such as New Romney. And if Gilbert Banaster did not write these two compositions for this kind of choir, they were nevertheless appropriated for this kind of usage during the time that he was alive.

Poetry in Magdalene Pepys 1236

By looking more closely at some of the other contents of this book it is possible to gain further insights into the kinds of texts which were considered – perhaps by John Tuder – to be appropriate companions to Banaster's compositions in the Magdalene manuscript. There are various fascinating entries in this manuscript which are not musical compositions. None of these other contents comment directly on Banaster's own life or on his works for that matter, but they do help to fill in the picture of the cultural context in which he was living and producing his music, and the contexts of belief and of textual production in which he lived.

---

[100]   Charles, 'Pepys MS 1236', p. 70. Another version is found in BL Eg. MS 3307.
[101]   Fenlon, *Cambridge Music Manuscripts*, p. 112.
[102]   Fenlon, *Cambridge Music Manuscripts*, p. 114.
[103]   Charles, 'Pepys MS 1236', p. 70.
[104]   Fenlon, *Cambridge Music Manuscripts*, p. 112.

There is way too much to talk about with regard to the content of the Magdalene manuscript, and its inclusion of observations on the use of powdered snake skin, auspicious days for bleeding and forecasting the weather, and a long version of the 'well-known' poem *Stans Puer ad Mensam* (a treatise on the upbringing of boys in socially acceptable and decorous behaviour) render this little book worthy of careful consideration in its own right. There is a little space here, however, to pause to consider some of this manuscript's devotional poetry and also to make a brief mention of a couple of later (probably sixteenth-century) annotations, which provide evidence that the book was being used by at least one other person who was not the original scribe – perhaps one of the schoolboys.

One rather enigmatic annotation appears to indicate something about the repetitive use of this book and the familiarity of that reader with its contents: in the end margin after the end of a setting to the Latin Gloria is written 'many times have I bene in'.[105] This might reflect the boredom of a schoolboy once again rehearsing the same Gloria. However, it could also be an unfinished entry which is seductive of over-interpretation (rather like the 'I can't go on' forged suicide note in Agatha Christie's *The Moving Finger*, torn from a memo which Miss Marple realises had originally continued with some fairly inconsequential information).

Towards the end of Magdalene Pepys 1236, the hand of the main scribe (perhaps John Tuder) has transcribed or invented a poem in English which appears to take the theme of old testament prophecies, addressed to the people of Jerusalem, concerning the coming of Christ.[106] There are three verses each of seven lines, or there should be – the third verse appears to have been cut short, or erased, and has only three lines, the last of which is very faint. Each of the three verses has been given a sort of title to the right of the poem text, in red ink; the first is called 'Jeremias', the second 'Ysayas' and the third 'David'. The mood of the poem is of an instruction (to the people of Jerusalem) to behold, or listen to, or believe, the prophecy of Christ's coming, as this will bring the hope of salvation. In a rougher and larger hand, taking up the space the David poem would have used if it had completed its seven lines, is a five-line annotation as follows:

On a crucifix
Why not the picture of our dying lord
As of a friend nor this nor that & adored
Does not the Eternal law command that thou
Shalt even as well forbeare to make us bowe [107]

The sentiment of this annotation is not entirely clear. Does it make some comment on the use of images, or icons, particularly the crucifix? Is it referring to the forbidding in the 'Eternal law' (Old Testament law perhaps) of the use of icons? It

---

[105] Magd Coll MS Pepys 1236, fol. 64r.
[106] Madg Coll MS Pepys 1236, fol. 127v.
[107] Magd Coll MS Pepys 1236, fol. 128r.

could be that this annotation was written into the book at a time when attitudes to traditional Medieval Catholic uses of imagery in worship were being criticised. It is a wonder that this book with its primarily devotional contents which are so expressive of the liturgical priorities of Medieval Catholicism survived the destructive zeal of the Reformation. It would be even more of a marvel if it had actually been in the hands, and under the pen, of an annotator who felt strongly about this.

The other poem I want to mention here is also fairly close to the end of the book and written in the main scribe's hand. It is 'macaronic' which means it is written in a mixture of languages – Latin and English in this case. It is quite long – seven verses with between ten and twelve lines in each verse, and its subject is an address to the Virgin Mary in praise of her. It begins:

> [R] egina Celi and Lady letare
> Lemyng sely & in place of lyght
> Quia quiem meruisti portare
> ye ben sett sempit'ne in his syght
> Resurexit as he sayde to the
> By miracle of his grete myght
> In to hevyn ascendyd w+ humanyte
> above the orders of angelys bryght
> Gloryouse lady gete us that ryght
> to the ryall mansyon unto be nome
> After the deth when we be done
> Maria virgo virgini[108]

> [Queen of Heaven and lady of joy
> Dear sweeting and in place of light
> As deserving mother of him
> you have been eternally set in his sight
> Risen as he said to thee
> By miracle of his great might
> Into heaven ascended with humanity
> Above the orders of angels bright
> Glorious lady get us that right
> To the royal mansion unto be set
> After death when we are sent
> Mary virgin of virgins]

Like *My Feerfull Dreme* this poem is representative of the Medieval tradition of affective piety, although it leans more towards one of the traditional form of affectivity which might be described as a kind of intensity of praise for the beauty and sweetness and extreme holiness of the Virgin, rather than one concerned with

---

[108]   Magd Coll MS Pepys 1236, fols 98v–99r. The 'R' of Regina is missing, and there appears to be a large space left as if it were to be an illuminated initial.

the bitter, sorrowful, and painful emotions of the Passion which *My Feerfull Dreme* represents. As a whole, the poem also runs, chronologically, through an important set of Christian events, from the annunciation of Christ which is mentioned in verse two ('Our holy lorde on the was hydde / by hyryng of an angeles horn'[109]), to his death in verse five ('Crist for us that jewys dedde kelle'[110]), to after the ascension in verse six ('As the splendaunt sonne syteth in space / so shewyth yo[r] symylytude mos glorius'[111]). This is a rather self-conscious composition which appears, like others of its type, to enjoy playing with words and sounds, across its macaronic range. For example verse five begins:

O dulcis diamonde deyt' damesell
d'na mu'di thow delyka dame [112]

[O sweet diamond dainty damsel
ruler of the world thou delicate dame]

In many ways it has nothing whatsoever to do with the life of Gilbert Banaster. But then again, it is strongly expressive of a tradition in Medieval Catholicism which Banaster himself also engaged with in the composition or setting of his carol, *My Feerfull Dreme*. As such, a glance at this poem helps to elaborate on the picture that is being built of Banaster's likely cultural – and in this case particularly his religious – sensibilities and tastes. Indeed it seems that Banaster may have been interested in enhancing the 'affective appeal' of his apparently more secular setting, *O Maria*: he may have employed the boy's voice in this story of the Visitation with the purpose of eliciting those notions of 'pre-pubescence and innocence' which were configured around the unbroken voice.[113] For all his potential to produce new forms of music which might be considered to anticipate the next generation of early Renaissance cultural interests, Banaster's devotional works tend to implicate him in the very traditional world of Medieval Catholic affective piety. A world which, as the annotator's query about iconoclasm might suggest, was already in transition and – shortly after Banaster's death – to be fundamentally altered.

---

[109]   Magd Coll MS Pepys 1236, fol. 99r. 'hyryng' is 'hearing'.

[110]   Magd Coll MS Pepys 1236, fol. 99v; 'dedde kelle' is probably a dialectically influenced spelling of 'did kill'.

[111]   Magd Coll MS Pepys 1236, fol. 99v.

[112]   O dulcis diamonde deyty damesell / domina mundi delykat dame.

[113]   Williamson, 'Royal Image-Making', p. 257, here discussing suggestions made by Christopher Page.

Chapter 4

Elizabeth Philip

Introduction

This chapter is concerned with Elizabeth Philip, a 'silkwoman' who was skilled in the production and styling of silk and other fabrics for garments, and who supplied materials and made costumes for the household of Henry VIII. I first came across her in what is known as the 'Revel Accounts', produced during the reign of Henry VIII, and with particular frequency during the years c. 1510–1530, as recorded by household staff.[1] It seems that this Tudor court and household was constantly engaged in celebratory displays of wealth and artistic prowess. Accounts for the painting of streamers and flags to festoon the royal vessels and ships leave no doubt that during the early decades of the sixteenth century, all the towns and villages along the Thames experienced the visual impact of the court's symbolic displays of its own might and military prowess.[2] The Revel Accounts, along with the accounts drawn up for jousts and other entertainments, give fairly detailed descriptions of the raw materials purchased in terms of the quality, place of production, and price. They also provide some wonderful descriptions of the styles of the costumes required for the particular types of characters which were involved in these sumptuous events.

The records associated with the various departments of the royal household which were involved with the storage and production of apparel and costume, such as the Wardrobe, give a fascinating glimpse into the involvement of otherwise unrecorded individuals (such as Elizabeth Philip), in the construction of the identity of this most excessive and sumptuous Tudor court. Unfortunately, however, there is never so much surviving evidence about the lives of these kinds of people as there is about those who were of higher status or of greater renown during their lifetimes, and this is particularly the case with women. But this should not prevent attempts to reconstruct aspects of these people's lives. The collection of biographies in *Medieval London Widows, 1300–1500*, for example, reconstructs the lives of a set of women who are otherwise lost to history but who have emerged from one specific source of evidence. Despite the fact that '[N]one of these sources tells us as much as Margaret Paston's letters or Margery Kempe's autobiography',

---

[1]   See for example NA E 36/227; and BL MS Eg 2605 fols 16v, 34v ff.
[2]   BL MS Stowe 146, fols 112r–113v, 124r–v.

attempts to follow these threads of evidence might, nevertheless, give us access to economic and personal elements in these women's lives.[3]

In the case of Elizabeth Philip, the royal household accounts provide not only some access to the role and skills of such women, but also an insight into one person's role in the machinery of skilled workers and makers who enabled and provided for Henry VIII's desires to consume and to display, as part of the process of constructing the myth of the English Tudor Dynasty. The lives of the numerous other women (and men) who are also named in these accounts, might also provide a profitable thread of evidence for understanding the importance of the humble producers, artisans, and servants who lay behind the façade of Tudor royal courts, households and their myth-making.[4]

Silk and Silk Workers in England

Silk work in England has already received the attention of scholars studying the work of women in fifteenth- and sixteenth- century England; this is partly because, in this period, silk work was primarily an occupation for women. A seminal essay on the subject of London silkwomen in the fifteenth century, for example, was written in 1933 by Marian Dale.[5] The work required to produce the decorative designs associated with silk apparel was very skilled. This is evident from the six to seven years required for an apprenticeship.[6] London also seems to have been an important English centre for silk work in the fifteenth and sixteenth centuries. Girls apprenticed to London silkwomen in this period came from some distance including Norfolk, Buckinghamshire, Lincolnshire, Warwickshire, Bristol and Northampton.[7] The apprentice agreements for silkwomen are much like the agreements made for the trades occupied by men. A list of the duties and responsibilities for each of the parties (the apprentice and the master or mistress) are set down. It was a silk apprentice's duty, therefore, to 'cherish' the interests of her master and mistress, not to 'waste' their goods or merchandise without permission, to 'behave well' and not to 'withdraw unlawfully' from their service.

---

[3]   Caroline M. Barron, 'Introduction: the Widow's World', in Caroline M. Barron and Anne F. Sutton (eds), *Medieval London Widows, 1300–1500* (London and Rio Grande, Hambledon, 1994), p. xvii.

[4]   A large-scale prosopographical survey of these subjects is needed.

[5]   See Marian K. Dale, 'London Silkwomen of the Fifteenth Century', *Economic History Review*, 1st Series, 4 (1933): 324–35, pp. 328–9; Anne F. Sutton and P.W. Hammond (eds), *The Coronation of Richard III: The Extant Documents* (Alan Sutton, Gloucester, 1983), pp. 65–6.

[6]   Dale, 'London Silkwomen', 325; she cites fifteenth-century examples of apprenticeship agreements: National Archive (Ancient Deeds) C 2314 and C 1176. See also NA C 146/1240 for a mid-sixteenth-century example.

[7]   Dale, 'London Silkwomen', 325; NA C 146/1240.

The master or mistress promised to 'teach, take charge of, and instruct' the apprentice, or 'cause her to be instructed'.[8]

Silkwomen made silk thread or twined silk from the raw silk imported from the Italian reelers in 'fardels' or 'papers'. The thread was produced by craftspeople called 'throwsters' and this was sold by the ounce or pound. The thrown thread was used to make small goods of the kind which Elizabeth Philip frequently provided to the royal household. These include 'corses', 'ribbons', 'tassels', 'fringes' and 'laces'.[9] Many of these goods were more like silk cords than the flat openwork which we associate with lace although the type of work now understood as 'lace' also became fashionable in the sixteenth century. The cords could be woven in with gold or silver thread. Venice and Lucca produced particularly prized gold thread, but Cyprus thread was another type which was slightly cheaper and made of gilded animal membrane. The 'Gold of Venice' or Venice Gold often mentioned in the Revel Accounts and provided by Elizabeth Philip is probably this sort of woven cord work.[10]

The importance of silk trading and working, the value of the products and the relatively high regard of the women involved in this trade is indicated by the various law suits and petitions which involve silk products and silk trading in the fifteenth and sixteenth centuries. This includes various acts of parliament which concern the rights of silk workers throughout this period. As part of Marian Dale's investigation of the 'economic position of women at that time', she provided evidence for the role of silkwomen as artisans and traders in their own right rather than as wives or widows working for or on behalf of their husbands.[11] She suggests that by 1368 London silkwomen were 'sufficiently organized, and important' to present a petition to the mayor regarding the protection of their English trade against the importation of foreign goods.[12] And, between 1455 and 1504, there were five further acts protecting the English trade of silkwomen, as well as 'menne and women of the hole craft of Silkewerk of the Cite of London and all other Citeis, Townes, Boroghes, and Vilages of the Realme of Englond'.[13]

The Popularity of Silk

Between the fifteenth and the seventeenth centuries there were other ways to learn about the craft of silk work than through apprenticeship. There survive in the British Library some sets of written 'directions' for making various sorts of laces;

---

8   Dale, 'London Silkwomen', 325–6.
9   Sutton and Hammond, *Coronation*, pp. 65–6.
10 For all of this detail see Sutton and Hammond, *Coronation*, pp. 65–6.
11 Dale, 'London Silkwomen', 334.
12 Dale, 'London Silkwomen', 324.
13 Dale, 'London Silkwomen', 324–5. This act was made in 1482. Dale points out that some of these petitions may have been part of a wider anti-alien movement.

one of which dates from the fifteenth century.[14] This text is described in the Catalogue of Harleian Manuscripts as being for laces which were 'in Fashion in the times of Kings Henry VI and Edward IV'.[15] It includes various patterns and shapes of lace such as round and broad, flat and thin; some of which is bordered on one or both sides, some multicoloured and some made of single colours. There are also directions for how to weave various laces of heraldic patterns such as 'chevron' which are the kinds of designs that must have been learned by heart for someone working for the royal households. All the laces in the manual are made by winding particular threads around certain fingers of each hand. The directions begin by telling the reader how each finger is classified. Judging by the descriptions, which are short but quite complicated, even the basic making of lace was a process requiring a good degree of skill and concentration; and also a process which had its own specialist vocabulary.[16] Some of the laces needed two people, so four hands.

The perception of silk as an important commodity seems to have provoked an interest in this material and its production in other spheres: for example at the end of the sixteenth century, so a little later than the silk working discussed in this chapter, Thomas Moffet found inspiration to write quite a long poem using the subject of silk (and the stages of its production by silkworms).[17] His 'loving muse' found his poem wandered through numerous figures from classical mythology in his discovery of what the table of contents describes as '[D]ivers opinions how and when silke was first invented and worne'.[18] This poem is not really so much about attitudes to silk as it is about a certain style of late sixteenth century poetry which revelled in making classical references in order to explore ancient origins and how these might relate to the contemporary nation. Nevertheless it is interesting that silk was a worthy vehicle for such a poetic excursion.

The Lives of Silk Women in England

A chapter in the biography of a fifteenth-century silkwoman has recently been

---

[14]   The manuscript is BL MS Harl 2320. See E.G. Stanley, 'Directions for Making Many Sorts of Laces', in Beryl Rowland (ed.), *Chaucer and Middle English Studies* in honour of Rossell Hope Robbins (George Allen & Unwin Ltd, London, 1974), pp. 89–103, p. 89–90 on the date of the manuscript; this is mentioned in Sutton and Hammond, *Coronation*, p. 66, n.74.

[15]   Stanley, 'Making Laces', p. 89.

[16]   See Stanley, 'Making Laces', pp. 90–91, on attempts to follow the instructions to produce a lace; and pp. 89–94 on the Medieval vocabulary of lace-making.

[17]   Thomas Moffet, *The Silkewormes, and their Flies: Lively described in Verse by T.M. a Countrie Farmar, and an apprentice in Physicke. For the Great Benefit and Enriching of England* (London, 1599); this is STC 17994 consulted at Early English Books Online. I am grateful to my colleague, Dr Jayne Archer, for providing this reference.

[18]   Moffet, *Silkewormes*, fol. A 2 for the table of Contents; fol. B 3 for the 'loving muse'.

written.[19] This concerns Alice Claver who lived in London and died in 1489. She was a businesswoman in her own right while she was married to her mercer husband, as was allowed by the customs of London in the fifteenth century.[20] As Anne Sutton points out, this was an ideal partnership as mercers dealt in luxury goods, dealing with the Italian merchants based in London and selling these on to the city's silk traders.[21] Claver continued trading after the death of her husband and must have had quite a substantial business, which included a considerable network of trading contacts and business associations with other silkwomen in the city.[22] Some of these connections, as well as her wealth, are reflected in the bequests she made in her last will and testament.[23]

Elizabeth Philip followed in the footsteps of fifteenth-century silkwomen such as Alice Claver. Indeed, Elizabeth may well have been an apprentice to a skilled woman of this generation of silk workers. Although the specific role of 'Royal Sikwoman' was not created until the reign of Mary I, women such as Claver and Philip appear to have fulfilled this function.[24] Claver supplied goods for the households of Edward IV, Richard III, and Henry VII. This involved trading with the officers of 'The Great Wardrobe' of the royal household. She appears in the records for transactions involving the sale of sewing silk, silk corses, 'streyte' (narrow) ribbon, single and double laces, as well as the blue silk, lace, and buttons for the garter robe of the Duke of Ferrara. She is also recorded as having provided laces, tassels and buttons of blue silk and gold for garnishing various books belonging to Edward IV. And, in 1483, she provided large quantities of silk and gold fringe as well as sewing silks and ribbon (14d per ounce for English work and 2s per ounce for Venetian material). For Richard III, Alice Claver provided twelve tufts of silk and gold thread for decorating his coronation gloves, as well as great laces of purple silk and gold thread of Venice and tassels and silk buttons for the purple velvet coronation mantles of Richard and his queen at a cost of 63s 2d each. For these ceremonies she was also paid 60s for the white silk and gold lace used for the Queen's mantle during the coronation procession through the streets of London. For Henry VII, Claver provided some red silk ribbon as well as some silk fringing and gold thread.[25] One of the female associates named by Alice in her will, who was perhaps a servant or an apprentice, is called Elizabeth Atkinson. It is tempting to wonder whether this Elizabeth could have been the unmarried Elizabeth Philip.

---

[19] Anne F. Sutton, 'Alice Claver, Silkwoman (d. 1489)', in *Medieval London Widows, 1300–1500*, pp. 129–142.

[20]   Sutton, 'Alice Claver', p. 130.

[21]   Sutton, 'Alice Claver', p. 130.

[22]   Barron, 'Introduction: The Widow's World', p. xxxiii.

[23]   Sutton, 'Alice Claver', pp. 132–5.

[24]   See Sutton and Hammond, *Coronation*, p. 65.

[25]   For more details of the evidence for Alice Claver's work see Sutton, 'Alice Claver', pp. 137–8; also, Sutton and Hammond, *Coronation*, pp. 65–6.

The Culture of Fashion, Excess, and Revelry in the Household of Henry VIII

Wardrobe

There was plenty of work for a silkwoman working for the royal household of Henry VIII, particularly perhaps in the early years of his reign. Accounts which relate to the royal household department known as the 'Wardrobe' of Henry VIII provide a clue to the immense amount of clothing and apparel as well as other accessories which were in this king's possession. A large book kept in the British Library, for example, details all the King's 'ryche stuff' remaining in his 'standynge warderobe of Robes withyn the Towne of London', between 1521 and 1526. Just one sample page of this book gives some idea of the sheer amount of apparel, its fine quality and its value.[26] The page under the heading of 'Gowns, Shamers, Frocks, Mantelles, & Glaudles Furred', for example, lists sixteen gowns to a value of over £3000. This includes a few individual garments valued at around £400, and made of various colours (browns, purples, white, black, crimson) in fabrics such as velvet, silk, and satin, and often lined with expensive furs such as ermine or sable, and decorated with silver and gold work fashioned by skilled smiths.[27] Some of the entries on this page also hint at the continual refashioning of these items: a gown of white 'cloth of gold of damask', for example is listed as having previously been furred with sable – the sable had been removed the previous year and put onto a 'new gown' of sarcenet (fine soft silk). In another section of this inventory entitled 'Diverse Small Parcelles' are items such as a banner 'for a trumpet' with lace and tassels of silk; thirty-five banners of white sarcenet with the cross of St George; a little pouch 'well wrought with a girdle with tassels of silke & golde'; eight short narrow pieces of black satin embroidered with needle work and layers of 'gold of Venice' and two bundles of 'Carlisle Laces'.[28]

Revels

Rapid Production Rates
The accounts which relate to the organisation and provision of materials and scenery for the various entertainments, known as the 'Revel Accounts', provide an insight into the excessive demands that were put on the makers to produce extraordinary costumes and settings for the various tournaments, pastimes, 'disguisings' and ceremonies which were devised, probably under the pressure of a tight deadline, by people such as Harry Gyllforth and William Cornyshe. The sense of urgency which pervades these accounts indicates that much of this work was

---

[26]   BL MS Harl 4217.
[27]   BL MS Harl 4217, fol. 2r.
[28]   BL MS Harl 4217, fol. 22r.

required at short notice. For the Epiphany revels of 1511, a 'hill summit with a golden branched stock crowned with roses and pomegranates' was required. Out of the hill would issue a 'Morryke' danced by the King's young gentlemen, and also a lady. A large quantity of paint, hogs' bristles for paint brushes, paper for sculpting, and material was needed. This includes stuff to dress the fool and 'fourteen buckled leather garters with bells for the Morryke' (which sounds like the trappings for what is now called 'Morris dancing'). The 48lbs of candles 'for nightwork' betray the pressured conditions under which this scene was produced. The hire of seventeen dozen bells 'while the gentlemen learned to dance' gives a clue to the hasty and noisy practising in preparation for the revel. The payment of 2s in 'house rent where the stuff was wrought', with 12d for 'reeds to strew the house again' and 8d for 'cleaning it' implies a crowded scene of frantic paper-folding, embroidering, cutting and dance practice.[29] With not much recovery time for the makers, just one month later on 12 and 13 February, the accounts record that there was a joust of honour for which 'a forest was constructed within the house of Black Friars, Ludgate'. This involved a 'pageant' (which refers to a pageant wagon) which was 26ft long, 16ft broad and 9 ft high. It was garnished with artificial:

> hawthorns, oaks, maples, hazels, birches, fern, broom, and furze, with beasts and birds embossed in sundry fashion with foresters sitting and going on the top of the same and a castle on the said forest with a maiden sitting thereby with a garland and lion of great stature and bigness, with an antelope of like proportion after his kind drawing the said pageant or forest.[30]

The boughs and stalks were covered in thousands of silk flowers each individually sculpted, 2400 turned acorns and hazel nuts added to the scene, together with yellow, brown or green costumes for the forest men and the various maidens accompanying the lion and antelope. The antelope is sometimes described as an 'olyvant' (elephant?) throughout this account, as if the enormous proportions have begun to affect the scribe's imagination. Not satisfied with that, on the same two nights a revel was held at White Hall, Westminster, for which a pageant called 'The Golden Arbour in the Arch Yard of Pleasure' was devised by William Cornysh.[31]

Another indication of the fast turnaround required of the household staff is the entry written in 1520 concerning the masques at the manor of Havering-at-Bower in early September 1519. On 23 August 1519, the King sent for Gibson to order that 'letters be prepared' to send to William Botre, a mercer, for the provision of 'silks and other stuffs' to make twelve 'Almain ['German'] coats', six green and

---

[29]   *Letters and Papers Foreign and Domestic in the Reign of Henry VIII*, [hereafter *L.P.*] various eds. (London, Longman & Co, 1862–1932), vol. 2, part 2, p. 1494.

[30]   *L.P.*, vol. 2, part 2, p. 1494.

[31]   *L.P.*, vol. 2, part 2, pp. 1495–6. See Chapter 5 this volume.

six yellow satin. The green coats were to be decorated with gold scales 'like those of a dragon or a sturgeon' and the yellow coats were to be decorated with silver scales. Various other items for minstrels were also to be provided, and all of it to be transported to New Hall in Essex for the evening of 3 September. There was, therefore, less than a fortnight between the writing of the letters to the merchant presumably based in London and the acting out of the scene in Essex.[32] And, for the jousts held in June 1520, at Guines in France, for which whitethorn trees were constructed on a platform or carriage of twenty foot square, Elizabeth Philip provided 7lb of sleeved silk at 16s as well as 'whipping wires' with leaves and flowers set onto them. She provided these, in London, on 16 May, just nine days after the King had proclaimed his plans for this joust. This sort of timescale for the preparation of various fiddly pieces of decoration strongly suggests that she had a number of makers working for her. [33]

Recycling Revels

Although the symbols and heraldic emblems required for specific pageants and jousts were each very significant and meaningful – and indeed they needed to be meaningful enough in their own right that spectators would know what they represented – yet the items themselves were not treated with great respect. Rather, once they had been used for the specific joust or revel whose story they related, they were often dismantled and transformed for the next fantasy scenario. Large stores of costumes were kept by the wardrobe department for re-fashioning according to the storyline or theme of subsequent festivities. In 1510, for example, when the King sent for Richard Gibson to arrange for a revel at Richmond on 14 November, a quantity of stuff was left with Gibson by Harry Wentworth, 'gentleman usher and master of the revels', which included 'old disguising gear, satins and sarcenets'. And on 15 November the same year, it is recorded that Richard Gibson acknowledged receipt of 'two war chests' full of garments of various fashions.[34] On other occasions, there are accounts for the payment of people to re-work, or 'translate' old outfits into a new fashion. The set of embroidered designs required for the jousts at Guines, along with a number of others, was to be 'ripped' and re-made into a set of costumes with a much greater focus on harts, falcons, hearts, white roses, pomegranates, and St George. In March 1521, a quantity of materials was delivered from the King's wardrobe in order to provide for the planned jousts to be held in May of that year to celebrate meeting the French king at Calais.[35] This included 22 yards of 'white tissue damask gold', 13 yards of 'black tissue damask gold', about 68 yards of white tissue Venice Gold and some three hundred and 50 yards of cloth described as 'silver damask silver plain'. Materials provided from the wardrobe to dress the King's staff included

---

[32] *L.P.*, vol. 3, part 2, p. 1550.

[33] *L.P.*, vol. 3, part 2, pp. 1552–3.

[34] *L.P.*, vol. 2, part 2, pp. 1492–3.

[35] BL MS Harl 2284, fol. 22v.

over forty yards of 'damask gold' and 'damask silver'. And materials provided from the store for the 'maskers' in 1522 included

> First a purple tissue of Venice Gold 17¼ yards
> Item in crimson tissue of Venice Gold 43 yards
> Item in black tissue of Venice Gold 16¾ yards
> Item in russet tissue of Venice Gold 16¾ yards
> Item in crimson tissue of Damask Gold 8½ yards
> Item in russet cloth of gold in the Calais-style 34 yards
> Item in purple cloth of gold Calais-style 30 yards
> Item in crimson cloth of gold after Calais-style 68 yards
> Item in green cloth of gold Calais-style 61 yards
> Item yellow cloth of gold Calais-style 10½ yards
> Item in purple cloth of gold in Venice Gold 16 yards
> Item in cloth of gold damask gold yellow 84 yards
> Item in cloth of silver of damask 150 yards

Elizabeth Philip's Appearances in the Royal Household Accounts

Revels

Elizabeth Philip appears frequently in Revel Accounts dating between about 1510 and 1536. She provides raw materials for making costumes, and also acts as a skilled seamstress fashioning particular outfits. Her appearances in records from the beginning of the reign of Henry VIII, suggest that she may well have already been working for the royal household of Henry VII in some capacity, possibly as an apprentice. An early mention of her occurs in the Revel Accounts for the festivities at Richmond on 14 November 1510. These were planned on the 8th of that month. Alongside the stuff already available to him, Richard Gibson bought various fabrics for the apparel of twenty-eight lords and ladies and six minstrels. This includes satins, velvets and sarcenets of various colours to be made into bonnets, 'Almain ['German'] doublets', jackets, minstrels' apparel, dresses and girdles. Amongst this list is thirty-two ounces of 'Venice Gold' bought of 'Mistress Ellsebethe Philypp to make seventy two tassels for the white and green garments, ribbon for the ladies' garments and the King's bonnet; £3 12s 4d was paid for 'workmanship' on the whole order, part of which would have gone to Elizabeth.[36]

For Christmas Revels in 1514, Elizabeth Philip provided Venice ribbon at 4s 6d a piece, six dozen ribbon points, at 8d the dozen, the German-style mantles, four caps of white velvet of German-style, four blue and white satin gowns and bonnets for the mummers, four blue and white damask coats and bonnets for the 'drumbyllslads' (drummers?) and crimson and green satin for the 'taborets and

---

[36]　　*L.P.*, vol. 2, part 2, p. 1493.

rebecks' (tabret and rebec players).[37] On 19 and 20 May 1516 the King held jousts of honour at Greenwich. This involved another huge amount of outfitting for people of both noble and humble rank. On the first day, large amounts of blue damask, satin, and sarcenet were required so that everyone except the lords could be dressed in blue (this includes 'honest persons of the stable', waiters, armourers and trumpeters).[38] On the second day, when the King wore a blue ensemble, set wrought with leaves in gold, most of the more humble members of the household were required to wear yellows. Quite a large proportion of the material for both these days appears to have been required for the horses' costumes, including saddle coverings and other accessories. Richard Gibson is recorded as having purchased 388 ounces of gold damask at a cost of £90 3s 4d from Florentine Woodward, George Seneske and Elizabeth Philip, to be used for the king's coat. In addition these three people provided 'a long tassel for the horses' throats', fringes for stirrups, 211 ounces of Venice Gold, £16 2s 10d worth of silk tassels; and 93¾ ounces of Kollen (Cologne?) gold and silver for the apparel of the Earl of Essex and Nicholas Carew (this appears to be slightly lower-grade material because the accounts remarks that this was provided instead of 'rich stuff which could not be gotten nor had').[39]

For further celebrations during the summer of 1520, Elizabeth Philip also provided more materials, made various amounts of fringing, and supplied eleven pieces of 'Paris Ribbon' 40 yards in length, each at 4s a piece, as well as material for the making of hose for the king's footmen, and twenty four pairs of made-up hose for the armourers. By this time, the quality of her work – and the work of what must have been a considerable workshop – seems to have been valued over other suppliers as it is recorded that these items were to be used 'on this side the sea and beyond the sea'.[40]

Intersections with Iconic Moments

The accounts which include Elizabeth Philip also, by chance, touch on some iconic themes from the reign from the popular history of this monarch. For example, on 15 March 1513, in the same entry as records the fee for 'lodemanshippe of *The Mary Rose* into the Temmys' (60s), is the record of an outstanding account for the materials used for the disguising on 'Twelve night last'. Elizabeth Philip is described here as 'Mrs. Philippe, silkwoman' and paid £6 2s 2d. No further details

---

[37] *L.P.*, vol. 2, part 2, pp. 1500–1501. A tabret is a small drum, like a timbrel; a rebec is a kind of fiddle.

[38] *L.P.*, vol. 2, part 2, p. 1507.

[39] *L.P.*, vol. 2, part 2, 1507–8.

[40] *L.P.*, vol. 3, part 2, p. 1555. See also *L.P.*, vol. 4, part 1, pp. 844–7. New Year's gifts in 1526 included a shirt, six coifs and six handkerchiefs by Mrs Phillipps (p. 845).

are given about what Elizabeth did for this although alongside her name in this account are also a 'throwester' who was paid 103s 7d and 'another silkwoman' paid 41s, which indicates that Elizabeth was probably working on the next stage of the production from the throwing, and may have had a lower-paid assistant.[41] There are also some rather poignant entries concerning the execution of Anne Boleyn and the subsequent reckoning of her goods and debts which took place in early December 1536. On the point of her death Anne Boleyn owed to 'Mrs Curtes, Mrs Kelingem, and Mrs Philips, silkwomen, £7 12s 10d'.[42]

Wardrobe

Unfortunately mention of Elizabeth Philip in the wardrobe inventories of Henry VIII during the period when she appears to be most actively involved with providing for the revels, jousts and pageants, remains elusive.[43] Although these records are often listing and describing items of clothing with no reference to the maker, there are also a number of references to cloth being sent to a specific named individual in order that they might produce a particular garment. It is noticeable, however, that nearly all these named individuals are men. Names mentioned with particular frequency include William Buttry, Geram Bowdice William Hilton (often described simply as Hilton), William Hosyer, John de Parys, and Richard Gressam. One woman who is mentioned in this set of accounts, and who was involved with providing for the revels at the same time as Elizabeth Philip, is Christiana Warren. On 18 July 1517 she was commissioned 'by the Kinge's graces owne commaundement' to make nine purses for himself and also for the Queen. For this she was provided with various yard and half-yard lots of velvets in russet, purple (for the Queen), and black.[44]

Distribution of Wares into the Community

The workmanship of skilled seamstresses such as Elizabeth Philip was not confined to a private world of élite celebration behind the walls of royal palaces. The large numbers of performers required for many of these events meant that numerous of the very humble servants of the royal household, and perhaps their children, were required to take part in the pageants. In order to take part, they needed to have the correct costumes provided for them. Although there were vast stores of old costumes, on a number of occasions the outfits were distributed to both the noble and humble members of the royal household.[45] After the revels

---

41   *L.P.*, vol. 1, part 2, p. 1503.
42   *L.P.*, vol. 10, pp. 382–3.
43   I refer specifically to the inventories found in BL MSS Harl 2284 and 4217.
44   BL MS Harl 2284, fol. 32r
45   *L.P.*, vol. 2, part 2, p. 1493.

finished on the night of 14 November 1510, for example, the account reports that much of the apparel was given away to the people who had worn it for the disguising, and the Master of the Wardrobe was left with just three sleeveless ladies' garments of crimson and satin.[46] An account written in February 1520, which refers to the revels held on 3 September 1519 at New Hall in Essex, states that all of the costumes for this occasion were 'given to the wearers. Nothing remained'.[47] Elizabeth Philip had provided a quantity of green material including thirteen yards of ribbon for 'lacing bonnets and knitting vizors' for one of William Cornysh's 'pastimes' performed during the New Hall celebrations. This had a weather theme and included a cast drawn from the children of the chapel playing parts such as 'Sun', 'Moon', 'Winter', 'Wind' and 'Rain'. Elizabeth's materials, together with her workmanship in the form of '482 ounces of flat gold and flat silver' which she had woven into fringes at 3d per ounce, therefore, became the property of the performers, both adults and children.[48] What did the more humble people do with these items which were probably constructed from much finer materials than they usually enjoyed? Perhaps they wore them for their own special occasions, or re-used the cloth to make outfits more appropriate to everyday life. Or maybe the costumes were treasured and converted into heirlooms to which stories of the experience of performing for the King were attached.

Sometimes the dispersal of the rich materials and costumes produced and provided by the army of makers like Elizabeth Philip seems to have become a free for all of grabbing, tearing, and stealing rather than a sedate process of distribution. Such a mêlée occurred after the 1515 Epiphany revels. The accounts report that 'in the press of people', the 51 yards of blue and red 'tartron' (an expensive fabric, probably a silk[49]) which was used on the pageant structures was 'cut away, rent, and torn by strangers and others as well as the King's servants … and letted not for the King's presence' [and not left alone despite the King's presence].[50]

Elizabeth Philip's Life and View on the World

Concerning evidence for the rest of Elizabeth Philip's life, the royal household accounts are almost silent. Details such as whether she was married or widowed, had children, what age she was and so on, are all unknown. I am inclined to think that she was probably at least in her 50s by the later references to her work for the

---

46   *L.P.*, vol. 2, part 2, p. 1493.
47   *L.P.*, vol. 3, part 2, p. 1551.
48   *L.P.*, vol. 3, part 2, pp. 1550–1551.
49   See, Hans Kurath and Sherman M. Kuhn, *Middle English Dictionary* (Ann Arbor, University of Michigan Press, 1954–) gives this definition, adding that this fabric may have originally been exported from Tartar.
50   *L.P.*, vol. 2, part 2, p. 1502.

royal household in the 1530s. She had been providing for the revels for over
twenty-five years by 1536, and she must have spent around six to seven years as an
apprentice at the beginning of her career, and then it is possible that she spent some
years after that improving her skills and building up her reputation in order to be
suitably qualified to supply finely wrought fabrics and costumes to the royal
household.[51] There are just two possible clues as to her domestic life. In 1526, a
'Mrs Phelippes' is named as one of the Queen's maids, to be provided with
lodgings in the King's household.[52] And, in the list of court expenses of 1536 there
is mention of a 'Mr Phyllipes the hardwareman', who was paid £5 19s 3d; it is
conceivable he could be Elizabeth's husband..[53]

Politics, Identity, Myth, and Display

The various celebratory events at the royal household were very much concerned
with displaying the prowess and wealth of the Tudor royal household, and many of
the occasions celebrated specific victories and particular diplomatic occasions
where foreign magnates and officials were visiting the royal court. For the visit of
the Emperor Charles V, on the 4 and 5 of June 1522, Elizabeth Philip provided
materials for a medley which involved the construction of various mountains
covered in gold and decorated with hearts and a number of 'bards' (a decorative
covering for a tournament horse) embroidered with various decorations of a
fantastic and chivalric nature. One decoration, for example, was to depict knights
on horseback riding upon mountains of gold with broken spears in their hands and
ladies coming out of clouds casting darts at the knights, the same ladies were to be
bare above the waist and covered only with the clouds. Elizabeth provided 44
ounces of Venice Gold cords at 4s 6d per ounce for the King's 'bard' and apparel,
as well as 207½ ounces of silk points and cords, at 14d (per ounce) for nineteen
more bards and apparels.[54]

Elizabeth Philip was not herself in command of the master-plans for these
events. She was probably never involved in planning meetings with those
individuals such as the Master of the Revels whose role it was to conceive of the
whole effect. And she may not have been a witness to many, or any, of the final
performances. But she was probably present on those hectic occasions of last-
minute sewing, costume fitting, and rehearsing such as the preparations for the
Morris dancing spectacle of Epiphany 1511. Whatever the extent of her
experiences of the final show, Elizabeth – like other workers and servants of the

---

[51]   See, for example, NA C1/658/10 and NA C146/1240, for details of the
apprenticeship period for other silkwomen in London in the late fifteenth and early sixteenth
centuries.

[52]   *L.P.*, vol. 4, part 1, pp. 866–7.

[53]   *L.P.*, vol. 10, p. 325.

[54]   *L.P.*, vol. 3, part 2, pp. 976–7.

royal household – was involved in making costumes and providing material for a truly cosmopolitan range of pageants.

Fashion and Identity

Elizabeth Philip provided costumes of particular national fashions for some stories and jousts; she provided materials and decorations to make the effect of numerous mythological and real animals; and she provided costumes in ranges of colour combinations which were designed to be symbolic of different national and fantastical jousting factions. In 1522, for example, in the presence of various foreign dignitaries such as the Prince of Orange, alongside various of the English nobility, there were also revels devised by William Cornysh, for which Elizabeth Philip provided 91 ounces of red silk cords at 14d (per ounce) in order to make borders for eight 'Italian mantles' of crimson satin with gold neck ties. She also provided Venice Gold woven into 'tristam knots' at 23s 4d, eight headdresses of damask gold at 3s, 12 yards of white sarcenet at 4s, three pieces of Cyprus satin at 3s which was to be used by the ladies at Windsor when they wore the headdresses and three gross of points at 4s a gross for fashioning sleeves, cloaks, bonnets and buskins.[55] Whether or not such Italian fashion was popularly worn about the court in this period, the fact that Elizabeth Philip was charged with making these costumes clearly indicates that she was not only aware of this national style but also skilled in the production of costumes relating to the same.

Sensitivity to matters of national identity is often expressed through the descriptions of the costumes. A maker such as Elizabeth Philip must therefore also have been acutely aware of the ways that distinctions of fashion and style represented those issues of national and regional identity which were of great interest to the Tudor monarchy during this period of turbulent international relations. Partly, references to other nations or towns when describing materials relate to the identification of specific fabrics, such as the various kinds of silks named after their place of production. For example, material is often described as being from Bruges or Venice, which were important places of cloth production in this period. Other references to nations appear to refer more to national styles of dress, or at least national modes of fashioning, such as 'Spanish work'. On 7 March 1519, for example, there was a 'maskalayne' described as being 'after the manner of Italy', followed by a joust on 8 March at Greenwich. Forty-six people were involved in all and their costumes, which were provided by Elizabeth Philip together with Christiana Warren, included ladies' petticoats of 'Spanish Work', masking hoods, hats and bonnets as well as items for the King's saddle and other 'necessaries for tilting', wire for skirt hoops and ostrich feathers to a sum total of £60 7s 3d.[56] Fifty-two yards of 'cloth of gold' were also re-used from the King's store for this occasion.[57] So this event employed a mixture of national themes to

---

[55]   *L.P.*, vol. 3, part 2, pp. 976–7.
[56]   *L.P.*, vol. 3, part 1, pp. 34–5.
[57]   BL MS Harl 2284, fol. 18r.

create its effect: it was styled after the manner of one nation's custom (Italy), while some of the costumes were worked in the fashion of another nation (Spain). The pageants, jousts, masks and other celebrations often also involved the playing out of battles between imagined factions and so specific colour-schemes of costumes were also used to symbolically represent these different types of identity. Artisans such as Elizabeth Philip therefore had a particular perspective on the ways that real issues of international diplomacy as well as real issues relating to the production of materials may be reflected in, and experienced through, the fantasy- world of masques and pageants.

Tudor Myths of Identity

Some pageants seem to have used a 'culture contact' theme as a device to create their action. A pageant called 'The Pavyllyon in the Plas Parlos', for example, seems to have used colour, costume, and also musical sound to act out a scenario of what happens when 'strangers' encounter each other (and perhaps, according to the title, speak in various languages). Soon after the excesses of the Christmas Revels for 1514, the King decided to hold new revels for Epiphany 1515 'as the court was full of strangers, French, Spanish, German'.[58] For this there was a pavilion on a 'plas' or stage of crimson and blue damask, with a gold crown and a bush of roses on the top, and hung with 'blue tartron'. At the four corners of the stage area were four brickwork towers with a lord in each dressed in purple satin embroidered with gold wreaths and the letters H and K. Six minstrels stood on the towers and made 'strange sounds', with sackbuts, shawms, viols and so on, dressed in blue and white damask. At the foot of the castle structure were two armed knights with swords in their hands guarding the place. After the explanation of this pageant by William Cornysh and others, there entered three armed knights in yellow satin to the noise of drumming at which a fight ensued between the two sets of knights. The entry of six wodwos (wildmen) separates this tournament, and some ladies wearing crimson satin (who were not mentioned before) are rescued.

The pageants' attention to issues of 'culture contact' makes a comment on what were contemporary concerns in national and international politics. The symbols and emblems which signal these current themes are sometimes also mixed with symbols and icons relevant to the ancient identity of the English nation. In the description of the various equipment and costumes re-used for the revels and jousts of May 1519, for example, are a collection of embroidered coverings for 'bardes' which are described in a list as follows:

> the arms of England and France; England alone; France alone; King Arthur; Brut; Cadwallader; England, France and Spain; England, France and Hainault; England and France 'payned' with France and Navarre; Ireland, Wales, Normandy, and Cornwall; and 'the lion of England powdered with imperial crowns, clouds and suns.[59]

---

[58]   *L.P.*, vol. 2, part 2, p. 1501.
[59]   *L.P.*, vol. 3, part 2, p. 1550.

The ordinary people who formed the machinery of the royal household's culture of fantasy and revelry were key to the production of this display of current and ancient symbols of national identity. Through her skilled workmanship and specialist occupation, Elizabeth Philip would have acquired knowledge about current politics, international relations, as well as ancient history, and key historical figures in the myths of English or British identity.

***

Despite being only a very small element in the fashioning machine of the Tudor royal household with its multitude of workers involved in the production of very many events focusing on display, symbolism, and representation, Elizabeth Philip had special access to Tudor concepts of national identity, its politics, and its symbolic representation because of her special knowledge and skill as a silkwoman.

Chapter 5

The Anonymous Witness

Introduction

In 1501, Prince Arthur – the son of Henry VII and heir to the English throne – was married to Katherine of Aragon. This involved a flamboyant set of ceremonial events in London to welcome the arrival of the princess and her entourage during October and November of that year. A number of the pageants were held in public spaces of the city so that the whole community might witness the making of this political alliance. The accounts of this extraordinary celebration focus on the drama and pageantry of the event, whilst also marking an important political moment for the Tudor dynasty.[1] Just five months after these joyous celebrations, came the tragedy of the young prince's death – he was just a teenager. Whether on the sidelines as an ordinary commoner of London (or England) or as a part of the royal household closely involved with the preparations for the festivities followed so soon by the mourning, anyone who experienced this tragedy would have found the sequence of events imprinted on their memory. The marriage alliance was so important politically, for the continuation of the royal dynasty but also for the preservation of a fragile peace, that it really did have colossal implications for the lives of the wealthy and noble as well as for the townsman and the pauper. So once witnessed, it should be assumed that other events during those individuals' lifetimes – family ceremonies or other public festivities – would always have been held in comparison to this extraordinary year of contrasts.

Various versions of the celebrations and the funeral service survive. One set of accounts is particularly detailed and provides a unique record, sometimes in the first person, of what turns out to be an emotionally turbulent voyage between the extremely joyful celebrations for the perpetuation of the dynasty and the tragic loss

---

[1]   Sydney Anglo, 'The London Pageants for the Reception of Katharine of Aragon: November 1501', *Journal of the Warburg and Courtauld Institutes*, 26, 1/2 (1963): 53–89.

of that hope.[2] Another account, intended for wider public consumption by the anonymous witnesses to these events, was printed in 1500.[3]

The Accounts of the Heralds

We do not know who wrote these accounts although there are some definite possibilities. The Herald who wrote the funeral account, for example, has been given a name by some scholars: using codicological evidence this part of the text has been attributed to William Colbarne, but there is some doubt about this identification and its significance for the account in general. The manuscript of the Heralds, which is almost certainly a combination of various witnesses' viewpoints, records the experiences of watching a bemusing array of pageantry and mourning. The accounts are written in a combination of styles, although many of the details provided follow official patterns for the recording of heraldic and ceremonial events by officials of the royal household.[4]

The information provided in the Heralds' accounts includes detailed descriptions of the various wagons, devices, and allegorical characters required to stage the pageants at a number of places throughout London. Some of the poetic scripts used to describe the tableaux scenes are also recorded. The accounts therefore provide access to some of the themes used in this kind of celebration, indicating the court's dramatic interests in cosmology, astrology, hagiography, ancient tradition, ancestry, and national identity. Each pageant was designed to produce a very vivid spectacle which would have had an instant visual impact on the observer; each also has layers of much more complex allegorical meaning which relies on increasingly in-depth biblical, philosophical, and cosmographical knowledge. The descriptions of these pageants also indicate that the new forms of expression and representation of the early English Renaissance may have been at least as confusing to the spectator as they were wonderful.

At the heart of this pageant sequence is the message that Prince Arthur is a representative of virtue and honour. The portrayal of St Ursula and St Katherine in the first pageant sets the scene for the complex of cosmological, dynastic, biblical and literary references that celebrate the honour of the marriage alliance. For this first pageant, to be held at 'the great bridge of London', the princess and her

---

[2]   See *The Receyt of the Ladie Katheryne*, edited with an Introduction by Gordon Kipling, Early English Text Society (Oxford, OUP, 1990), pp. xxxi–xlii for a discussion of the manuscript(s). There is also a record of the events in *The Great Chronicle of London* – see, *The Great Chronicle of London*, ed. A.H. Thomas and I.D. Thornley (Gloucester, Alan Sutton, 1983), pp. 294–326.

[3]   *A Remembraunce for the Traduction & Mariage of the Princesse Kateryne Doughter to the Right High and Right Myghty Prince the Kinge and Quene of Spayne as Here in Articles it Dothe Ensure*, STC 4814 (Published by Pynson, London, c. 1500).

[4]   Kipling, *Receyt*, pp. xlv, lxi.

retinue from Spain, together with a 'right semely company of the Kinges Grace' including a number of dukes and lords, all processed on horseback from St George's Field, and through Southwark.[5] The pageant tabernacle itself was set up 'on the myddes of the bridge' and made of 'two flouers, assemblant unto tweyne rodeloftes'.[6] In this double-storey stage there were two seats; on the lower floor was a woman holding a wheel (to indicate St Katherine), surrounded by 'many virgins' and on the upper seat there was another woman 'in likness of Seint Ursula', also surrounded by a multitude of virgins.[7] Above both these storeys was a picture of the Trinity and on each side were what seem to be small display boxes, described as 'tabernacles', six in all, decorated with the traditional French inscription 'Onye soit que male pens' ('Evil be to him who evil thinks'), together with regal red roses each having an angel on the top decorated with symbols for the Trinity, St Ursula, and St Katherine. The walls of the storeyed stage were painted with hanging curtains of 'cloth of tissue, blue and red'. And in what seems to be a signpost pointing towards the stage at the middle of the bridge, there were two 'grete postes' carved from wood and painted in gilt, decorated with ostrich feathers, red roses and portcullises, each also displaying a red lion rampant holding a vane painted with the arms of England.

In many ways, the first pageant sets the scene for the remaining five. Speeches are uttered by the two saints as a sort of dialogue which is also directed towards the princess. They at once welcome the young Spanish woman to London whilst asserting a set of auspicious genealogical connections and proposing this marriage alliance as one which will bring not only the worldly benefits of temporal honour but also the more spiritual rewards of perpetual glory. This first pageant indicates the important connections between the saints, various cosmological bodies, and the prince and princess, using what Sydney Anglo described as an 'intricate and closely knit group of name parallels'.[8] The figure of Ursula was considered a British saint, as described in Geoffrey of Monmouth's history of the foundation of Britain. Ursula's first speech makes reference to her membership of the Lancastrian lineage, which she also connects to that most famous other Arthur, 'the wise, noble, and vaillaunt kyng / That in this region was furst of his name'.[9] Ursula also goes on to provide some cosmographical connections between her name and the name of the constellation Ursa Minor which, she explains, is adjacent in the skies to the constellation called Arcturus (a name sometimes used for Ursa Major, a group of seven stars). At the end of this speech, Ursula also affirms the connection between Arthur the sixteenth-century prince and 'the ffyrst Arthur' by proposing that as the second Arthur now succeeds the first, so Princess Katherine succeeds Ursula (presumably intended to imply that Katherine would from that

---

5   Kipling, *Receyt*, p. 12.
6   Kipling, *Receyt*, pp. 12–13.
7   Kipling, *Receyt*, p. 13.
8   Anglo, 'London Pageants', 58.
9   Kipling, *Receyt*, pp. 15, ll. 100–101.

time on have a role as an important British figure). The potential for audience confusion is, I think, clear.

As Sydney Anglo points out, there is also a much more complicated set of references embedded in these name parallels and these are associated with the connections between Arthur, Arcturus, and the seven-star group called The Pleiades. This set of connections has its source in the Old Testament book of Job, and the interpretation of this by Gregory the Great which explores the symbolic importance of the number seven, including seven rays shining from the middle of the heavens over the whole of Holy Church as represented in the apocalyptic visions of St John by seven candlesticks, and the possibility that this represents the 'Spirit of Sevenfold Grace' which shines forth from the axis of truth itself. According to Gregory, The Pleiades represents the saints who continue to illuminate the world despite its darkness. Gregory goes on to propose that whereas The Pleiades represents the New Testament, Arcturus represents the Old Testament; Arcturus therefore represents a prophetic voice and ultimately, through various twists of meaning concerning the Trinity, the Four Cardinal Virtues, and the seven-fold gifts of the Holy Spirit, leads to the implication that the constellation of Arcturus represents the Christian life of virtue. I am sure that many of the onlookers in early sixteenth-century London would not actually make all those connections

The remaining five pageants continue in the same vein. The second, which also introduced some general themes, took place at 'Grasechurch Street' in the widest part of the street and involved a castle, called 'The Castle of Portcullises', built over the water conduit there and made of a real stone base of about four feet high with a timber structure above that covered in a canvas painted to look like stonework. The script takes the form of a conversation between allegorical characters called Policy, Virtue and Noblesse. Noblesse proclaims that it is his role to bring Katherine to virtue, a trait already present in her noble blood. This way she will attain honour and be a better ruler of the commons.[10]

The third to sixth pageants have more specific focuses all of which elaborate on the cosmological theme introduced in the first. The third, called 'The Sphere of the Moon' positioned at the conduit in Cornhill, was housed in a mock-brick building with pretend marble pillars and all manner of bright coloured heraldic designs. Above the stage was an astronomical table known as a 'volvell', designed to give various information required for astrological readings such as hours, days, months, years, zodiacal signs and so on. The four characters giving speeches were Raphael the Archangel, Alphonso the astronomer king, Job the prophet and Boethius the philosopher. The mood of this pageant is a foretelling of the success of this marriage alliance based on the auspicious astrological conjunctions of Katherine's and Arthur's births. It includes references to various sources including the Old Testament marriage of Sara and Tobias, and Chaucer's translation of Boethius's

---

[10]   Kipling, *Receyt*, pp. 15–20.

Consolation of Philosophy, as printed by Caxton in the 1470s.[11] In the fourth pageant, the '*Sphere of the Sun*', which was at the Great Conduit on Cheapside, the centre piece was a celestial body like the sun. A central figure seated in the middle of the 'sun' represents Prince Arthur and, as Job describes in the third pageant, he is sitting in 'the Sun of Justice'. Through a series of visual and verbal connections, Arthur is here identified with Christ the Redeemer.[12] The fifth pageant, called the 'Temple of God', has as its main focus the throne of heaven on which sits the Father of Heaven. God and another character called Prelacy then expound to Princess Katherine on the doctrinal principals and the mysteries of marriage. There is some suggestion that the King of Heaven also represents the earthly King, Henry VII, and at the end, the figures from the second pageant (Policy, Noblesse, and Virtue) are mentioned again as elements in the marriage between Katherine and Arthur. The final pageant, 'The Throne of Honour', was built at the entrance to St Paul's Cathedral, and it forms an extended allegory on the themes of honour and virtue which have already appeared in the earlier pageants.[13]

The prevailing cosmic theme, which draws on ancient and biblical literatures, may have been influenced by Henry VII's taste for Burgundian culture.[14] Some of the pageants described here were probably the innovative early creations of the flamboyant revel-maker William Cornysh who is the subject of Chapter 5.[15] Sydney Anglo suggested that the heralds making the written record of these events may not have fully understood all the references, such as, for example, the connection between the Sun of Justice, Christ, and the Prince, in the fourth pageant.[16] But if this is the case what hope was there for the ordinary spectator to actually follow the complex multi-layering of references? Who watched these extraordinary, complicated, and virtuosic displays of allegory and drama? Who understood them? In other words, what impression did the ordinary spectator gain of 'early English Renaissance' culture from these dramatic expressions and performances? Certainly, the Spanish visitors may have struggled with the English speeches, despite the provision made for them by Latin captions, or 'distichs' carried by each of the main speakers – these would be rather like cartoon speech bubbles, carried by the speaking figures.[17]

In the course of the detailed descriptions of literary form, the Herald recording the marriage pageants also happens to describe London as he saw it in use for these performances, providing excellent access to topographical and architectural details

11   Anglo, 'London Pageants', 70–71.
12   Anglo, 'London Pageants', 75–6.
13   Kipling, *Receyt*, pp. 33–5.
14   Gordon Kipling, *The Triumph of Honour: Burgundian Origins of the Elizabethan Renaissance* (Published for the Sir Thomas Browne Institute, The Hague, Leiden University Press, 1977), Chapter 5.
15   Kipling, *Triumph of Honour*, pp. 100–106.
16   Anglo, 'London Pageants', 77.
17   Anglo, 'London Pageants', 86.

of this capital city, including the width of its streets and the existence of various water courses down some of these main thoroughfares. The Herald recording the jousts following the marriage service also took in the marvels of Richmond Palace, where the party stayed for some celebratory hunting. His detailed descriptions of the rooms of the palace are of architectural interest and also provide access to the experiences of this man – who one must assume was quite accustomed to the splendour of royal palaces – which sometimes amount to awe. Not least in the description of Richmond Palace is the rehearsal of the raft of ancestral portraits lining the banqueting hall. These are described as follows:

> In the wallys and siddys of this halle betwene the wyndowes bethe pictures of the noble kings of this realme in their harness and robis of goolde, as Brute, Engest, King William, Rufus, Kyng Arthur, King Henry – and many other of that name – King Richard and Kyng Edward and of thoes names many noble waryours and kinges of this riall realme with their fachons and swordes in their handes; visagid and appeiryng like bold and valiaunt knightes, and so their dedis and actes in the chroniclis right evidently bethe shewen and declared emong thes nombre of famous kinges.[18]

These descriptions re-iterate a theme which pervades the celebrations for Prince Arthur's life and indeed the mourning at his loss: like the immense display of lineage going back to the Brut, the prince is seen as a celebration of Englishness that ties the sixteenth-century court of Henry VII with the mythical foundations of the English nation. The anonymous Herald's first person account, therefore, provides access to one individual's experiences of the overwhelming joy and sadness wrought by the excessive display and pageantry of a court seeking to legitimate its identity within the Renaissance world. This joyous excess marks a sharp contrast with the words of the Herald who sums up the distraught ending at the funeral ceremony for Prince Arthur, the new English hope:

> The orisons said by the Busshop of Lincoln, also sore weeping, he set the crosse over the chest and cast holiwater and erth thereon. His Officer of Armse, sore weping took of his cote of armes, and cast it alonges over the chest, right lamentably. Then to have sen Sir William Owdale, Comptroller of his Household, sore weeping and criying, toke the staff of his office by bothe endes and over his own hed brake it, and cast it into the grave, and in likewise did Sir Richard Crofte, stuard of his Howshold, and cast his staff broken into the grave, and in likewise did the gentilmen husshers their roddes. It was a pitious sight, who had sene it.[19]

The funeral service indicates the bitter sadness at this tragedy and the ways this sadness is ceremonially performed. The record of the marriage ceremony signals

---

[18] Kipling, *Receyt*, p. 72.

[19] Kipling, *Receyt*, pp. 92–3.

the hopes for the future of this Tudor dynasty and, perhaps, the interest of the court and its pageant writers in new fashions of representation.[20]

A Witness to the Ceremonies

As I have suggested, there are a number of different accounts of the marriage ceremonies. Interestingly, one of the versions indicates a desire that the spectacular events should be more than simply a celebration of a royal marriage by the élite of the royal household and court. In order to include the ordinary people in this celebration of Early English Renaissance culture and ideals, a printed pamphlet of the plans for the ceremony, called *A Remembraunce for the Traduction & Mariage of the Princesse*, was circulated around London in the year 1500.[21] In the remainder of this chapter, I will explore some moments in the biography of one unknown reader of this pamphlet, an anonymous witness to the events.

The Anonymous Reader

The reconstruction of moments from a biography of an anonymous reader is on deliberately tenuous ground. The purpose of this exercise in writing biographical moments is to explore a range of interpretive issues that are always present in those reconstructions of the past which attempt to understand the experiences and perceptions of the people living in that past. My use of the *Traduction* pamphlet explores some of the interpretative issues specifically concerned with the ways that different forms of knowledge interact in the formation and memorisation of an experience which is significant. In this case, I am concerned with how the anticipation of an event which is informed by reading a pamphlet might interact with the experience of witnessing the actual events of the marriage festivities. This kind of investigation is faceted and unresolved because it deals in various levels of a process of construing the nature of one unknown individual's experience of different 'events'. The first step is to understand how the anonymous reader may have reacted to the pamphlet. This interpretative exercise involves an investigation of reading practice. The basic question here is: how would this pamphlet be understood by a reader in c. 1500? The second step is to assess the relationship between the reader's anticipation of the events as described by the pamphlet and the spectator's experience of the events as they happened in London in 1501.

---

[20]   Kipling, *Triumph of Honour*, pp. 97–8.
[21]   *Remembraunce for the Traduction & Mariage*; Kipling, *Triumph of Honour*, pp. 173–4.

Reconstructing Reading Practice

In recent years, there has been a revived interest in investigating how people read in the past. 'The History of Reading' has developed as a discipline in its own right.[22] Nevertheless, recoveries of reading practice in the past are still in their infancy. This is especially the case when it is the reading practices of the general public that are being investigated, rather than those of a specific named individual. To attempt a reconstruction of how an anonymous reader may have read the *Traduction & Mariage* involves investigating how his or her imagination may have been engaged influenced during the act of reading the pamphlet. Such an investigation, which works in the realms of the imaginative reconstruction of likely reactions, is very different from the investigation and recovery of a known individual's reading activities.

When an individual Renaissance reader is known, it is possible to read elements of that reader's character, for which there is other surviving evidence, into an analysis of his or her reading experience; it is possible to assume he or she found certain aspects of a text particularly interesting because they relate to preoccupations in the rest of his or her life; and it is possible to expect that reader to have a specific style of reading based on his or her own educational background.[23] When reconstructing the reading experience of an unknown reader in the early sixteenth century there is, in general, no such specific information to apply to the investigation. However, there are certain parameters which help to inform the analysis. Firstly, it is important to imagine the specific conditions of literacy and attitudes to text which are appropriate to the chronological period. In this case, it is worth bearing in mind that in the sixteenth century there was relatively less reading matter available to the average reader than there is today, although the existence of this pamphlet indicates that small cheap 'news' texts were in circulation during this period. The fact that this is a printed pamphlet is, of course, notable as it was produced within the first fifty years of printing in England. However it would be a mistake to think that the fact of its being printed is

---

[22] See, for example, Roger Chartier and Guglielmo Cavallo, *A History of Reading in the West* (Cambridge and Oxford: Polity Press, 1999); and see Elisabeth Salter, ' "The Dayes Moralised": Reconstructing Devotional Reading, c. 1450–1560', in Elisabeth Salter and Robert Lutton (eds), *Pieties in Transition: Religious Practices and Experiences, c. 1400–1640* (Aldershot, Ashgate, forthcoming 2006).

[23] See, for example, Lisa Jardine and Anthony Grafton, *From Humanism to Humanities: Education and the Liberal Arts in Fifteenth- and Sixteenth-Century Europe* (London, Duckworth, 1986). See, especially, chapter 1 on 'Ideals and Practice', where in pp. 9–13 Jardine and Grafton address 'what actually went on' in the classroom of Guarino Guarini of Verona. See also p. 161 for the intention of this volume to get to grips with 'humanist *practice*' rather than its theoretical and idealistic promises. Also, William Sherman, *John Dee, The Politics of Reading and Writing in the English Renaissance*, Massachusetts Studies in Early Modern Culture (University of Massachusetts Press, Massachusetts, 1997).

an inherent element in its wide circulation; plenty of small texts were in circulation in manuscript prior to the use of printing.[24] Another issue which helps to narrow down the likely experience of reading this pamphlet is to consider what other literatures the anonymous reader may have encountered. He or she probably had access to a religious book or books, perhaps in the form of a service book either in manuscript or in print, and he or she may also have seen, bought, and read some of the single-leaf devotional texts that were circulating in this period.[25] As a member of the London civic community, the reader is also likely to have had access to various forms of administrative literature, most probably some sort of account records. This latter type of literate activity does not discount women, although it was probably more often men that dealt with the texts associated with business; and, ultimately, it is probably reasonable to assume that more men than women encountered the *Traduction & Mariage* pamphlet.

There are two main sources of evidence for the reading experience of an unknown reader of a specific text in a particular cultural context. These are: evidence found within the structure of the text as it was produced by writer (and printer); and evidence added to the text by a reader in the form of reader annotations. The former kind of evidence is very useful for reconstructing the reader's experience not only of the meaning of the text but also of using the object itself. Such evidence includes the text's contents, page layout (for example, the use of headings, paragraph marks, cross-references and so on), use of images, mode of expression (for example if it is abbreviated like a list or written in dense paragraphs); the latter includes annotations in words which make a direct comment on the text, the addition of emphases at certain parts of the text (such as underlining, crosses in the margin, the use of 'Nota Bene' at a particular word or section); the addition of material which is apparently irrelevant to the subject of the text (details of a monetary account, a list of dates or other form of memo, pen scribblings and so on); and assertions of ownership which most often occurs in the form of an individual's name and perhaps some phrase such as 'this is his book'. Some of these elements of the *Traduction & Mariage* pamphlet are now explored in the following paragraphs with the intention of being able to recover something of the relationships between the expectations that the pamphlet sets up for the reader and how this informed the experience of that reader as a witness to the events of the marriage festivities which were followed by the tragic death of the Prince.

---

[24]   For seminal work on literacy and the circulation of documents, see Michael Clanchy, *From Memory to Written Record: England 1066–1377*, 2nd edn (Oxford, Blackwell, 1993).

[25]   See, for example, Mary C. Erler, 'Devotional Literature', in Lotte Helinga and J.B. Trapp (eds), *The Cambridge History of the Book* (Cambridge, CUP, 1999), vol. 3, '1400–1557', pp. 495–525.

Figure 4.1 Woodcut image from *A Remembraunce for the Traduction & Mariage of the Princesse Kateryne*

The Woodcut

The first set of information about the ceremonies that the reader encounters is the woodcut on the front leaf of the pamphlet [see FIG. 4.1]. It depicts the marriage ceremony between Katherine and Arthur which, the pamphlet later informs its readers, was to be performed by the Archbishop of Canterbury in St Paul's Cathedral. Although the image could be taken from a generic woodcut of a marriage ceremony (printers often recycled woodcuts for the illustration of a range of different texts), this one definitely appears to illustrate the particular subject of this pamphlet and was probably therefore produced for this text (and possibly re-used on various occasions after that). The prince and princess are central in the foreground; he clasps her right hand with his right and they face each other whilst also being angled slightly outwards towards the reader. Behind them facing directly out (almost as if addressing the reader from a pulpit) is the figure of a bishop in full regalia or 'pontificalibus' as it is described in the pamphlet text.[26] He

---

[26] *Remembraunce for the Traduction & Mariage*, fol. Avii.

holds his fingers in the traditional pontifical poise – the first and second fingers pointing outwards. Surrounding the tableau of the central three figures are eight people – four men standing to the side of and behind the prince and four women in similar positions to the men but on the side of the princess. The eleven people are all standing very close together. It is almost as if they are pressed into the frame of the woodcut, but also presumably the woodcut designer intended to give the impression of a collection of individuals all involved in one intensely important event.

The male and female supporters are represented as being dressed in their finest clothing. The woodcut pays much attention to the details of the women's long pleated dresses, the men's fashionable gowns which are open at the front and brought together at the waist by a girdle. The prince's gown is left open at the front rather than being secured by a belt, to reveal more of his patterned tunic as well as his tight leggings – perhaps this was thought to emphasise his strength and general manliness. All the sleeves are very full with wide cuffs, the dresses have long trailing pieces which each woman holds in her hands. All those assembled, except the prince, are wearing a hat. The men are sporting various styles of cloth cap (the bishop, of course, has a mitre), the supporting women are wearing varying styles of headdress with long pieces of material falling down their shoulders, and the princess appears to be wearing a small coronet. Alongside the focus on pleats and folds which emphasises the expensive amounts of material in each of these costumes, the woodcut also indicates that these fabrics were of varying patterns. This is signalled (particularly on the men's outfits) by the clear difference between a bold diagonal stripe, a narrow vertical stripe and a more complicated swirling pattern on the prince's tunic.

The background to the woodcut also appears to be carefully designed to reflect the plans for the occasion. At the rear left of the frame is an archway which, by being filled with a blank white space, looks as if it leads out into a distinctly different location from where the assembled party stands. By contrast, the remainder of the backdrop is covered in various styles of broken lines which are representative of different types of brick, stonework or wooden boarding, and this is broken up by vertical lines which look like pillars, and also by a couple of small arched windows with what looks now like the distinctive diamond pattern of Tudor glass. All of these combinations give the effect of a number of small recesses being behind the party of people which might be chapels, all clad with different building materials. Finally the floor is decorated in a bold black and white tiled arrangement reminiscent of so many fifteenth- and sixteenth- century northern European paintings of interiors. The chequered flooring adds to the sense that this is a rather fine and fashionable ensemble in a grand place which the pamphlet informs the reader is St Paul's Cathedral. All of these details on this small black and white woodcut image present an enticement for the reader to turn the page and peruse the written information which presents the plans for this important event, beginning from the arrival of Princess Katherine at Southampton, to the departure after the marriage of the party and its royal, spiritual, and civic entourage down the Thames in a convoy of boats.

The Written Text of the Pamphlet

The tone of the written text is rather like an itinerary of proposed events. The pamphlet runs chronologically through the events from arrival to departure after the wedding, and the various sections are separated out with phrases traditionally used in legal and administrative documents such as 'In Primis' and 'Item', which are themselves highlighted by customarily used paragraph marks. In addition, there are also some headings to signal certain aspects of the organisation such as 'By the quenes comaundement' and some which are addressed to a particular administrative group in the household's organisation such as 'Clerke of the Werkis by the over sighte of master comptroller' and 'Master Secretary and the Maister of the Rolls'. This structure immediately encourages the reader to imagine a well-orchestrated plan with a clearly defined set of requirements.

The text begins by describing each of the parties of people the princess must meet as she moves towards London (the different 'metyngs' are itemised in the text). Details of the numbers of people involved at all stages are also provided with precision; this includes the numbers of attendants to the princess at her landing, the numbers of gentlemen and yeomen, the numbers and types of horses to follow the princess. Costume and equipment is also described in some detail with a particular emphasis here on what is appropriate for different status groups or 'estates'; this includes the types of official staves the yeomen and gentlemen will hold, and the types of chairs and litters to be used for carrying the princess and her lady attendants. The fourth meeting is to be with the mayor of London and certain citizens of London. The King's counsel and the mayor are to 'devyse the maner therof with all the solempnytes & ceremonyes necessary for the honour of the cyte and of the feste'.[27]

There follows various precise information about the choreography of the processions, particularly once the princess has entered into London, and specifically concerning the route taken into and through St Paul's Cathedral on her arrival there the day before the wedding ceremony. The pamphlet proposes that she be conveyed 'through the high stretis of London in such case accustomed to the west dore of the churche of poules …' and that she be met there by the Bishop of London accompanied by 'as many miters of his diosise as he can get attende' to receive the princess at the west door and then 'with the quere of the churche processionally to goo byfore hir to the hygh aulter'.[28]

The choreography and arrival of dignitaries for the actual marriage service, which it is proposed should be on a Sunday 'for the more solempnyte of the same', are then given with precision.[29] This includes some elements of timing with a

---

[27]   *Remembraunce for the Traduction & Mariage*, fol. Avi.
[28]   *Remembraunce for the Traduction & Mariage*, fol. Avii.
[29]   *Remembraunce for the Traduction & Mariage*, fol. Aviii.

suggestion that the service should begin 'somewhat before' 9am;[30] as well as arrangements for the arrival of various dignitaries, including the Archbishop of Canterbury and other bishops and abbots of his diocese together with every other bishop and abbot of the parliament, in an entourage of boats escorting the King from Westminster Palace. The arrival at St Paul's of the prince himself is also described including the choreography of his entry into the church 'at the fourth dore next west warde to our lady of grace in the body of the church', and from there to be conveyed to 'the haute place' (high place) to be made before the consistory in the body of the church.[31] The pamphlet points out that various precedents for the construction of the high place had been set at other royal occasions such as coronations and the baptism of the King's children. This certainly reasserts the significance of this particular marriage ceremony by placing it in the ceremonial and visual context of these other dynastically significant occasions.

The processional route for the princess is also described such that on leaving the great door of the bishop's palace, accompanied by 'greate astatis of lordis and ladies', she is to make her entry through the great west door and go to the same high place. The pamphlet appears to anticipate some crowd control issues at this point as it proposes:

> Item for the more easy comynge of the seide princesse. It is devised that barris shalbe made from the seide palleis gate unto the seide gret west dore of the churche. And from the saide grete weste dore so all alonge the churche to the quere dore of the same.[32]

As the princess walks between the great gate and the high place, the pamphlet proposes that trumptes 'stonde on loft over the same west dore' and 'blowe contynuelly'.[33]

Aspects of the service itself are then described, with a focus on the ceremonial rather than on the details of liturgy. This includes a memorandum about the design of the high place which is to be built by the Clerk of the Works: it should be designed that the prince and princess are able to escape from what, the implication is, could be a lengthy service and observe the ceremony from the bishop's palace. This involves the making of a back door in the consistory which 'may be sone doone and at litell charge'.[34] There follows a brief consideration of how the banns of marriage should be taken and then a query concerning whether the princess needs to be given away by the custom of Spain as she would by English custom. If she needs to be given away then 'who shall gyve the pryncesse as bride Is to be respyted unto further knowledge be had who shall have comissuon from the kinge

30   *Remembraunce for the Traduction & Mariage*, fol. Aviii.
31   *Remembraunce for the Traduction & Mariage*, fol. Bi.
32   *Remembraunce for the Traduction & Mariage*, fol. Bi.
33   *Remembraunce for the Traduction & Mariage*, fol. Bii.
34   *Remembraunce for the Traduction & Mariage*, fol. Bii.

and quene of Spayne so to doo'.[35] The pamphlet glosses over what actually happens at the high place where the matrimony occurs, merely furnishing this crucial phase in the legal proceedings with the vague sentence that 'whan all shalbe fynysshed that is to be done upone the saide haute place for the matrimory', then the prince and princess will descend and process hand in hand straight through the church and through the quire to appointed places at the high altar where high mass will take place. Minstrels are to play continually during this procession from their positions 'on hight in the vawtis of the church'.[36] It seems that the high mass may also be a lengthy process as provision is once again to be made for the prince and princess to have 'some place secretly to resort unto' if necessary during the mass. The remainder of the description of this section is now lost.

The final portion of the pamphlet as it survives gives information about the departure from the church by barge and boat. The text indicates that the dignitaries, both temporal and spiritual, will require to be transported – although most of the detail in this section actually focuses on arranging the convoy that is to be provided by the mayor, aldermen, and citizens representing the different guilds and fellowships of London. The pamphlet suggests that this is the same procedure as is used annually for the oath-taking ceremony by the new mayor at the King's exchequer in Westminster. This ceremony entails all the aldermen and every craft guild and fellowship dressing in the 'clothe of theire crafte'. The convoy would provide a very colourful spectacle travelling down the Thames but as the comparison the pamphlet makes with other civic occasions suggests, not a sight which was unique to this royal occasion.

The pamphlet also points out that because of the 'kinges determynacion to go to westmynster by water' that all these London residents need to make sure that they make preparations for using their great boats and 'ship boats' because the barges and boats that they usually use for this kind of ceremonial occasion 'muste of necessite nowe serve for the lordes them selfe'.[37] The final paragraph provides a few details of how the water transport is to be orchestrated, and instructs that the boats containing the various dignitaries, the mayor and the London crafts should 'hover and attende' the king's barge at Baynard's Castle, and then:

> all the other bargis and botis to rowe by the kynge after the kynge and aboute the kynge as the space of the river with thebbe or flowe as gode ordre shall leede them to the tyme his grace shalbe landyd at the greate brydge of westmynster and no barge nor bote to lande but suche as shalbe assigned [...] And after that done all other bargis and botis not apoynted to lande shall departe to their lodgynges with the kynges special thankes [38]

---

35 *Remembraunce for the Traduction & Mariage*, fol. Biv.
36 *Remembraunce for the Traduction & Mariage*, fol. Biv.
37 *Remembraunce for the Traduction & Mariage*, fol. Ci.
38 *Remembraunce for the Traduction & Mariage*, fol. Cii.

Reactions to the Pamphlet

One might imagine that this pamphlet was designed to be an announcement for the eagerly anticipated arrival of the princess into the city, and into England. Certainly other evidence indicates that there was mounting excitement during that year, and that there were several deferrals and changes in the plan subsequent to the printing of this pamphlet's version of events. *The Great Chronicle of London*, for example, records that on St Francis' day, 4 October 1501, the first certain tidings came to the mayor of the landing of Dame Katherine the daughter of the King of Spain. This, the entry stresses, was now definite as news of her landing at Plymouth (not Southampton as initially planned and recorded in the *Traduction & Mariage*) on 2 October had been brought from the King. Up until that certain news 'many tymys ffleing Rumours Ran that she was landid sundry tymys beffore'.[39] Does the pamphlet of 1500 count amongst these 'rumours'?

The intention of the pamphlet, however, does not seem solely concerned with stirring up its readers' excited anticipation of the extraordinary sights which the marriage pageants would present. Rather, it seems to show a prevailing tendency to record and detail the administrative arrangements necessary for the day. In its format it may well borrow from various recorded narratives of such plans which were produced by officials of the royal household. Indeed, some of the headings which refer to the responsibilities of specific offices and the references to other documentation such as rolls which contain lists would seem to confirm this.[40] The attention to administrative details might not seem the most exciting elements of the occasion to the modern reader, but it would probably be a mistake to assume that a sixteenth-century reader would hold the same view. The fact that much of the attention to organisation focuses on ensuring that appropriate precedents are followed is perhaps indicative of the expected readership for this pamphlet. The concern with the appointment of individuals responsible for specific aspects of the organisation; the ordering of specific status groups in the processions; and also the ways that all the information is recorded all seem to cater for a reader who is accustomed to and interested by issues associated with ceremonial conduct.

Perhaps one of the methods used by this pamphlet in the transmission of information is to talk to the reader in a language he (or maybe she) understands: the language of administration and civic organisation. At the same time, the extent of the organisation involved for the welcoming of the future Queen into England and her passage to London is, of course, on a much greater and grander scale than most readers would have previously experienced. So, it is feasible to think of the pamphlet as taking the reader on an imaginative journey which uses his (or her) own relatively small-scale experiences of civic organisation and the vocabulary of administration, accounting, and status, in order to help him (or her) to engage with

---

[39]   *Great Chronicle*, p. 298.

[40]   See, for example, *Remembraunce for the Traduction & Mariage*, fol. Aiii; and Kipling, *Receyt*, pp. xlv, lxi.

the organisation of this extraordinary, unique, and politically very significant occasion. In fact, on the surviving copy of this pamphlet in the British Library, there are some annotations which suggest that one reader at least was prompted to think about his (or her) own administrative dealings in response to the pamphlet. At two places on this text, there are annotations relating to administrative affairs, although unfortunately both of these are fairly faint. The first details, in Latin, the dates of some courts (*curia*) during the reign of Henry VII;[41] the second, also in Latin, appears to concern an account for some goods purchased, perhaps for some kind of celebration (*jocund* ...), for which the name 'Master John Tyrell' occurs several times.[42] The fact that these annotations are in Latin is of interest. It indicates that this reader is literate (in Latin). But more interestingly the reader's use of both a conventional language and format for recording administrative details suggests that the tone of the pamphlet seems to him (or her) to be appropriate to such additions. In other words, this pamphlet is prompting the anonymous reader to think in administrative terms. But why would the pamphlet and those who commissioned its publication wish to engage the reader in this way?

It seems very possible that this pamphlet represents a concerted effort to encourage the civic community of London to feel included in the royal ceremonies in order that they might cooperate. This cooperation included the provision and preparation of their boats on account of the king's 'determynacion' to go to Westminster by water. The pamphlet makes the point, finally, that whereas the barges and boats belonging to the spiritual and temporal lords were usually used to serve the said city at the presentment of the Mayor, on this occasion the lords themselves would require these barges (which we might assume are the better boats) for themselves. Whilst seeking the cooperation of the members of the civic community, then, the pamphlet also clearly indicates that their help should be seen by the townsmen as a favour repaid.

But organisation and administration, however interesting to the anonymous readers of London, are not the sole focus of this pamphlet. The woodcut image provides a glimpse of the marriage ceremony itself and seems to be attempting to portray this as an occasion of finery and grand surroundings. Perhaps this is intended to whet the reader's appetite for imagining the great occasion. Perhaps also it might encourage the reader to imagine, in an aspirant way, what it must be like to rub shoulders with the people of great estate – the kinds of people who would be converging on the city for this momentous occasion of the marriage of Princess Katherine with Prince Arthur.

The pamphlet certainly endorses the entitlement of the anonymous witness to see the ceremonial high-spot of the proceedings in St Paul's when the prince and princess are to be joined in matrimony. The description of this episode clearly

---

41   *Remembraunce for the Traduction & Mariage*, fol. Ai.

42   *Remembraunce for the Traduction & Mariage*, fol. Cii. There also seems to be some attempt to turn this information into a rhyming couplet. On the subject of rhyming annotations see Salter, ' "The Days Moralised" ', pp. 159–61.

indicates that the central group of the prince and princess, with the cardinal and ministers, should stand on the 'gode large space' which forms the stage of the high place all together, with no one else standing higher up the steps of this structure than is necessary. Bishops, abbots and officers are put in their relative social positions here by the information that they may stand 'lower up on the sayde steppis of the haute place'. But significantly the reason given for these gradated standing positions in the pamphlet is specifically, 'therby there growe none Impedyment to the sight of the people'.[43] Presumably, when it came to the actual occasion, the crowds would be too great to enable everyone to squeeze into the cathedral, so the pamphlet's goals for inclusiveness might never actually be realised.

By giving details about the ceremonial and processional elements of the arrival and the marriage service itself, the anonymous witness is included in the most significant elements of this occasion in both political and religious terms. The arrangements for this marriage, therefore, might also cause the reader to think about this subject more generally. Indeed, one annotation which is now rather obscured in the tight binding (probably written by the same reader as are the administrative annotations) is a whimsical rhyming ditty on some subject associated with love. This has been written on pages which discuss the meeting of the princess with the mayor and citizens of London with due ceremonies for the honour of the city. This is a section of the pamphlet, therefore, which specifically involves witnesses like the anonymous reader so it may be significant that he (or she) has chosen to annotate here. It is not possible to make out the whole of it but it appears in part to read as follows:

Yor lovers names ys butt[s?] fresche }} but whyll I leve the wryt shall I
Woht gifte in wrytyng ys desyre   }} farewell my frende adieu […][44]

Conclusion

In the pamphlet, the anonymous witness had access to administrative information, details about precedent, and the elements of ceremonial display required for various social hierarchies to honour foreign royalty. The reader was also furnished with information about the spiritually and politically vital elements of this occasion in the form of the arrangements for the matrimony ceremony, and his or her right to be involved in this as a spectator was positively endorsed. All this information would have impinged on his or her sense of personal identity and social position in relation to the nobility and royalty involved in the ceremonies. It may also have informed the witness's own views about the organisation of future events and celebrations during the remainder of his or her life. The administrative and

---

43   *Remembraunce for the Traduction & Mariage*, fol. Biii.

44   *Remembraunce for the Traduction & Mariage*, fol. Av.

organisational emphases of the pamphlet also seem to have encouraged at least one anonymous reader to think about other administrative issues as well as to muse poetically about love and the writing of love ditties. Nothing in this pamphlet, however, seems to have prepared the reader for the experience of being a witness to the pageants. Information about the content of the pageants, the records of which themselves offer a seductively first-person style of account, is not provided in any detail by this pamphlet, although the intention that the anonymous reader should be a witness to these extraordinary events is signalled.

Chapter 6

William Cornysh

Introduction

William Cornysh, Master of the King's Chapel in the reign of Henry VIII, has been described as 'the most considerable figure in the history of Early Tudor court revels'.[1] Cornysh did have a fascinating career and may have played an important role in bringing new forms of drama to the English royal court. But this attribution does not consider the experiences and views of William Cornysh himself. In the light of a new interpretation of a piece of personal evidence concerning the death and life of William Cornysh, this Chapter re-examines the biography of this composer, poet, and dramatist and in so doing examines one man's experiences of that culturally transitional phase known as the 'early English Renaissance'.[2] The resulting impression is of a man whose cultural creativity oscillated between innovation and tradition. Cornysh maintained an interest in the traditional late Medieval forms of belief and representation whilst also investing in the new forms of cultural expression and display required for a Renaissance court.

William Cornysh is known today for two main reasons both of which are associated with his role as Master of the King's Chapel. Firstly, he is famous for his involvement in the spectacle and pageantry of the Tudor royal courts of c. 1494–1522/3, and secondly he is known for his activities as a composer of both secular and religious music, some of which survives today.[3] Of all the people whose lives are considered in this book, this individual has probably already received the most attention. A pioneer of such attention, in connection with his work on the drama of the sixteenth-century English royal courts, is Sydney Anglo. It was he who described Cornysh as 'the most considerable figure in the history of Early Tudor court revels'.[4]

---

[1]   Sydney Anglo, 'William Cornysh in a Play: Pageants, Prison, and Politics', *Review of English Studies*, 10/40 (1959): 347–60, p. 347.

[2]   See Introduction, Chapter 1, for a discussion of this.

[3]   Sydney Anglo, *Spectacle, Pageantry and Early Tudor Policy* (Oxford, Clarendon, 1969); Fiona Kisby, 'Officers and Office-Holding at the English Court: A Study of the Chapel Royal, 1485–1547', *Royal Musical Association Research Chronicle*, 32 (1999): 1–61.

[4]   Anglo, 'William Cornysh in a Play', 347.

Elements of the reconstruction of William Cornysh's life have been pursued before. Some aspects of these reconstructions relate to areas of uncertainty about the identity of this figure. One persistent area of uncertainty concerns the question of whether there existed one or two William Cornyshes.[5] This confusion appears to be particularly relevant when it comes to deciding on the authorship of the musical compositions attributed to 'William Cornysh'. The new version of the lives of the William Cornyshes in the *Oxford Dictionary of National Biography* helps to clarify some of these uncertainties by adding more:

> The attribution of certain works to one William Cornysh junior in a manuscript of (apparently) 1501 discloses the existence at that time of an older composer of renown from whom the younger man needed to be distinguished. Eight major compositions attributed simply to William Cornysh were included in the Eton choirbook, a collection of Marian votive antiphons and Magnificats compiled between about 1502 and 1505; four survive complete, the remainder being incomplete or lost. The style of the surviving music is characteristic of a mature composer of the 1480s and 1490s, expansive in concept, ornate in detail, and requiring of its performers much virtuosity of vocal technique; it thus appears to be the work of a man born in the 1440s rather than thirty years later and (as first proposed by David Skinner in 1997) may be attributed to the elder William Cornysh. These works were well known and widely copied. (Further lost works attributed simply to Cornysh may be the work of either the older or the younger man of that name.) [...] certain settings of Lady mass sequences copied for the choir of King's College, Cambridge, in 1508/9 may well have been his work rather than that of his earlier namesake, as also may have been the four-part masses and single six-part mass recorded among that choir's repertory in 1529.[6]

The premise in this Chapter is that there were two William Cornyshs, that they were quite possibly father and son, and that the one whose life is considered here, 'the younger', was responsible for the pageants for which evidence survives today, although probably not for all of the musical compositions.[7] The life of William Cornysh as a revel writer has attracted particular attention. In a self-consciously modest article written in 1959, for example, Sydney Anglo suggested that he would 'fill in one or two gaps in our knowledge of Cornysh's career' and 'draw attention

---

[5]   See, W.H. Grattan-Flood, *Early Tudor Composers: Biographical Sketches of Thirty-two Musicians and Composers of the Period* (Oxford, OUP, 1925), 20; *The Dictionary of National Biography*, vol. 4 (London, OUP, 1887, repr. 1960), pp. 1172–4. Grattan-Flood proposed one, suggesting that a John Cornysh was the father of one William with the birth date of roughly 1468. For a recent discussion of this confusion see Kisby, 'Officers and Office-Holding', 51–2; and for a recent dispute of the existence of the two Williams see David Skinner, 'William Cornysh: Clerk or Courtier?', *Musical Times*, 138 (1997), 5–15.

[6]   The entry for William Cornysh in the *Oxford Dictionary of National Biography*, by Roger Bowers, is available at http://www.oxforddnb.com/view/article/6347.

[7]   For further confirmation of this premise see, Kisby, 'Officers and Office Holding', 51–3.

to three sources that have been overlooked in this connexion'.[8] The article is then divided into three main sections corresponding with its title: pageants, prison, and politics. Each section examines a new piece of evidence, or new information about a known piece of evidence, concerning the life of William Cornysh. Anglo's analysis and interpretation of the 'new' evidence for Cornysh's life in 1959 was very much concerned with tracing sources, and providing and correcting factual information about the career and life of this Tudor individual. A desire to 'fill in the gaps' seems to imply that a life, and the act of reconstructing it, is like a jigsaw puzzle: something whose reconstruction can be completed. One central approach to the writing of biographies in this book, however, is that biographical reconstructions are inevitably partial. This is particularly the case here because the people whose lives are being reconstructed lived several centuries ago; and also because they are not the best known figures – the royal, noble, or infamous.

William Cornysh as Pageant-Designer

Various well-known sources of evidence survive for Cornysh's involvement with the revels and pageants of the royal household in the very late fifteenth and early sixteenth centuries. He was involved in the production and performance of 'disguisings' and pageants late in the reign of Henry VII and on into the reign of Henry VIII when he became Master of the Chapel. Cornysh's involvement with the design of pageants and revels in the reign of Henry VII has been seen as significant by historians of the drama because it indicates his role as an innovator of dramatic style in the fifteenth century. The first appearance of Cornysh in the records appears to be in the Twelfth Night celebrations of 1494, and the second major event was the marriage ceremonies of Prince Arthur in 1501.[9]

The Great Chronicle of London provides evidence of Cornysh's early involvement with the pageantry of the royal court. The earliest of these dramatic appearances for which evidence survives is a scene occurring at Westminster Hall where gathered together are various dignitaries of London, and the King and Queen. *The Chronicle* tells it as follows:

> then about xj of Clok In the nyght, afftyr the kyng was comyn Into the hall with dyvers ambassadours of Fraunce, & of Spayn, and the Quene wyth hyr ladyes & Gentylwomen, and every astate was assygnyd unto theyr standing, Anoon cam In the kings players and shewid a goodly Interlude before the kyng. But or they hadd ffynysshid theyr play Cam In Ridyng oon of the kyngys Chapell namyd Cornysh apparaylid afftyr the ffygure of Seynt George, and aftir ffolowid a ffayer vyrgyn attyrid lyke unto a kyngys dowgthyr, and ledyng by a sylkyn lace a Terrible & huge Rede dragun, The which in Sundry placys of the halle as he passyd spytt ffyre at hys mowth And when the said Cornysh was

---

[8]   Anglo, 'William Cornysh in a Play', 347.

[9]   Anglo, 'William Cornysh in a Play', 348–50.

cummyn before the kyng he uttyrd a certayn spech made In balad Royall, aftyr ffynysshyng whereof he began This antempn off Seynt George, O Georgi deo Care, whereunto the kyngys Chapell which stood ffast [by] answerid Salvatorem Deprecarem, ut Gubernet Angliam, And soo sang owth alle the hool antempn with lusty Corage, In passe tyme whereof The said Cornysh avoydid wyth the dragon, and the vyrgyn was ladd unto the Quenys standing, ...[10]

Apart from the pageants in celebration of Prince Arthur's marriage to Katharine of Aragon in 1501, the bulk of evidence for William Cornysh's involvement with revel-making survives from the reign of Henry VIII.[11] Various account books detailing the expenses for the revels of the first quarter of the sixteenth century provide evidence for payments made to Cornysh for his work on a range of pageants at the royal court during this period. His main involvement with these events is generally thought to date from 1509, when he took up the office of Master of the King's Chapel.[12]

There are plenty of well-known surviving accounts of these Tudor revels, sumptuous events involving various staff of the royal household, their children, and the young choristers of the chapel as well as Cornysh himself.[13] A recurring impression received on reading the many accounts of the revels is the centrality of William Cornysh to these events. Of course as Master of the Chapel he had a significant role in these productions but over and again, even in what one might expect to be impartial accounts of expenditure, there are little details of information concerning William Cornysh. These details build a picture of a somewhat flamboyant man very much at the centre-stage of these revels.

Near the beginning of his involvement with the court of Henry VIII, for example, on 12 and 13 February 1511, Cornysh devised a pageant called 'The Golden Arbour of the Arch Yard of Pleasure'.[14] This was a typically sumptuous event, which involved the creation of an arbour and an orchard on a 'pageant' (a

---

[10]   *The Great Chronicle of London*, ed. A.H. Thomas, and I.D. Thornley (London, 1938), 251.

[11]   For further details of all Anglo's 'new' sources, see Anglo, 'William Cornysh in a Play', 347–8. Another source of evidence for Cornysh's role in designing revels and pageants is found in a letter written by a Spanish Ambassador who accompanied Charles V to England in 1522. The letter describes the political pageant organised by Cornysh for this occasion, adding significant details to the account provided by Edward Hall in his chronicle.

[12]   J. M. Manly, 'The Children of the Chapel Royal and their Masters', in *The Cambridge History of English Literature*, vol. 6, 'The Drama to 1642', Part Two, 279–92 (Cambridge, 1932, repr. 1966), especially 281–4; Kisby, 'Officers and Office holding', 51–3.

[13]   See, for example, *Letters and Papers Foreign and Domestic of the Reign of Henry VIII, Preserved in the Public Record Office, The British Museum, and Elsewhere in England* [hereafter *L.P.*], 21 vols, 2, Parts 2 and 3, Part 2, arranged and catalogued by J.S. Brewer (London, 1864–7).

[14]   *L.P.*, vol. 2, part 2, p. 1495.

wagon) which was moveable. The pageant was 'sett and wrought with kindly flowers, as rosys, lyllys, mary gollds, gelofers, primroses, kowslyps' and more; and the orchard was 'sett with horenge trees, ponygarnat trees, happyll trees, per trees, ollyf trees'.[15] Twelve lords and ladies sat in the arbour, and seven minstrels sat outside it playing 'strange' instruments; about thirty of the chapel children also stood on the pageant (wagon). In front of this structure, on the steps, stood various people disguised including Master Cornysh, together with a 'Master Kaan', and the 'Master Sub Dean'. Fourteen yards of material (type unspecified) was provided for a 'gown and bonnet' made for Cornysh 'in which he played one of his parts'; Master Kaan was to receive a 'half gown' which required seven yards. 46½ yards of green satin were also provided for the same pageant 'for another gown for Cornysh'. And 952 cut-out letters of H and K, using sixty-eight yards of material, were set onto Cornysh's and Kaan's Gowns. The dignitaries also had Hs and Ks made of gold leaf sewn onto their garments. The list of letters includes 259 of H weighing 89 ounces and 218 Ks weighing 81 ounces, and another 24½ ounces of gold letters together with hearts. The King, for example, had 887 pieces (presumably Hs, Ks, and hearts) sewn onto his garment. Although Cornysh's Hs and Ks were probably not of gold, it seems that he was not going to miss out on this opportunity to indulge in wearing a highly decorative costume or, in fact, two costumes.

The evidence of the pageants produced during Cornysh's term as the Master of the Chapel, c. 1509–22/3, indicates that the visual effect of the performances was considered of vital importance, apparently over and above any attribution of a textual narrative or 'story-line'; titles of the plays or pageants often being left unrecorded. In a play found in the accounts of 1520, for example, the names of the characters are given without any direct clarification of the story being portrayed. It was recorded that those of Cornysh's 'children' (the choristers) who played 'the sun', 'Winter', 'Wind' and 'Rain' should be provided with large quantities of gold and silver damask.[16] This pageant has been attributed to various authors including John Rastell, although there is no mention of him in the *Letters and Papers* account, the pageant here being described as 'Cornysh's pastime'.[17]

Apparently befitting what has been described as a new emphasis on Burgundian style, there is also frequent attention to the choreography of these events and its musical accompaniment. In the '*Garden de Esperance*' performed at Greenwich in 1516, for example, six brightly dressed knights and ladies walked through the garden in order to bring the pageant to the hall, accompanied by the 'noise' of minstrels. When the procession ended the 'personages' descended and danced before the King, Queen and assembled court. In the 'Troylus and Pandor' medley

[15]   *L.P.*, vol. 2, part 2, p. 1496.

[16]   *L.P.*, vol. 3, Part 2, pp. 1550–1.

[17]   *L.P.* vol. 3, Part 2, p. 1550; for this attribution of a play Rastell in c. 1520 entitled *The Nature of the Four Elements,* see Alison Weir, *Henry VIII King and Court* (London, Cape, 2001), p. 91.

of 1515, it is recorded that three 'strange' knights (made strange by their red and yellow costumes) fought six castle knights (dressed in green and white) in a battle which involved firstly 'certain strokes' made with spears and then a 'fair battle of xii strokes' done with 'naked swords'.[18]

Although there is a general lack of evidence for speeches and plots, when the existence of words is recorded there are recurring instances of Cornysh's involvement not only in the production of these speeches but also in their performance. This would seem to run contrary to suggestions that the poetic monologue went out of fashion in this period.[19] But whatever was the fashion, the involvement of Cornysh in these speeches indicates that he was a central character in the spoken aspects of these pageants. And seeing as he devised these pageants himself, we must surmise that he chose to put himself at centre-stage in order to perform these opening speeches. At the Eltham-based Epiphany Revels of 1515, for example, Cornysh and two other gentlemen of the chapel began the performance by first declaring the intent of the pageant 'by process of speech'.[20] And, at the start of the *'Garden de Esperance'* in 1516, it is recorded that Master Cornysh (alone) 'showed by speech' the effect and intent of the pageant, '... so declaring his purpose'.[21] These examples are indicative of one of Cornysh's important roles as an explicator of the purpose of the pageant, which might otherwise seem like a rather mysterious array of scenes. Cornysh also occurs in the record when other parties have speeches, such as at the Castle pageant of 1515, when the queen appeared out of the castle with her six ladies and they made speeches after the 'device of Mr. Cornysh'.[22] There followed a melodious song, played from the towers of the castle by minstrels dressed in long garments of white and green Bruges satin, presumably providing musical accompaniment for the action that lacked words.

The accounts of the revels conjure up images of excessive events, spectacularly colourful and sparkling outfits with strange dances, scenery and music. William Cornysh would often be present at the start of the play to explain the ensuing events, and then he might take several parts. As in 1515, when for the 'Troylus and Pandor' extravaganza he needed a mantel and a bishop's surcoat of yellow sarcenet in order to play 'Calchas' and also a garment of black sarcenet with a bonnet and a coat of armour, for parts unspecified. The black ensemble might have been his costume for playing 'the herald'.[23] For his explication at the beginning of the *'Garden de Esperance'*, Cornysh was apparelled like a 'stranger' in a gown of red

---

[18]   *L.P.* vol. 3, Part 2, p. 1505.
[19]   Gordon Kipling, *The Triumph of Honour: Burgundian Origins of the Elizabethan Renaissance* (The Hague, Leiden University Press, 1977), p. 102.
[20]   *L.P.* vol. 2, Part 2, p. 1501.
[21]   *L.P.* vol. 2, Part 2, p. 1509.
[22]   *L.P.* vol. 2, Part 2, p. 1505.
[23]   *L.P.* vol. 2, Part 2, pp. 1505–6.

sarcenet with a coat of arms on it, his horse 'trapped' with blue sarcenet.[24] The importance of music, the need for Cornysh's explanations and the general lack of evidence for scripts tends to suggest that these events largely relied on visual spectacle in conjunction with the explications of William Cornysh. This hints at the importance of using systems of colour-coding for the various ornate costumes in order to make symbolic battle-factions and other elements in the story of each pageant (insofar as they had a story). These coding systems would need to be sufficiently understood by the observers for the pageant to be enjoyed, and retain a measure of mystery for their wonderment.

William Cornysh as a Dramatic Innovator

There is a tendency in biographical accounts of William Cornysh's life to proclaim him as an innovator of new forms, and therefore as a 'Renaissance man' in the sphere of drama. The second early appearance of Cornysh as a revel-maker, at the marriage ceremonies of Katherine of Aragon and Prince Arthur in November 1501, for example, has been considered particularly important as an early example of the introduction of new forms of dramatic representation in England.[25] Particularly of interest to historians of the drama is the complexity of Cornysh's pageants in these ceremonies. Sydney Anglo, for example, views these 'early' dramatic productions as 'ancestors' to the masque plays of the seventeenth century. In *Spectacle, Pageantry, and Early Tudor Policy,* he wrote about William Cornysh's important role in the formation of Henrician Court revels as follows:

> amidst the series of pageant entertainments presented for the celebrations of 1501, William Cornysh [...] introduced his multiform spectacle, combining music, poetry, *débat*, combat, scenic display, and dance. This complex spectacle was adopted during the early years of Henry VIII's reign – when Cornysh, as Master of the Children of the Chapel Royal came to the fore as deviser of court entertainments – and is the direct ancestor of the mask which reached its apogee at the courts of James I and his son Charles I.[26]

William Cornysh has therefore been viewed as an originator of a new form of dramatic production – a type of production that probably had its very early emergence in 1494, when Cornysh burst into Westminster Hall dressed as St George; and which was displayed in the full glory of the new form at the set of

---

[24]   *L.P.* vol. 2, Part 2, p. 1509.

[25]   Anglo, 'William Cornysh in a Play', 350; Francis Grose and Thomas Astle, *The Antiquarian Repertory* (London, Jeffery, 1808), vol. 2, pp. 296–319; and see Sydney Anglo, 'The London Pageants for the Reception of Katharine of Aragon, November 1501', *Journal of the Warburg and Courtauld Institutes,* 26 (1969), 53–89; also see Kipling, *Triumph of Honour,* especially Chapter 5.

[26]   Anglo, *Spectacle,* p. 118.

pageants organised for Prince Arthur and Katharine of Aragon, in 1501.[27] More recently, it has also been proposed that there was a significant transition in style even in the seven years between the 1494 and the 1501 events, and that this transition relates directly to the involvement of William Cornysh in pageant design and innovation: Gordon Kipling suggests that Cornysh's involvement as the *designer* of the 1501 pageants (rather than his role merely as a player in the 1494 disguisings) sees a significant change involving the introduction of Burgundian-style pageant cars and the closer integration of the various elements of speech, performance, and dancing.[28]

It is interesting to speculate the extent to which recent assessments of Cornysh's role as an innovator have been informed by the already established myths of this man's role as a Renaissance innovator. These myths have been circulating for quite a while. An early edition of *The Cambridge History of English Literature*, for example, used evidence from the better-known period of Cornysh's artistic production (c. 1509–1522/3), to also describe him as a significant innovator of dramatic form. In what seems a rather over-confident claim, this now rather aged volume says:

> If the 'story of Troylus and Pandor', performed by [Cornysh] and the children before the king at Eltham, Christmas 1515, was written by him, he may be regarded as the earliest known dramatiser of romantic fiction [...] It seems therefore only fair [...] to regard Cornysh as a pioneer in the production, if not the composition, of romantic drama.[29]

When Cornysh is being hailed as an innovator of new forms of pageant which looks forward to the seventeenth century, he is being viewed as if he were a cog in the great wheel of pageant history. He is also seen as a sort of dramatic genius whose innovations looked forward to a period beyond his own. This way of assessing Cornysh's life pays very little attention to his own perceptions and experiences and it does not really consider anything of audiences' experiences of the pageants at the time that they were produced. Instead this view tends to impose importance on Cornysh as a significant player in the evolution of dramatic forms. By contrast, the recent definitive description (in the *DNB*) of William Cornysh's life which includes an assessment of the importance of Cornysh's role as an innovator rather dampens those earlier claims to his genius. Roger Bowers states:

> Within his very limited circle of courtly pursuits Cornysh in his own time was probably a man of some consequence. In the longer run, however, most of his accomplishments appear but transitory. Renaissance ideals had as yet reached neither English music nor English letters; Cornysh was a late Medieval figure who was merely quite good at quite a number of things which on the whole proved to have little long-term future.[30]

---

27 See, Kipling, *Triumph of Honour*, especially Chapter 5.
28 Kipling, *Triumph of Honour*, pp. 102–4.
29 Manly, 'The Children of the Chapel Royal and their Masters', p. 283.
30 http://www.oxforddnb.com/view/article/6347.

Neither of these ways of describing Cornysh's important role in the development of drama and Renaissance ideals (as the foresighted genius or the ultimately inconsequential figure), attempts to access Cornysh's own experiences of being an innovator and the contemporary perceptions of him in this role. These ways of describing Cornysh's important place in the development of drama, therefore, do not attempt to access his own experiences of designing and producing pageants at the royal court.

William Cornysh's Last Will and Testament

There is a different piece of evidence which is relevant to William Cornysh's life and this does provide some clues about his personal interests in performance and his attitudes to drama. By looking at this piece of evidence it becomes possible to re-examine his role in the creation of pageants in relation to his own attitudes to drama and performance. The piece of evidence for Cornysh's life (or rather his death) that I wish to examine in this chapter is his last will and testament. Insubstantial as a single testamentary document may on the surface seem in itself, I hope to show how and why this particular last will and testament provides significant access to the character and concerns of this extraordinary man, during both his life and in his death. So my intention is to use this will document to embellish our knowledge of this individual, particularly because it provides significant information about his own attitudes to, and perceptions of, performance.

Cornysh's last will and testament was registered amongst the testamentary records for the Prerogative Court of Canterbury in the early sixteenth century.[31] The existence of this document has been known for a relatively long time, although it has often not been examined in much detail or not considered of significance. It was not mentioned in the entry on Cornysh in the 1887 edition of the *Dictionary of National Biography* (reprinted in 1960) but it was mentioned in Frank Harrison's account and description of the Eton Manuscript, in *Musica Britannica,* produced 1956–58.[32]

Where Cornysh's last will and testament has been mentioned, by scholars in the recent and less recent past, there has tended to be either a disregard for its significance or what might be termed a 'mis-regard' based on readings of this text which are incorrect. An early example of 'mis-regard' is found in Grattan-Flood's biographical account which bewails the uncertainties of Cornysh's life ending with a triumphal flourish that, '[o]ne thing is certain, his will was proved on December 1523'.[33] The will was actually proved in October of that year, a minor correction but one that is symptomatic of the lack of careful attention this document has received. A much more recent 'mis-regard' of the will document is found in the

[31] NA PROB 11/13/96v–97.
[32] Frank Ll. Harrison, *Musica Britannica*, vol. 10 (Stainer and Bell, 1967): 16.
[33] Grattan-Flood, *Early Tudor Composers*, p. 22.

New Grove Dictionary of Music and Musicians which states that Cornysh 'was buried in the rood church of East Greenwich'.[34] Cornysh requested his burial in the 'chapel of the rood' in the church of East Greenwich and not, as this transcription indicates, in the 'rood' church where 'rood' seems to imply the 'plain' or 'common' church of the same place. The significance of this correction is explained below. Neither is it the case that Cornysh was definitely buried in East Greenwich at all. The will document provides evidence of his request for burial at this location and not the fact of its happening. This is a point which reflects the way of approaching textual sources such as the last will and testament for their provision of significant evidence for the personal expression of hopes and attitudes and not necessarily for evidence of certain kinds of 'facts' or real occurrences.[35]

The evidence of Cornysh's last will and testament provides a clue to something more than the retrospective attribution of this man as a 'most considerable figure in the history of Tudor court revels': it adds to the possibilities for understanding William Cornysh's own personal perceptions of performance. Taken in the context of the well-known evidences for Tudor court pageantry alongside other of his cultural productions such as poetry (and his possible musical compositions), this document enables the reconstruction of some of Cornysh's own perceptions of issues associated with performance. The juxtaposition of these evidences seems entirely appropriate as they concern that most closely defined kind of context, the creative output of one man. But the outcome of putting them together, as a collection of 'contingent evidence' which all relates to this one life, does not result in a single view of one individual's programme of cultural innovation and production. What transpires is evidence which hints at the plurality of tensions and fissures in William Cornysh's attitudes, suggesting a man whose career was surrounded by questions and doubts: What constituted a performance? What types of performance produced truthful representations? What was the place of innovative and of traditional forms of cultural expression? What should be Cornysh's own role in all these productions?

William Cornysh's last will and testament provides evidence for his distinct and individual ideas about performance or theatricality – ideas which he chose to convey, for posterity and commemoration, in an unusual request for a final memorial. Most of Cornysh's will document is entirely unremarkable, it is also quite short. It was made on the second day of January 1512, just over ten years before he died. The will gives a few details about his family indicating that he was

---

[34] *The New Grove Dictionary of Music and Musicians,* ed. Stanley Sadie, vol. 6, 'Claudel to Dante' (London, Macmillan, 1977–2001), p. 493.

[35] For more consideration of the uses of the last will and testament as evidence see 'Katherine Styles', this volume. See also Elisabeth Salter, *Cultural Creativity in the Early English Renaissance: Popular Culture in Town and Country* (London, Palgrave Macmillan, 2006), Chapter 1; for a comparable attitude to a different but similar textual source see Nathalie Z. Davis, *Fiction in the Archives: Pardon Tales and their Tellers in Sixteenth Century France* (Oxford, OUP, 1987).

married to Joanne and that at the date of making the will, he probably had several
children living, both male and female; his first son and heir being called Henry.
These details of family are generally given in connection to his property bequests,
which centre on unspecified lands and tenements in Greenwich. This version of the
will document was proved (in October 1523), indicating that it was the final
written legal form of his wishes. Apart from the details concerning the
maintenance of various saints' lights in the church at East Greenwich, including
one particular lamp in the Chapel of the Rood in the same church, there is a
disappointing lack of evidence for Cornysh's cultural and spiritual tastes. He
bequeaths no books, musical compositions or other similar items. However, amid
this very average summary of a man's life there is one extraordinary request, which
is as follows:

> I will that there be made a Tombe of Bryke over me and a stone upon it and a border
> aboute the same *for people to knele upon of half a fote high* ...[36] [my emphasis]

Taken in the context of the career of William Cornysh as a performer and designer
of pageants and other dramatic events, I hope to show that this very unusual
commemorative request is in fact very significant. It is an invitation for a
performance. The particular precision of Cornysh's bequest makes his memorial
very unusual. But his is not a precision relying on exact requirements for the order
of service and how his mourners would behave, as is found in so many other
similar documents written at this time. I suggest that this request is much more
concerned with the emotional affect of the memorial on its 'audience'. Being such
an unusual testamentary request, this piece of evidence also shows how personal a
sixteenth century last will and testament could be, expressing in this case the very
particular interest of this individual in issues of performance.[37] This
commemorative request is therefore symptomatic of the extensive knowledge
Cornysh had of audience reaction through his vast experience of producing
dramatic effects during his career at the royal court. It was also produced at the
apogee of his career at the Tudor royal court and so should perhaps be seen as
evidence of Cornysh looking forward to this final performance whilst at the height
of his creative career.

Juxtaposing the Pageant and Will Evidences

Cornysh's pageants used well-known stories and scenarios that would have been
understood as a dramatic form by the audience and he may have combined these
with some new forms of dramatic representation. The audience would presumably

---

[36]   NA PROB 11/13/96v.
[37]   That it is unusual is not a claim that this request is entirely unique, although I have
not come across another one.

have understood much of the content of these performances because of the clear symbolic clues, employing the colour coding of popularly recognised signs. But alongside these devices of visual theatre, William Cornysh assumed a crucial role as the describer and explainer of the elements of these events which might not be so transparent to an audience, perhaps because of their new dramatic forms.[38] Through his explications, William Cornysh performs the role of the explainer of cultural transition. He self-consciously acted as a mediator, on behalf of the audience, and in so doing he perpetuated a tradition of using the preliminary monologue.

The central and multiple roles of William Cornysh in these pageants, and his self-ascribed role as a cultural mediator, should be taken in the context of the new evidence for his personal request for a commemorative performance at the point of his death. In William Cornysh's memorial, the 'people' who come to kneel at his tomb are not only the participants in a carefully orchestrated drama as one might expect given his lifetime experiences with dramatic representation. But in addition to this 'the people' seem actually to be invited to be responsible for the creation and production of this quasi-theatrical performance.

For this memorial setting, Cornysh is unable to begin with his customary explication of the pageant's meaning and intention. Instead, by making this testamentary request, he is providing the stage for 'the people' that come to kneel there. In effect, Cornysh encouraged and allowed his mourners to devise and create their own performances. No words were necessary; Cornysh was no longer there to provide them. So perhaps he envisaged that the sight of people kneeling at the tomb or the experience of kneeling there would have produced enough dramatic effect.

Presumably, Cornysh's intention was that when people arrived at the Rood Chapel in Greenwich, the legends of 'William Cornysh, Master of the King's Chapel' would be well known, so they ought to have had performance in mind as they knelt on the ledge of 'half a foot high'. This suggests he had a different perception of himself than Roger Bowers' description of the transitory figure of little long-term consequence.[39] Perhaps Cornysh intended that during the performance of his memorial, the 'people' might find themselves reflecting on their other experiences of commemoration – of friends and family – many of whom would have been local to this church and the community of Greenwich. Perhaps he was providing a performance space for these Greenwich people, where they might reflect on the more traditional (and quintessentially Medieval) performative acts of memorial like prayers at saints' shrines or obituary devotions.

Whatever were the reflections of these 'people' and whatever Cornysh envisaged such reflecting might entail, the early date of his will (made in 1512)

---

[38] Kipling, *Triumph of Honour*, pp. 110–111; on the reception of other such events see Susan Crane, *The Performance of Self: Ritual, Clothing and Identity During the Hundred Years War* (Philadelphia, Philadelphia University Press, 2001), p. 3.

[39] http://www.oxforddnb.com/view/article/6347.

shows that some eleven years before his death he had made this request which handed over the control of the final pageant to his spectators. This raises a question as to Cornysh's own impression of the significance of his role as explicator of the court pageants: Did he have doubts about his role as cultural mediator? Of course, he does not entirely hand over to 'the people' all the control for this final performance: he planned for his memorial tomb to remain a very significant, silent, presence in this particular town of Greenwich – a town that had become central to his career as a pageant designer for the royal court; a place which also later became key to the claim that this man was a central figure in the history of early Tudor revels.

Cornysh as Poet

William Cornysh wrote a poem entitled *A Treatise bitwene Trowth and enformacion*.[40] The tag attached to this poem being: 'In the Fleete by me William Cornysh otherwise called Nysshewhete chapelman with the moost famose Kyng Henry the viith, his raigne the xixth yere the moneth of July ...'.[41] The *Treatise* is written in Rhyme Royal, like the verses uttered by St George in 1494. There are twenty stanzas in all, beginning with four introductory verses of complaint about how a man may be convicted by false information, and followed by sixteen verses under the separate heading of 'A Parable Betweene Enformacion and Musike'. According to Sydney Anglo, these sixteen verses 'argue by musical metaphors, that the author had been wrongfully accused'.[42] In fact, on closer inspection, there are some very interesting traces in this poem that begin to reveal something of the creative and personal tensions experienced by Cornysh in the early English Renaissance.

The confusion surrounding this poem involves a long trail of transcription and error which centres on John Stowe, the editor of the *London Chronicle*, and what Anglo deduced to be a wrong attribution to Cornysh of a scurrilous poem written at the beginning of the reign of Henry VIII. This scurrilous poem, found in *The London Chronicle*, is an attack on Sir Richard Empson, who is sometimes described as 'Henry VII's unpopular extortioner'.[43] Anglo convincingly proves, from its date and other manuscript evidence, that this 'opprobrious' poem is almost certainly a separate one from the *Treatise* written by William Cornysh in 1504. Stowe's mis-attribution, probably became even more confused when E.K.

---

[40]   Anglo, 'William Cornysh in a Play', 347, 353–7; the edition of the poem used in this article is the printed one, found in John Skelton, *The Pithy Pleasaunt and profitable workes of maister Skelton, Poete Laureate, Nowe Collected and newly published ANNO 1568* (London, Scolar, 1970), unpaginated.

[41]   Anglo, 'William Cornysh in a Play', 353.

[42]   Anglo, 'William Cornysh in a Play', 354.

[43]   Anglo, 'William Cornysh in a Play', 353.

Chambers then proposed that Cornysh's *Treatise* was 'doubtless the satirical ballad on Empson referred to by Stow'.[44] The rubric on Cornysh's treatise has not helped matters here, as the mysterious, 'A.B. of E, how C. for T. was p. in p.' it was suggested, in the old version of the *Dictionary of National Biography*, meant, 'A Ballad of Empson, how Cornysh for Treason was Put in Prison'. Some alternatives for this 'troubling rubric' have since been proposed such as, 'A Ballad of Enformacion', with the possibility that the second half reads 'How Cornysh for Trowth was put in Prison'.[45]

There have been some doubts concerning Cornysh's authorship of this poem. One major doubt arises because of the appearance of this poem in the *Pithy and Pleasant* collection of Skelton's works, printed in 1568. However it is worth mentioning the indication that contemporaries considered Cornysh up to the challenge of such poetry. In another of the scurrilous poems in *The Chronicle of London*, Cornysh is mentioned as a poet in the same rank as Chaucer, and his contemporaries Skelton and More.[46] The convincing quality of Sydney Anglo's arguments which involve proving and disproving the various provenances and correcting the earlier mistakes, particularly of John Stowe and E.K. Chambers, has enabled more recent scholars to attribute this *Treatise* poem to William Cornysh without any hesitation.[47]

Attempts at interpreting the poetic metaphors in Cornysh's *Treatise* include some considerable interest amongst musicologists as far back as the eighteenth century in the musical metaphors used throughout the *Treatise*; a verse discussing the four colours of music received some particular attention: [48]

Colours of Musyke
In Musyke I have learned iiii. colours as this
Blake, ful blake, verte, and in lykewyse redde
By these colours many subtill alteracions ther is
That wil begile one tho in cuning he be wel sped
With a prike of Indicion from a body that is dede
He shal try so his nombre with swetnes of his song
That the care shalbe pleased, and yet he all wrong

---

[44]   Anglo, 'William Cornysh in a Play', 354; E.K. Chambers, *The Elizabethan Stage*, vol. 2 (Oxford, Clarendon, 1923), p. 29.

[45]   Anglo, 'William Cornysh in a Play', 354.

[46]   See *The Chronicle of London*, p. 361, for this 'scurrilous poem' directed against John Baptist Grimald, one of Empson's henchmen; Anglo, 'William Cornysh in a Play', 357.

[47]   See, for example, Kisby, 'Officers and Office-Holding', 53; also Bowers in http://www. oxforddnb. com/ view/ article/6347.

[48]   Anglo, 'William Cornysh in a Play', 355; Anglo cites one eighteenth-century commentary on this verse in particular, which includes a full transcription of the poem: John Hawkins, *A General History of the Science and Practice of Music* (London, 1776).

It should be noted that it is actually quite difficult to appreciate the sense of this particular stanza in relation to the whole poem, although this is a verses that indicates the detailed interest of William Cornysh in musical sound, style and perhaps a technical vocabulary, as musicologists have noticed.[49]

The ballad has also been treated with that particular brand of disdain of the nineteenth century canonical scholar: in 1843, for example, Alexander Dyce described it as a 'very dull poem'.[50] And very recently, Roger Bowers' suggestion that 'Cornysh's writing lacks any conspicuous elegance' is hardly complementary. Although this *ODNB* biography does admit that the poem's 'use of imagery drawn from musical experience is of great interest', and that, 'the concepts he conveys were generated with a noteworthy degree of intelligent imagination and perceptiveness'.[51]

The use of musical metaphors throughout the *Treatise* is hardly surprising given Cornysh's role in the royal chapel and his expertise as a composer.[52] However, what is more interesting is Cornysh's use of musical metaphors to present what seems to be a very serious moral argument concerning the use, representation, and reception of truth. Taken in the context of the will evidence for William Cornysh's personal interests in performance and representation, this poem becomes worthy of a re-consideration.

The underlying theme of the whole poem is reflected in the theme of truth and its manipulated representation and reception as explored in the 'Parable of Music' section of the poem. This is addressed in the opening four stanzas, which are concerned with two main issues relating to the nature of truth and the nature of information. The first concern is that information might mislead a man who reasons its meaning wrongly and therefore does not fully understand what is right. Here, Cornysh uses the image of a stumbling blind man who should not be blamed for not seeing. The second concern, however, is with the wilful misuse of information, which he calls 'fals informacion' or 'evell information'. Cornysh uses the image of a jury misleading a judge on purpose: the judge must accept the jury's verdict using the information of these people who 'maketh their malice [that] mater of the power / and cruelly without conscience right or pity / Disgorge their venome'. But he warns of the later punishment of such deeds and the consequent

---

[49]   Anglo, 'William Cornysh in a Play', 355; Hawkins, *General History of Music*, pp. 180–181.

[50]   Alexander Dyce, *The Poetical Works of John Skelton* (London, Thomas Rodd, 1843), pp. 117–8.

[51]   http://www.oxforddnb.com/ view/article/6347.

[52]   http://www.oxforddnb.com/view/article/6347: Cornysh's job as Master of the Choristers is described as follows; 'The duties of this very exacting job extended to teaching fundamental music theory and notation, highly developed techniques of singing, all the intricacies of the liturgy, the basic Latin needed for their comprehension, and the vocal parts to be sung by the boys in the polyphonic repertory, including, for instance, masses by Robert Fayrfax, John Taverner, Hugh Aston, Thomas Ashwell, and John Marbeck.'

forgetting of their 'soules doloure / When, *dies illa , dies ire*, shalbe their songe'. It is the production and result of this false information, which occupies much of the rest of the poem.

The use of musical metaphors to make Cornysh's argument about false information appears to focus on the idea that a musical instrument owns an essential truth, but a wrong manipulation of this truth occurs through the improper or careless playing of the instrument, as is indicated by this opening stanza of the 'parable' section:

> The examples
> Musike in his Melody requireth true soundes
> Who setteth a song, should geve him to armony
> Who kepeth true his tuenes may not pass his sounds
> His alteracions & prolacions must be pricked treuly
> For musike is trew though minstrels maketh maystry
> The harper careth nothing but reward for his song
> Merily soundith his mouth when his tong goth all of wrong

The musical instruments mentioned in the poem are the harp, the song (or voice), the clavichord, and the trumpet. So, for example, Cornysh suggests the clavichord is essentially a tuneful instrument in itself, it 'hath a tunely kynde', but because the instrument is tuned to the player's mind, it may become 'mistuned' according to what its player is thinking, the outcome being that the mistuned clavichord 'shall hurt a trew song'. Similarly with the trumpet, if it is over-blown its tuning will go wrong and Cornysh advises that we should, 'blame none but the blower' for this poor tune.

> A clavicorde
> The clavicord hath a tunely kynde
> As the wyre is wrested hye and lowe
> So it tuenyth to the players mynde
> For as it is wrested so must it nedes showe
> As by this reson ye may well know
> Any instrument mistunyd shall hurt a trew song
> Yet blame not the clavicord *the* wrester doth wrong

> A trompet
> A trompet blowen hye with too hard a blast
> Shal cause him to vary from the tunable kynde
> But he that bloweth to hard must suage at *the* last
> And fayne to fall lower with the temperat wynde
> And then the trompet the true tune shall fynde
> For an instrument over wynded is tuned wrong
> Blame none but the blower, on him it is longe

The four stanzas covering the four different instruments are summarised by a fifth as follows:

> True counsell
> Who plaieth on the harpe, he should play trew
> Who syngeth a songe, let his voice be tunable
> Who wresteth the clavicorde mystunyng eschew
> Who bloweth a tro*m*pet let his wind be mesurable
> For instrumentes in them self be ferme & stable
> And of trouth, wold trouth to every manes so*n*ge
> Tune them then truly for in the*m* is no wronge.

Here again is the proposition that music and the musical instruments are inherently truthful; it is the people who play them, tune them wrongly, blow them too hard and so on who are responsible for the music going awry. This idea, as illustrated through musical metaphors, links with the themes addressed in the opening four stanzas. The message appears to be, therefore, that it is through people's misrepresentation of the 'truth' that 'false information' comes about. But significantly, Cornysh explores and expresses this theme through a metaphor reliant on the issue of performance. The resurgence of this issue seems to corroborate Cornysh as a man who considered very seriously the nature of performance, both in terms of his career but also in terms of his own life (and death), and also, the *Treatise* would suggest, in relation to the formation of moral meaning.

Towards the end of this poem, Cornysh presents a further discussion as a sort of dialogue on the different levels of truthfulness inherent in different styles of music. What he appears to be expressing, here, is the idea that music of a complex kind or 'cumbrous songe' actually masks the truth. Information, who appears to be responsible for this over-complex style is 'so curious in his chanting / That to hear the trew plainsong is not possible'.

> Truth
> I assayed theis tunes me thought them not swete
> The concords were nothing musicall
> I called masters of Musike cunyng and discrete
> And the first prynciple whose name was tuballe
> Guido Boice John de Murris, Vitryaco & them al
> I prayed them of helpe of this combrous songe
> Priked with force and lettred with wronge

> True answere
> They sayd I was horce I might not synge
> My voice is to pore is it not awdyble
> Informacion is so curyous in his chauntyng
> That to here the trew plainsong, it is not possible
> His proporcions be so hard with so highe a quatrible

And y playn song in the margin so craftily bou*n*d
That *the* true tunes of tuball ca*n* not have *the* ryght sounde

In this poem, Cornysh appears to be suggesting that polyphony amounts to false information. Written in 1504, at what is generally assumed to be the height of English polyphonic style, this criticism of such a form of expression is perhaps surprising. Taken in a general context of contemporary tastes in music, Cornysh's suggestion about the malign effects of polyphony seems significant. His support, through poetry, for more simple styles of musical expression is less surprising when the more personal context of the surviving evidence of his own musical compositions is examined.[53] His compositional style for secular songs has been described as exhibiting 'a degree of balance and poise belying its simplicity of structure', the inventive jollity of the songs of rustic merry-making complementing the reflectiveness of the songs of *fine amour*. Secular songs attributed to him such as *Adieu Mes Amours* have been thought to represent 'the birth of the secular song of the English Renaissance'.[54] Yet, a distinctively 'Medieval' four-part setting of a meditation on the Passion of Christ, called *Woefully Arrayed*, is also attributed to this William Cornysh. He probably wrote this in 1502, and was paid 13s 4d for his trouble by Elizabeth of York. According to Bowers, this carol exhibits a 'precociously skilful response to the mood of the text'.

Woefully Arrayed

The poem *Woefully Arrayed* almost certainly existed before Cornysh set it to music. It is a meditation on the Crucifixion in which the voice of the poem is Christ speaking from the cross. It is similar in its affective strength to the poem, *My Feerfull Dreme*, set by Gilbert Banaster, although the speaker is a different character from the Passion story. *Woefully Arrayed* should probably also be considered as representative of the popular literatures of affective piety which circulated in this period. The four verses of *Woefully Arrayed* tell of events immediately leading up to and during the Crucifixion, with continued references to the meaning and purpose of that sacrifice, and continued chastisements towards 'man' to listen empathetically to this story of woe, and 'be not hard-hartid'.[55] The poem moves in and out of different time-frames throughout, from the narration of what the Jews did (With sharpe corde sore fretid, / The Jewis me thretid, / They mowed, they grynned, they scornyd me'.[56]) in the first verse; to a present tense

---

[53] *The New Oxford History of Music* [hereafter *NOHM*], vol. 3, 'Antiphons by Fayrfax and Cornysh' (Oxford, OUP, 1954), pp. 318–319, 346–347.

[54] *NOHM*, vol. 3, p. 304.

[55] John Stevens, *Music and Poetry in the Early Tudor Court*, Cambridge Studies in Music (Cambridge, CUP, 1979), p. 370, Verse Stanza 1, l. 2.

[56] Stevens, *Music and Poetry*, p. 370, ll. 6–8.

description of the pain of being on the cross at the beginning of verse 2 ('Thus Nakyd am I nailed, O man, for thy sake'[57]) which changes quickly to a past tense command that the reader should remember these pains ('I love the, then love me; why slepist thou? Awake! / Remembir my tendir hart-rote for the brake'[58]); to a narration, by the dead Christ, of his sacrifice in verse 3, ending with a question of 'What might I suffir more / Than I have done, O man, for the?'[59] And there is a final plea on the part of Christ to man that he should 'Cum when thou lyst, welcum to me!'.[60]

Cornysh's four-part setting of a poem surely embedded in a Medieval tradition of affective devotions is itself meditative. John Stevens suggested that it is 'the clearest possible example of a poem being chosen for setting for non-musical qualities'.[61] The music appears to be sensitive to the horrific story which is narrated in this poem. The focus of the musical phrases on the syllables of the poem gives it an almost stately air. Cornysh also embellishes the affective experience of the text by staggering the moment at which the parts sing a specific line.[62] So, using similar techniques to Banaster's, Cornysh places emphasis on particular words and phrases: the word 'scorned' for example is uttered at three separate moments, the highest part taking this word a whole musical phrase before the other parts, the alto and bass parts singing the word together, and the tenor part one beat before them.[63] The separation in pitch of alto and bass makes the listener also hear that simultaneous 'scorned' twice. Simultaneous singing of specific words and phrases is also used for similar emphasis: verse 3's 'I love thee; then love me', for example, is sung at the same time by three parts, with the bass joining together for the second of these two strong assertive phrases.[64] Cornysh, like Banaster, also employs some sustained melisma which serve to emphasise a particular word, as in the refrain on both the key words 'woefully' and 'arrayed'.[65]

Seen in connection with the view of William Cornysh as an innovator who introduced new styles of pageantry, his attitudes towards musical style as presented in his compositions are sometimes consistent with a man who was eager to try new forms of cultural expression. His metaphorical use of ideas about musical composition, however, as expressed in his poem do not so much indicate the thoughts of someone excited by the new, but rather a man critical of the current fashions and styles. Perhaps he was seeking a new and better mode for the

---

57   Stevens, *Music and Poetry*, p. 370, Verse Stanza 2, l. 1.

58   Stevens, *Music and Poetry*, p. 370, ll. 3–4.

59   Stevens, *Music and Poetry*, p. 370, Verse Stanza 3, ll. 7–8.

60   Stevens, *Music and Poetry*, p. 370, l. 9.

61   Stevens, *Music and Poetry*, p. 371

62   I am using a modernised transcription for this analysis, in: 'Early Tudor Songs and Carols', ed. John Stevens, *Musica Britannica*, 36 (1975): 92–97.

63   Stevens, 'Early Tudor Songs and Carols', 94.

64   Stevens, 'Early Tudor Songs and Carols', 95.

65   Stevens, 'Early Tudor Songs and Carols', 92–7.

representation of the truth which at once anticipated changes occurring twenty years hence and also looked back to the older forms of plainsong before it became encumbered by polyphony. At the same time as exploring new possibilities for musical compositions which move away from the traditions of Medieval polyphony (perhaps for pragmatic expediency), this William Cornysh was also using elements of polyphonic style in his settings for the distinctively emotional devotional poetry of Medieval traditional affective piety.

Conclusion

There appear to be some pleasing coherences in the personal and public attitudes of William Cornysh towards performance, innovation, representation, and truth. But it would be a mistake to assume that these issues are representative of the seamlessly meaningful programme of cultural production and creativity of a man whose primary aim was to innovate and experiment with forms of representation. This is despite the retrospectively imposed view of Cornysh as a 'most considerable figure in the history of early Tudor court revels'.[66] Indeed the view of Cornysh as critical of the current fashions rather than eager for the new, which emerges from his poetic use of musical metaphors, begins to indicate some of the fissures in any programme of cultural innovation motivated by a single desire to promote new forms of cultural expression. But his return to the older structures of plainsong may indeed reflect his Renaissance drive to look back to previous forms of expression (although one might have expected plainsong to be associated with the 'Medieval' rather than the 'antique' which formed a popular focus for Renaissance cultural investigations).

If the performative context of William Cornysh's personal burial request is taken into consideration, some further fissures in this picture of coherence appear. The commemorative request does seem, on the surface, to corroborate evidence for Cornysh's life-long interest, even obsession, with issues of performance. But there are other resonances in this document, which are ill at ease with the idea of Cornysh as an innovator in all spheres of his public and private cultural life. The request to be buried in the Rood Chapel does indeed appear to allow space for the innovation of 'the people' who come to kneel at the ledge, but this innovation is framed within a very traditional setting of late Medieval Catholicism. Cornysh's request for the veneration of a number of lights in the church attests to this, as does his insistence on the continued preservation of the lamp in the Rood Chapel, by his heirs. He gives 12d. to each of the lights of The Rood, Our Lady, Our Lady of Pity, St Anne, and St James; and he adds several reminders concerning the maintaining of the lamp in the Rood Chapel by his widow and her heirs, that it should burn 'both day and nyght'. These requests made in 1512 are the wishes of a man deeply

---

[66]   Anglo, 'William Cornysh in a Play', 347.

entrenched in the traditions of the late Medieval Catholic orthodoxy and not of the man solely devoted to reform and innovation that evidence of his pageant designs, and more particularly the retrospective categorisation of his achievements in pageant design, might suggest.

One final look at the last will and testament helps to clarify the significance of this 'new' piece of evidence for understanding William Cornysh's career and his attitudes to performance. This testamentary request for the final commemorative performance is framed by some particularly significant clauses about the location of the tomb. These are clauses indicating that not only was performance personally very important to William Cornysh even in his death wishes, but also that Greenwich held a very special place in this aspect of his life and career:

> my body to be buried in the body of the chapel of the rood within the same towne of estgrenewich *yf* I happen to deceas within the same towne or nygh to the said towne or elles my body to be buried in some other church or church yard or other holy place where it shall please god item I will that *if* [I] be buried in the said chapel of the rood within grenewich aforesaid Than I will that there be made a tombe of bryke over me with a stone upon it and a border aboute the same for people to knele upon of half a foote high.[67] [My emphases]

---

[67]   NA PROB 11/13/96v.

Chapter 7

Katherine Styles

This chapter focuses on the way that one surviving piece of evidence for the life of Dame Katherine Styles leads to fascinating details concerning one early sixteenth-century woman's social and family networks, transitional attitudes towards piety, interest in fashionable goods, reading habits, and concern about the preservation of her heritage for her many children and grandchildren. Katherine was relatively wealthy by the time of her death, and had substantial networks of family and kin. The surviving evidences of these add to the possibilities for reconstructing this life. Dame Katherine Styles made her will on 8 August 1530 and it was proved just over a year later on 16 October 1531. She was married three times, to men of successively increasing status. This is stated plainly in the opening clauses of her last will and testament.[1] The will document provides access to what seems a peculiar world of complicated family allegiances and interactions. This involves Katherine, at that significant point in her lifecycle, in making transactions and confirming requests made by each of her three husbands on behalf of various of her children and godchildren.

Katherine's last will and testament is a central piece of evidence in this biographical analysis. That a text in preparation for death can be the only surviving evidence of an individual's life is an interesting paradox. There are many issues associated with the interpretation and use of a will document as evidence for a person's life. Crudely speaking there are two main schools of thought on their uses, the negative and the positive. The negative school claims the will to be of relatively little use as a source of evidence for the life and attitude of the individual testator. This is because of factors such as the involvement of a scribe in writing the will text, the formulaic nature of the legal document, and the incomplete quality of the information it contains about the testator's wealth and property owing to the fact that it only records provision for *post mortem* inheritance. This is specifically indicated in Katherine's will where the provision of inheritance to her son William included a request of 'certeyne plate to be solde whiche is not here bequethid for the performaunce of this my will'. The positive school considers the will to be of great value because of the evidence it can provide – however partial the glimpse – about an individual's wealth and property as well as his or her attitudes to elements that constitute his or her identity such as religion, the ownership and giving of heirloom goods, and family or kin.

---

[1]   NA PROB 11/24/9/66v–67v.

Given that this chapter begins from one last will and testament, it is clear that I consider wills to be of great value. This is particularly the case when reconstructing the lives and attitudes of people who are otherwise lost to history. Relatively large numbers of these documents survive and they stretch fairly far down the social scale to townspeople and artisans, although not to the very poorest people. They can be found today in local record offices (for wills made in the local consistory courts) as well as in the National Archive in London (for wills of the more wealthy individuals often with property in more than one county, and proved in the Prerogative courts). The form in which most of these documents survives is in registers, which means they have been copied into a book from another version produced on a single sheet of parchment or paper. Wills are formulaic legal documents so they follow a specific format, and they are in general written by a scribe (although sometimes a document specifically records that it was written by the hand of the testator and this is copied into the registered form). There is a lot to say about the uses of wills as evidence which I will not rehearse here, although I base my use of this will on the experience of having read over a thousand such documents.[2] However, regarding the negative idea that these are merely formulaic documents controlled by the scribe there is one important issue to mention: wills are peppered with incidences of the personal expressions of the testator. These are found in the individualised descriptions of particular objects which have been selected as heirlooms, in the short narratives of a testator's personal circumstances which are sometimes present, and in the choices about religious commemoration. In many ways it is the very fact of the formulaic nature of these documents which brings to the fore these aberrant, individualised choices about the wording of the will. And it is because of these individualised words, phrases, and personal narratives that the will text provides a valuable glimpse, however partial, onto the lives and attitudes of people such as Katherine Styles.

Because wills are such individualised documents there is much to be gained from considering each document in its own right, although it is also beneficial to know what seems fairly ordinary and what seems unusual by making comparisons with other texts. Based on my experience, I would suggest that the will of Katherine Styles, although detailed and containing some interesting features, is not excessively unusual in any respect. Amongst her unexceptional bequests, however, there are many clues to her life and so with this in mind, I have reproduced Katherine Styles's will in its entirety in order to discuss some elements of it in more detail below. In the paragraphs following that, I explore some elements of the biography of Katherine Styles that may be deduced from this individual's last will and testament, together with those which survive of her family and kin.

---

[2]   For more detailed consideration of the last will and testament as a source of evidence, and its uses, see Elisabeth Salter, *Cultural Creativity in the Early English Renaissance: Popular Culture in Town and Country* (London, Palgrave Macmillan, 2006), pp. 13–20.

The Last Will and Testament of Katherine Styles

In the name of god amen. The viiith day of the monnythe of auguste in the yere of our lorde Jhu Criste a thousande five hundred and xxx and in the xxii yere of the Reigne of our Soveraigne lorde king henry the viiith. I dame Katherine Styles of Estgrenewiche in the countie of Kent *with*in the diocese of Rochester widowe late the widow of Sir John Style Knight deceased, and before that the wife of Edward Skern esquire also deceased and before that the wife of William Cooke late of the same town and Countie yoman in likewise deceased oon whos soules almighty god have mercye Remembring this transitory worke and unstedfast calling to my Remembraunce that every lyving Creatoure is mortall and muste have an ende and not purveyed of my testament nor will as yet made and now I being aswell in *per*fitt good and stedfast mynde and memorye as in bodily helth laud and praysed be allmyghty god make and ordeyne and devise this my present testament concerning my last will in man*er* and fourme hereafter ensueyng ffirste I com*m*ende and bequethe my soule to almighty god my maker and redeemer to *o*ur blissid lady sancta Marye mother and virgin and to all the celestiall company of heven. And my bodye to be buryed in the chapel at Sancte George and Sancte Anne *with*in the parishe churche of Sancte Alphey[ge] of Grenewiche aforesaid wherof I am *p*arishen*er* nexte unto the tombe or grave of my said firste husband William Cooke in place for my bodyie there ordeynid if it shall please god so for me to ordeyne or ells in some other holy or sanctified place where it shall please god to ordeyne at his beinng and high pleasure. Item I bequeath to the highe aulter of the same churche of EstGrenewiche for my tithes and offerings forgotten or negligently forgotten in discharging of my conscience againste god xxd. Item to the mother churche of Rof*fyn*s*is* [Rochester] xiid. Item to the lightes *with*in thys parishe churche of Estgrenewiche aforesaid that is to say to our ladye light *with*in the chappell one taper of one pounde of waxe to burne afore our ladye at *ser*vice tyme and to be mayneteynid by the space of all th^e hole terme of myn executoris life And I will that the testament and last will of my late husband Willi*a*m Cooke be in every thing doon according to the declaracon therof if *e*very thinge shalhappen of ygnoraunce by me not doon or to be doon in this my present life tyme as god defende. Item I bequethe to the brotherode of Saint George and Sancte Anne after my decease by the space of vii yeres every yere vis viiid as I paye nowe to be prayed for. And also I will that there be by the same space vii yeres twoo tap*er*s brennyng and to stand ov*er* my tombe and grave and to be lyght at *ser*vice tymes on the holly daye and at the broderode masse on the worky day. And one *p*ersonne to be lymytid or assigned to light the said tapers and the taper before our ladye having for his labour yerelye xiid quarterly to be paide. Item I will that myne householde and moveable stuffe excepte that whiche I entende to give by my life besolde by myne executour underwritten. And the monnye therof coming to be distributed for the *per*formaunce of this my testament and last will that is to say I bequethe to my sonnes children William Cooke vii of theym now being on lyve to *e*very of theym xls of lawfull corraunte monnye of Ingland. And if any of them decease before their porcion at yeres of discretion of xxi yeres or at their marriage be not delivered that then every of their porcions to be divided amongst them that shalbe onlyve. Item I bequethe to every oon of those doughters oone fetherbedd *with* bolster pillow covering a payer of blankets a payer sheetes and seeler and tester that is to say to Jane ii bras pottes vi platters vi dishes vi sawcers and a charger ii candilstickes a little silver salte coverid iii silver spones iii cusshynnes. Item to Ursula a fetherbedd a bolster a pillow a covering a payer of blankettes a payer sheetes seler and tester of saye a bras potte iii platters iii disshyes iii silver spones iii cusshynnes. Item to Anne Cooke a fetherbedd a bolster a pillowe a covering a payer of blankettes a payer sheetes a tester seler a bras potte iii platters iii dishes iii sawcers ii candilstickes iii silver spones iii cusshynes. Item to every of them a table clothe and a towel at the discretion of myne executours and to my husbande Styles doughter late Hewesters wif a table clothe and a towel of diap*er* with Katherine Wheles. Item to hir husband Water a ringe of goold whiche hir husband Hewster gave to my husband Style. Item to Jerome the sonne of Hewster if he be alive in money xxs. Item to my husband Styles sonne if he amend his conditions a fetherbedd a bolster a paire sheetes a quylte Covering and in money xxs. Item to Master Whitewanges wife if she ou*t*live me a Ring like a signet. Item to our lady of Walsingham after my decease a hoope of gold whiche was my wedding ringe. Item to my sonne William and to my doughter Emma Cooke his wif my best girdell with gilte harness and my beste beades of mother a pearle and my best gowne and my gowne of chamblett and a kertill of damaske and a Ringe of gold with a Turcas and a nutte silver parcel gilte with a cov*er* demi dossen spones a goblit with a cover parcel gilte And I bequethe to Edmond Skerme a standing cuppe of silv*er* parcel gilt whiche my husbande Skerme bequeathed him so that he deliver a bill of Sir John Styles hand, the whiche he hath for the same. Item to Robert Ustwayte gentilman a flat cuppe with a columbine in the bottom wherof he hathe a bill and the same bille to be delivered in likewise. Item to my sonne Thomas Cooke and to his wife my best gowne of clothe and a kirtill of Chamblett a girdell with a chayne a payer of bead*es* with gawdyes of silver and gilte a silver salte wi*th*out cover parcel gilte d*e*mi dossen silver spones a little silver potte cov*er*ed a maser and I forgieve hym all his obligaciones. Item to my ii sonnes a dossen cusshynnes wherof d*e*mi dossen carpitt warke and d*e*mi dosyne [?utrdo*r*] and my sonne William to chuse. Item I will myne executors take the Rent of my landes in Stepney m*a*rshe to William Cooke my sonne and to his assignes and also I will assigne certeyne plate to be solde whiche is not here bequethid for the p*er*formaunce of this my will by thadvise of myn executors and overseer whome I ordeyne William Cooke myne eldest sonne my sole executour and he to dispose for the helthe of my soule as he shall seame best to the pleasure of god by thadvise always of myn overseer whome I ordeyne constitute and make William Draper of this parrishe Esquier whome I give for his diligent labo*ur* to see this my present testament and last will p*er*fourmed xls his expens*es* to be boren by myne eecutour at all tymes & my said sonne William myne executour to have for his labour doying and p*er*fourming this my testament and wille xs. Item to my late s*er*vante John Hunter xxs. Item to my s*er*vante William a payer of sheet*es*. Item to every my godchildren being on lyve xld whose names are written in a bylle that is to saye M*aster* John Chesemans doughter a booke which was doctour Gawthorpe with clapses silver w*ith*oute monneye. Item to margarete Wilde xld to Eldertones doughter Margarete Hoptons sonne xls and to his mother a gowne of my wearing at the discretion of myne executour to Margery Reynolde Wyllys wif an other gowne of my wering and I forgive her all her debts owing to me. Item to Bettreslocke my s*er*vante a ring of golde with a stone and I forgeve hir suche duetye as she owith me. Item to Anne Reynolde late Arthures wife a payer of bead*es* of white aumber and I forgive her her debts. Item to Maister Bery of the chapel a golde Ring. Item I will have xii torches at my burying and monnethis mynd whiche I have redy in my house and after to be gevyn to the churche to pray for me and for my frend*es* soules. It*em* I bequethe unto the good freers xxs. Item I give unto Elizabeth Chubbyns in money xs and one kertill of chamblitte. Item to Katherine Cooke doughter unto Thomas Cooke xls to hir marriage and if she happyn to decease to Remayne to the nexte of his children ~~and~~ if he have any. Item I will that myn executour give to Godlucke for in the way of charytie and for Goddess sake xld. Item I will that my house be solde the whiche was Stauntes for to pay my debts if need be. Item I give Cristofer Baldewin my cosen one greate bras potte the whiche he hath in his keeping and a horse harnys. It*em* Also I will that the liili viis iiiid whiche is due unto me by the kinges grace my soveragn lord of the warres in Ireland under the right high and famous prince Thomas duke of Norfolk then being the Kinges leveten*en*te therto be received by my said Executour for the p*er*fourmaunce of this my last will humbly desiring the honourable lord*es* of the kinges moost honourable counsel to be unto hym ayding and assistaunte for the attending of the same. These witnesses William Draper Esquier Sir Richard Ridge curate there Sir John Morland John Hunter Elizabeth Whitwhange Den[nis] Dowe Hugh Stevenson and other &c

Transitional Piety

Katherine Styles produced her last will and testament in 1530, a period in England when religious expression and devotion was in the process of undergoing some major transitions. Testaments produced across the years c. 1525 to 1540 do frequently exhibit a fluctuation between overtly Catholic and apparently Protestant forms of devotion and commemoration. Katherine's transitional attitude to piety is signalled in her own will by her use of what might be considered 'proto-Protestant' phrases such as this in the opening lines: 'remembering this transitory worke ever in stedfast calling to my Remembrance that every lyving Creatoure is mortall and muste have an ende'.[3] This is matched with the equally traditional requests of late Medieval Catholicism, including a request to be buried in the chapel of St George and St Anne, in the parish church of Greenwich and the various obits, money for lights, and requests for the burning of wax tapers expected of a devout late Medieval Catholic. She also requests that, for the space of twelve years, 6s 8d be paid annually to the brotherhood of St George and St Anne, as has been paid during her lifetime.

A glance at the testamentary requests of Katherine's final husband adds colour to this picture of changing devotional loyalties in what constitutes a transitional period in orthodox piety. Sir John Styles, who made his will in 1529, also appears to be hedging his bets between the old traditions and the new ideologies.[4] He requests for his burial:

---

[3]   NA PROB 11/24/9/66v–67v; for a consideration of 'transitional pieties' in a regional context see Robert Lutton and Elisabeth Salter (eds), *Pieties in Transition: Religious Practices and Experiences* (Aldershot, Ashgate, 2007).

[4]   NA PROB 11/23/14/110r–v.

that it be doon without sumptuous costes pompe or pryde or great charges forasmoche as I doo well considere and knowe that my worldly goodes be of noo great value or substance first I will that immediately after my deceas myn executors doo cause a tirgintall of masses to be saide for my soule that they therefore doo paye tenne shilinges in money in caase that I do not the said trentall of masses to be saide before my deceas

John Styles' request to be buried in London at All Hallows Barking, next to his previous wives Katherine (an earlier Katherine) and Dame Elizabeth also adds to the picture of the complicated sets of loyalties existing for these multiply-married individuals. It might seem odd that Katherine chose to be buried next to her first husband who had died some twenty five years before her, rather than next to her most recent husband John Styles. Evidently, this had been planned for a while as she had a place reserved for her there. Such a request is actually not unusual in the sixteenth century, and so we must expect that it did not seem strange to Katherine and her family.

Humanist Connections

Alongside the apparently proto-Protestant sentiments at the beginning of her will, Katherine's interests in the newer ideologies of the early sixteenth century also seem to be signalled by one of her bequests. She gives a book to one of her goddaughters, described simply as 'a booke whiche was doctour Gunthorpes with claspes of silver'. The goddaughter is described as being Master John Cheeseman's daughter; the Cheesemans were a wealthy family resident in Greenwich.

Mention of a book in a last will and testament is always interesting because wills are not, in general, copiously endowed with book bequests – this does not mean that testators did not own any books. The gift of a book from one woman to another is specifically interesting in its own right because it hints that this older woman, Katherine, wished to encourage another, younger, woman in her reading. Katherine may have considered this to be part of her duty as a godparent.[5] Unfortunately the type or title of the book is not given in this instance. When the book in the bequest is identified it is most often a devotional work, such as primer, prayer book, or other specific religious title. Gifts of devotional books from woman to woman are also interesting because they hint at the formation of networks of female spirituality.[6] Although the book given by Katherine is not described explicitly as a devotional text, it is described as having been originally the

[5]   See, Mary C. Erler, 'Devotional Literature', in J.B. Trapp and Lotte Hellinga (eds), *The Cambridge History of the Book in Britain*, vol. 3, '1400–1557', pp. 523–5.

[6]   See Felicity Riddy, ' "Women talking about the things of God": A Late Medieval Sub-Culture', in Carol Meale (ed.), *Women & Literature in Britain, 1150–1500* (Cambridge, 1993), pp. 106–111.

possession of 'doctour Gawthorpe'. This description gives a clue now to its provenance, but it may well have given a clue then as to the nature of the book, because Doctor John Gunthorpe was an important English humanist scholar who also had connections with Greenwich and the royal court there.[7]

John Gunthorpe was educated at Cambridge University, and was a Master of Arts by about 1452.[8] He went to Italy with the purpose of attending humanistic lectures and learning rhetoric and Greek.[9] Around 1456, he and another English scholar, John Free, were attending lectures and being tutored by the Italian humanist at Ferrara called Guarino de Verona.[10] When he returned to England, some time after 1465, Gunthorpe was employed in various official roles in the households of Edwards IV and V, Richard III, and Henry VII; and also on diplomatic missions for these kings where his abilities in writing oratory speeches (some of which survive) were valued. He became the Dean of Wells in 1472.[11]

John Gunthorpe owned a substantial library of Latin and Greek prose and poetry in both manuscript and print by the time of his death. Alongside another famous English humanist called William of Worcester, Gunthorpe had inherited part of the library of John Free after he died in Italy in 1465.[12] Other books which belonged to Gunthorpe survive today in various UK and US libraries, some of which have his marginal notes based on Guarino's lectures, and others of which were his own translations of classical texts.[13] Some of Gunthorpe's library was housed in Jesus College, Cambridge, during the sixteenth century. He may have donated books to this college as well as to other institutions and individuals during his life. In this way he may have been responsible for spreading Italian knowledge in England, and also for inspiring others to go to Italy to further their education.[14] The book he gave to Dame Katherine Styles may have included some texts relating to his humanist interests, although it was probably a devotional book. This is a truly extraordinary man to have had contact with. He died in 1498, so Katherine's contact with him must have been in the first half of her life.[15] Perhaps he was her spiritual advisor.

Gunthorpe's mentions of the 'Ustwaite' family in his will also indicates that he had connections with the same group of kin as Katherine and her husband John Styles.[16] For example, Gunthorpe gives to a 'Robert Ustwaite' and his son Thomas

---

[7]   *ODNB*, http://www.oxforddnb.com/view/article/11752, by Cecil H. Clough.

[8]   Roberto Weiss, *Humanism in England During the Fifteenth Century* (Oxford, Basil Blackwell, 3rd edition 1967), p. 122.

[9]   Weiss, *Humanism*, p. 84, 123.

[10]   Weiss, *Humanism*, p. 107.

[11]   Weiss, *Humanism*, pp. 124–5.

[12]   Weiss, *Humanism*, p. 111.

[13]   Weiss, *Humanism*, p. 123, 126. One such book mentioned by Weiss is BL MS Harl. 2485.

[14]   Weiss, *Humanism*, p. 127.

[15]   NA PROB 11/22/11/181v–182r.

[16]   NA PROB 11/22/11/181v–182r.

all land and tenements in East Greenwich and also various other lands in the county of Kent. He also bequeaths £40 to a branch of this family resident in the city of Wells (he was a deacon at Wells Cathedral at the time of his death, and he requested to be buried there, where his memorial tomb still stands).[17] Katherine also mentions a 'Robert Ustwayte' in connection with a bequest made by her third husband.[18] The existence of these connections which are commemorated through bequests suggests that this could have been some sort of network of people who were interested in humanist ideas, perhaps under the direction of Gunthorpe. Katherine Styles may therefore have had knowledge relating to humanist concepts and perhaps this might have informed her apparently proto-Protestant tendencies. However, despite clues to her connections with progressive ideas and interests, Katherine also makes a number of overtly Catholic bequests which concern the fairly standard provision, at the start of the testament, of lights for obituary prayers at particular saints' shrines. There is also her very personal commemoration of devotion to a pilgrimage cult expressed through the gift 'to our lady of Walsingham' of 'a hoope of gold whiche was my wedding ringe'.[19]

Katherine's Wealth and Status

Will documents do not lend themselves to searches for definitive indications of wealth, even though they are produced in consideration of an all-important issue associated with wealth, which is the *post mortem* inheritance of money, land, property and goods. They do often provide clues to the nominal status of the testator, as rank or occupation is often given in the opening sentences of the will, after the testator's name. Katherine is described as 'Dame' in this context, and also in her third husband's will. The opening sentence of Katherine's will, which states the names of her three husbands and their successive increase in social rank (yeoman, esquire, knight), suggests that she was quite status conscious. In this regard it is interesting to note that she ascribes the status of 'yeoman' to her first husband, whereas this description is not used in his own will, made in 1505.[20]

The survival of the will of Katherine's first husband, William Cooke, means that the extent of the property she inherited on her first widowhood may be assessed.[21] This included all tenements and gardens he owned lying in Greenwich, and a range of different types of land (meadows, pastures, woods), along with rents pertaining to these types of land, in the 'townes and parishes' of Greenwich, Deptford, West Greenwich (Lewisham), Westshene (Richmond), Stebenhithe marsh in Middlesex and elsewhere in England. Quantities such as acreage or the

---

17   NA PROB 11/22/11/181v.
18   NA PROB 11/24/9/67r. This bequest is discussed below.
19   NA PROB 11/24/9/67r.
20   NA PROB 11/14/30/234v–5r.
21   NA PROB 11/14/30/234v–5r.

amount of rent are not given but this all sounds like a significant amount of land which would ensure that Katherine could live in comfort. Unfortunately the will of Katherine's second husband does not survive so it is not possible to assess how much wealth she inherited from him. Her third husband, John Styles, does not make very detailed references to his property, it is simply included in a generic bequest of the residue of his moveable and unmoveable goods which is to be inherited by Katherine. He does mention two small items of property, however, in bequests which are probably much more concerned with emotional ties than with the extent of his landed wealth. The first item relates to what must have been the Style family's place of residence when he was a child, in Tiverton, Devon (he gives this to his brother); the second concerns Katherine and it is the return to her of a gift she gave to him of a tenement lying 'in the backlane by Billingsgate in Estgrenewich', with the condition that after his decease she shall enjoy it 'in lik astat as that she had before that she gave the same unto me'. Perhaps she inherited this from her second husband.

Katherine's own will does not mention much land and property, indicating that most of it had probably already been inherited by her heirs as a *pre mortem* transaction and the rest was to be included in the request that:

> myne householde and moveable stuffe except the whiche I intend to give by my life besolde by myne executour underwritten. And the monnye therof coming to be distributed for the performaunce of this my testament and last will

Katherine does make mention of her rent in Stepney Marsh which is to be inherited by her son William; this is probably the same rent as was bequeathed to her (in 'Stebenhithe') by her first husband.

Material Goods, Heirlooms, and Identity

Some evidence for the life and experiences of Katherine Styles is available through the gifts that she bequeaths. These include silver ware, jewellery, devotional beads, a book, soft furnishings, and other household goods. The items are often small but quite precious. Katherine's gift to her daughter in law, Emma Cooke (described as her daughter), for example, consists of several pieces of jewellery (the rosary beads of 'mother a pearle' and the ring of gold 'with a Turcas'. Some of the items are described in detail using words which add to the emotional value of the bequest, such as the word 'best' used for the beads, the girdle and the gown. Other items and bequests appear to have a narrative concerning their ownership attached to them.

It is important to remember that the goods given in a last will and testament almost certainly do not constitute all the possessions owned by the testator. Rather, the items mentioned have been selected for a specific purpose which immediately implies that the ways the goods are described, and the individual to whom they are given, are of significance. This is specifically indicated in Katherine's will with the clause that 'I will that myne household and moveable stuffee excepte that whiche I entende to give by my life besolde by myne executour underwritten'.[22] It is also important to remember that although there were plenty of material goods available for consumption in sixteenth-century England – and this is particularly the case for a woman of reasonable wealth such as Katherine Styles, living close to London – yet the sixteenth century did not have the culture of mass consumption which probably developed more rapidly from the seventeenth century.[23] This means that material goods had a different kind of status in the sixteenth century than they do today; each one being more precious in its own right as an object.

A number of the bequests of heirloom goods made by Katherine are very standard in that they aim to provide for her children and grandchildren. She gives, for example, a set of bed and bedding to each of the seven grandchildren who are the children of her son William Cooke. Three of these children, perhaps all the daughters, are also given some further items such as brass pots, plates, dishes and saucers (probably in pewter), candlesticks and single items of silver ware. The clause about when these gifts should be given indicates that all of these grandchildren are under twenty one at the time of this bequest. Her determination to protect her family's interests and the wealth that she has accrued through her increasingly favourable marriages is indicated by these provisions for her grandchildren. This promise appears to be echoed in the will of her son, William Cooke, who requests that, 'my daughters have the full bequest that my mother bequeathed them'.[24] And Katherine indicates again the firmness of her resolve, even in her dying wishes, that her family should receive what it is owed through the posthumous grantof the wages he deserves for loyal service (of her third husband) to Thomas, Duke of Norfolk in the Irish campaign.

Katherine also provided for some of the more grown-up children in her network of kin. The person described as 'my husband stiles doughter', for example, is probably not one of Katherine's children, but a grown-up child from one of John Styles's previous marriages – she has certainly been widowed once already being described as 'late Hewsters wife'. She is bequeathed a 'table cloth and a towel of diaper with Katherine Wheles', which is a pretty sounding gift but not one which would provide, or is even symbolic of, the necessaries for a young woman setting up her dowry. But by giving this gift, Katherine is signalling her continued allegiance to that branch of her kin network which came about through her third marriage. The intricacies of these family networks are also indicated by the bequest which follows this, of a gold ring to the husband (called 'Water') of the person called 'my husband stiles doughter', with the explanatory clause, 'whiche hir

---

22   NA PROB 11/24/9/66v.

23   See, for example, John Brewer and Roy Porter (eds), *Consumption and the World of Goods* (London, Routledge, 1993); also, Lorna Weatherill, *Consumer Behaviour & Material Culture in Britain 1660–1760* (London, Routledge, 1988).

24   NA PROB 11/24/15/240r.

husband Hewster gave to my husband Style'. Actually, John Styles's own will confirms who all these people are. He mentions a daughter called 'Jane Water' who is married to a merchant and grocer called Edward Water in London; this Jane, who was evidently already widowed in 1529, had a son called Jerome Hewster.[25] It does indicate something about the way these kin relationships were perceived, however, that Katherine is in effect giving back to her step-daughter Jane Water's second husband (Edward Water) a ring which was initially given by Jane's first husband (Hewster) to Katherine's husband John Stiles. Perhaps the ring of gold is being used as an object capable of producing a thread of connection between these sets of kin who are not related by blood. And in so doing, maybe the ring fosters a network of connections and loyalties over time.

Some of Katherine's bequests hint that the business of gift-giving and the sharing out of inheritance has not always been a smooth process for this family. Several times, she makes reference to a 'bill' that the beneficiary must deliver in order to receive the bequest. The mention of these bills (written documents) appears to indicate that Katherine was very concerned to be very precise about the specific items which were already owed to, or which she wished to give to, specific individuals. The first of these concerns the bequest of a standing cup of silver and gilt to her son Edmond Skerme who must be the child of her second marriage. The text indicates that this cup was bequeathed to Edmond by his father, but the instruction is that in order to collect the item he must 'deliver a bill of Sir John Styles hand, the whiche he hath for the same'. Similarly, another beneficiary to receive such a bill is Robert Ustwayte who is not a member of the immediate family but is evidently part of a kin network. It concerns a cup, 'wherof he hathe a bill and the same bille to be delievred in likewise'. The third reference to a bill concerns the bequests to Katherine's grandchildren and implies that all their names are written in a 'bylle', and that there is also further information in this bill about the book to be given to Master John Cheeseman's daughter.

There is no explanation of this concern with written proof of bequests in Katherine's will. However the will of her third husband, Sir John Styles, does provide a possible explanation:

> And as for my sonne Richard Style my wille is that he shall not have any parcell or parcelles or porcion of my goodes moveable nor unmoveable forasmoch that he hath been chargeable and alwayes disobedient unto me and for his disobedience and mysdemeaner and for that I wolde namore encombered with him. I gave to him a porcion and theruppon before a Notarye in the towne of Anwarpe in Brabant and diverse merchantes of Inglond there being the said Richard made to me a quitaunce with condicion that never hereafter he nore noo manner of persone for him shall clayme or demande any parcell of goodes or thingis that belonge or apperteyn unto me

---

[25]   NA PROB 11/23/14/110v. These three individuals are bequeathed a new black gown each by John Styles.

Past and Present Identity and Loyalty

Because it is a summary of elements of an individual's identity from birth to death, the last will and testament often makes reference to particular geographical locations or commemorative sites that have been important during the lifetime of the testator as well as to other members of the family, sometimes in previous generations. Katherine's loyalty to the chapel of St Anne and to the brotherhood of St George and St Anne, for example, seems to relate back to her first marriage. This is suggested by her description of this burial place as next to that of her first husband, William Cooke, 'in place for my bodyie there ordeynid', and is confirmed by William's own request to be buried at this site in his last will and testament.[26] In 1505 when William made his will it was called the 'Chapel of St Anne' only, a difference in name which might reflect changing popularities of saints over the twenty-five years between his death and Katherine's. The chapel therefore seems to fulfil the role of a traditional family burial site for the Cooke family. It also received continued patronage in the next generation as signalled by the request of William Cooke, Katherine's son, to be buried there in the short and perhaps hastily produced will in preparation for what one must assume was his early death in 1532.[27] Katherine's burial request makes or rejuvenates a familial connection which might otherwise have seemed weakened by her successive marriages. But Katherine, like other spouses, is not able to reflect all the important connections of her three husbands. John Styles's clear intention to affirm his connections with the place of his birth, in Tiverton, Devon, for example, is signalled in a number of ways, but this is not pursued by Katherine in her will. His bequests to this area include the donation of his best and longest streamer of silk, which bears his coat of arms, to the parish church of St Peter in Tiverton 'where I was borne and cristoned'.[28] Katherine's choice to prioritise the geography of her connection with the Cooke family, appears to be a definite choice to make a connection with the family of her first marriage but this is also the family of her lowest status marriage. This seems like an interesting choice for a woman who appears to be very conscious of her rise in status.

***

Undoubtedly more difficult a task than the reconstruction of life and experience for the men in this volume, the study of Dame Katherine Styles, like that of Elizabeth Philip, provides a particular perspective on life in the early English Renaissance. Dame Katherine did not leave behind so many 'cultural productions' as the three men. However, the details provided by her own last will and testament, and the

---

26   NA PROB 11/14/30/234v–5r.
27   NA PROB 11/15/24/240.
28   NA PROB 11/23/14/110v.

other evidences of her family and social networks that this document brings to the surface, provide a valuable perspective on social status and opportunity, changing levels of wealth, issues of piety and ideology, and the effect of the three different husbands on the experiences woman had of the Early English Renaissance.

Chapter 8

William Buckley

Introduction

On the discovery of one significant piece of personal documentation, a collection of fragmentary evidences has emerged for the reconstruction of the life (and death) of William Buckley, an English schoolmaster who lived and worked in Greenwich and Cambridge in the first half of the sixteenth century. At one level, the evidence for William Buckley's life and cultural innovations fits snugly into the usual story, or the 'grand narrative' of the early English Renaissance. But focusing on this one man's experiences also brings to the surface nuances of the experience of being a Renaissance man: emotional responses, generous benefactions, hopes for the new dawn of scientific discovery, bitter disappointment and mourning at the loss of two young pupils. Reconstructing William Buckley's life therefore requires a consideration of sentiments often thought unacceptable in the writing of a narrative about life or lives in the sixteenth century. So when pieced together, the fragments of evidence emerging for William Buckley's life produce a biography that questions the usual way of telling stories about sixteenth-century society and Renaissance.

This story begins with an ending, the written record of the schoolmaster's death, in his last will and testament. The will provides clues about his family, social connections, property, learning, attitudes, and lifestyle. The trail from this schoolmaster's will, made in 1551, leads to: a learned mathematician with a political and philosophical commitment to education; a philosopher interested in body and soul; a poet commemorating the deaths of contemporary dukes and religious charismatics; a man with distinguished friends; a maker of ornate scientific instruments; and a family member who wishes to be commemorated by his mother, uncle, brother and father. These are all facets of one man's life, which undeniably provide some perspective on sixteenth-century society. These facets also happen to touch on themes often raised in the construction of overarching narratives of sixteenth-century history, such as English Renaissance; early print culture; poetic anthology; humanism; educational reform; neo-Platonism; improving literacy; scientific rebirth; godly family; Protestantism. And significantly, some interesting individual perspectives on these broadly defined terms are found in this single document.[1]

An outline structure for William Buckley's life-course is already available in various reference sources, which were constructed without the benefit of his will.[2] However, taking a closer look at the bequests in the will document opens up a selection of trails concerning this individual's personal experiences of Renaissance. I hope to show in this chapter the ways that the small fragment of new evidence, in the form of a single document, might stimulate alternative perspectives on the well-documented 'facts' about culture and society in the past.[3]

Writing this 'Biography'

This chapter is structured as a number of themed sections, each dealing with one aspect of the fragments which survive for William Buckley's life. In this sense it is a simple structure arising from the description of various fragments which themselves emerged because of the chance finding of the single piece of new evidence – the will document. However, by juxtaposing these themes and fragments, my intention is to explore the way that these pieces of evidence put emphases on the story of Renaissance which are different from those provided by the grander narratives of culture and society. The different themed sections interact with each other, thereby building a version of this Renaissance individual, which becomes a multi-layered impression of one man's experiences of life in the Renaissance. Aspects of William Buckley's character and attitude that are revealed include his interest in teaching at the elementary level, his excitement about new scientific discoveries, his distress at the death of his prodigious pupils and his gratitude for being provided an opportunity for his own education.

William Buckley's Will[4]

William Buckley's last will and testament is very similar to many such texts also found in the will registers of the Canterbury Prerogative Court in the sixteenth

---

[1]   See Carlo Ginzburg, *The Cheese and the Worms: The Cosmos of a Sixteenth Century Miller*, trans. John and Anne C. Tredeschi (London, Routledge and Kegan Paul, 1981). Here, Ginzburg proposes that in reducing the scale of observation, that which for another scholar could have been a simple footnote is transformed into a book.

[2]   See below for a discussion of these sources.

[3]   See Introduction, Chapter 1; and also Carlo Ginzburg, 'Microhistory: Two or Three Things I Know about It', *Critical Inquiry*, 20/ 1 (1993): 10–35, p. 29; Ginzburg cites Renata Serra's 'almost feverish' worries about the problematic relationships that individual documents have with reality.

[4]   NA PROB 11/35/88v–89r; the surviving version of the will was produced in July 1551, and proved in May 1552.

century.[5] It begins, after the customary greeting, with the date of production, 15 July 1551; then the subject's name and occupation, William Buckley, Schoolmaster to the King's Majesty's Henchmen; and his place of residence, Greenwich. Compared with others from the same period, the will is fairly short, even though it is extended at the end by a codicil. A number of associates receive bequests in the normal way. These include close family members and other associates. In general, the will follows the expected conventions. But the nature of the bequests and the names of some associates deserve detailed examination.

On closer inspection, the conventional structure of this will's narrative is speckled with unusual and significant clues. William Buckley does not specify his place of burial nor does he bequeath any money or property to a church or religious institution. This is not without comparison at this time in the wake of reforming attitudes to the Church's control over the afterlife.[6] However, there are some distinctly unusual references to body and soul, and the separation of these two elements of the individual at death. The text reads, 'my soule to almightie god and my bodye to be buried where yt shall please god *my soul to be separated from the same.*'[7] I have emphasised the unusual phrase, which appears to hint at a neo-Platonist philosophy of body and soul.

By the end of his life, William Buckley moved in illustrious circles. Because of his involvement with the royal court and his scientific connections, his biographical details are recorded by the *Dictionary of National Biography;*[8] and in a shortened form in the new *Oxford Dictionary of National Biography.*[9] Because his last will and testament had not been discovered, a question was left hanging over the date of his death in the older *DNB* account of Buckley's life. However, working from the records of his schooling at Eton College and his admission to King's College at the age of eighteen, Buckley's birth year may be calculated as 1519. On the basis of a normal life expectancy, these biographer-historians guessed that Buckley's life drew to a close in 1570–71.[10] The more recent *ODNB* account has dispensed with this caution, or (in its shorter form) with the wordage required to show the workings of approximated calculations about Buckley's likely death date which are based on normal life expectancy. Instead this more recent version

---

5   See the collection of such records in NA PROB 11.

6   For a consideration of preambles see Elisabeth Salter, *Cultural Creativity in the Early English Renaissance: Popular Culture in Town and Country* (London, Palgrave Macmillan, 2006), Chapter 6.

7   NA PROB 11/35/88v.

8   *The Dictionary of National Biography: From the Earliest Times to 1900* [hereafter *DNB*], ed. Leslie Stephen and Sidney Lee, 22 vols (London, Oxford University Press, 1917; repr. 1960) vol. 3, p. 215.

9   Thompson Cooper, 'Buckley, William (1518/19–1571)', rev. Anita McConnell, in *ODNB*, Oxford University Press, 2004 http://www.oxforddnb.com/view/article/3869.

10   *DNB* estimates 1570; for the estimate of 1571, see John Venn, *Alumni Cantabrigiensis*, Part 1, 4 vols (Cambridge, CUP, 1922–7), Part 1, vol. 1, '*Earliest Times to 1751*' (1922), p. 248.

has gone for the more assertive 'Buckley died in 1571'. Both of these accounts are incorrect. Buckley actually died in 1552. The poignant correction of this death date allows the discovery of a man who died more than twenty years before he had reached old age.

As a boy and as a young man, William Buckley was fortunate in the education that he received. And luckily, these educational establishments also have detailed records that provide a trace of Buckley's early life. Two of the biographical works that have entries for this promising young scholar suggest that he was born in Lilleshall, Shropshire. Sterry's *Eton College Register* and Venn's *Alumni Cantabrigiensis,* therefore, also suggest that Buckley's earliest education was at the school of Lilleshall Abbey, which is in Shropshire and survives today as a picturesque ruin.[11] Between the years c. 1532 and 1537, and from the age of about thirteen to eighteen, Buckley was educated at Eton College, probably as a 'King's scholar'. In August 1537 he left Eton to take up a scholarship at Eton's sister institution of King's College in Cambridge. He received a BA in 1541/2 and an M.A. in 1545.[12] The MA degree conferred on him the title of Magister, or 'Master', which is used in his testament.

The *DNB* (and the shorter *ODNB*), the Eton register, and the record of Cambridge students all have roughly corroborating sketches of Buckley's biography. Each discusses him with reference to three principal features of his life. Firstly, he is described as an author of mathematical textbooks; secondly, as a teacher of this subject to King Edward VI and his 'henchmen' or 'pages'; and thirdly, as an associate of the well-known John Cheke, scholar and schoolmaster to the young king; a man with controversial views about education and religion. There is one other biography of William Buckley on account of his influential involvement with scientific discovery. This is *The Mathematical Practitioners of Tudor and Stuart England* which indicates how important for the development of this discipline was his contribution to mathematics, and his own role as a 'mechanician' (or mathematical practitioner).[13]

Historians of science also mention some tantalising material evidence concerning Buckley's involvement with a London instrument maker called Thomas Gemini. Some of the instruments Gemini made survive today and these are described and discussed, together with his career, in Gerard L'E. Turner's recent study.[14] Thomas Gemini is known as an originator of the London trade in

---

11   Venn, *Alumni*, p. 248; and *The Eton College Register 1441–1698: Alphabetically Arranged and Edited with Biographical Notes by Sir Wasey Sterry* (Eton College, Spottiswoode, Ballantyne and Co, 1943).

12   *DNB*, vol. 3, p. 215

13   E.G.R. Taylor, *The Mathematical Practitioners of Tudor and Stuart England*, Institute of Navigation (Cambridge, CUP, 1954; repr. 1967), pp. 165–9.

14   Gerard L'E. Turner, *Elizabethan Instrument Makers: The Origins of the London Trade in Precision Instrument Making* (Oxford, OUP, 2000), pp. 3–20, 34–7, 95–111.

precision instruments, but what was William Buckley's role in this craft? As a 'mechanician' he may have calculated the date tables on these instruments.

William Buckley's Family and Friends

The nature of William Buckley's social connections and his social world may be investigated, in the first instance, by looking at his will. To his mother, Alice, one of his executors, he gave most of his bedding except his green coverlet kept at Greenwich and other bedding kept in Cambridge, which he gives to his nephew, William Coley. Buckley also gives his mother ten old 'angels' (an old English coin).[15] To his sister, Mary Bannister, Buckley gives two new sovereigns of 20 shillings and to his brother-in-law, William Bannister, a merchant at 'Lombardstreet', whom he elects the supervisor of his bequests and estate, he gives various items of clothing such as his 'hood storked with velvet' and his 'black shorte gowne furred with budge'. Clothing is also specified for his (unnamed) father, and his brother Geoffrey:

> Item to my brother Geoffrey a payr of new hose and satten jacket gardyd with velvet and my Riding cote gardyd with velvet and my white dublet of sakerlothe. Item to my father my Riding cloke and my hatt, too old black cotes, two old dublets of fustian and two payre of old hosen and anewe hole soverayne of twentie shillings and my studye gowne of rattes colour.[16]

This is the main extent of Buckley's bequests of domestic goods, but not the extent of his bequests to his family.

To his uncle and benefactor, Sir Edmund Woodsend, parson in Grendon, Warwickshire, Buckley gives all his other clothing and all his chests, except those needed to transport his books. He also returns to his uncle a silver goblet that he had loaned him in order that he could borrow money to study at Cambridge. And then apparently following in this tradition of supporting family members through education, Buckley's bequest to his own nephew is as follows:

> Itm I gyve and bequeathe to Willm Coley my nephew, child in Eton College, all my books and all my Instruments pertayning to study whether they be at Grenewich, at M*agister* Cheeks house in London at doctor Hatchers house in Cambridge or in the provests place there. Except such books and instruments as I shall dispose otherways by a bill subscribed with my own hand.[17]

---

[15]   In the *OED*, a noble is an old English coin showing St Michael the Archangel piercing the dragon, hence the term 'angel noble', or 'angel' for such a coin.
[16]   NA PROB 11/35/89r.
[17]   NA PROB 11/35/88v.

It is presumably this William Coley who is recorded by Venn as entering King's College Cambridge, although he probably failed to gain his degree. According to the Eton College register, Coley was expelled from King's because of his involvement with necromancy. The fate of the books and instruments of study that he acquired from his uncle and benefactor is presently unknown.

Alongside Buckley's nephew, it is his non-familial friends who receive the more intellectual bequests appropriate to a 'Renaissance man'. Most of these other named associates are connected with Cambridge, generally King's College. These bequests include:

> Item, to Mag*ister* Cheke my greate quadrant of brass with a saphea upon the backside with such of the best mathematicall books that he will chose amonges all my books.[18]

To a Master Wendy, Buckley gives his 'chart of Grece' and his 'chart of England' with a brazen sphere that is 'at Mag*ister* doctor Hatcher's house in Cambridge'. To Sir Temple, fellow of King's College Cambridge, he bequeaths his books '*horologiographien masteri*' and '*supplementum almanack cardani*'.[19] And finally to a Doctor Owen he bequeaths a book entitled, '*Calendarium historium & bibliatum de ratione temporum*'.[20]

Other beneficiaries are of elevated social status. The codicil begins with bequests to such friends:

> Item I give my sphere of brass unto my L*ord* Lisle. Item to Mag*ister* henry Syddney my little astrolabe wheron my name ys graven and my other brazen Instrument with wheles having a shippe in the back of yt and also *paulus jounus dehistoria sui temporis*.[21]

Buckley's 'my Lord Lisle', is probably John Dudley (1504–1553), Duke of Northumberland, and Lord Lisle officially between 1540–47. He held major landholdings in Shropshire (Buckley's natal county) and Staffordshire, amongst other places.[22] He also belongs to a family very much associated with the ownership of scientific instruments, although significantly it is the following generation of Dudleys who are usually considered most important collectors.[23] Buckley's gifts to John Dudley therefore provide a new perspective on this. 'Master Henry Sidney' is probably the son-in-law of Lord Lisle and the father of the well-known Philip Sidney of Penshurst Place, in Kent.[24] From this evidence, it

---

[18]   NA PROB 11/35/89r.

[19]   Not all the books have yet been identified, however the '*supplementu almanack cardani*' almost certainly refers to works of Girolamo Cardano.

[20]   NA PROB 11/35/89r

[21]   NA PROB 11/35/89r.

[22]   David Loades, *John Dudley: Duke of Northumberland, 1504–1553* (Oxford, Clarendon Press, 1996), p. ix, 48, 57.

[23]   See Turner, *Elizabethan Instrument Makers*, Chapter 5.

[24]   Loades, *John Dudley*, pp. 161,180.

appears that William Buckley was a man with a varied and distinguished social and intellectual network. It is not yet clear how he came to acquire such interesting friends and property, although he may have been related to a gentry family of Cheshire origins which may have brought him into contact with some of these men from the higher echelons of society.

Perhaps in William Buckley we have access to the quintessential educational reformer of this period: perhaps he was himself a product of new opportunities who sought to reform traditional structures. The early sixteenth century was indeed an exciting time for changes in educational possibilities and practices: provision of schooling was probably on the increase.[25] The 'new learning' associated with reforming attitudes to the church and social structure brought new opportunities and educational controversies.[26] Certainly by the early sixteenth century, Buckley's university, Cambridge, had gained the reputation as a centre for new learning. And, since its foundation by Henry VI in c.1440, King's College had a degree of independence from papal statutes, which may have enabled ideas of educational reform to flourish.

Education and Reform

In the sixteenth-century context of educational provision and reform, the commitment to reassessing methods of learning and teaching was recorded by humanist scholars and writers on education such as Erasmus, Vives, and John Cheke of Cambridge one of whose pupils was William Buckley.[27] The role of education as the path for all individuals to their own vocation was central to the social humanism and Protestantism of the sixteenth century.[28] The implication of

---

[25]   Nicholas Orme, *English Schools in the Middle Ages* (London, Methuen, 1973), p. 23 ff.; David Cressy, *Education in Tudor and Stuart England*, Documents of Modern History (London, Edward Arnold, 1975).

[26]   Joan Simon, *Education and Society in Tudor England* (Cambridge, CUP, 1966), pp. 120–1, 153, 204, 209; Rosemary O'Day, *Education and Society 1500–1800: The Social Foundations of Education in Early Modern Britain* (London, Longman, 1982), pp. 242, and 244–6 for Vives's views that education was a remedy against poverty and that expenditure on the education of the poor was a duty for civic magistrates.

[27]   O'Day, *Education and Society*, p. 66 ff., on the conversion of education in order to teach a Protestant ideology; and *idem*, p. 55 for the influence of Petrus Jordan and Wolfgang Ratchius's stress on the interaction of reading and writing in the learning process. This was adopted by Vives, which in turn was accepted by educationalists such as Brinsley, Coote and Mulcaster. Also, Simon, *Education and Society*, Chapters 2 and 3.

[28]   O'Day, *Education and Society*, p. 166 ff., and Simon, *Education and Society*, p. 63 on the acquisition of nobility through education; for Bucer's views on the related matter of educational discipline see Martin Greschat, 'Church and Civil Community', in David F. Wright (ed.), *Martin Bucer: Reforming Church and Community* (Cambridge, CUP, 1994), pp. 26–31. For related arguments about the pedagogical value of private confession see Amy

these ideas for the school and university syllabus was an invigorated emphasis on practical application to further the 'useful' use of knowledge.[29] This included: new vigour for the teaching of Greek and Latin and the imitation of rhetorical traditions; and new emphasis on reading practical tracts about husbandry, arithmetic for architecture, and astronomy for navigational techniques.[30] The use of the vernacular languages was also encouraged: Vives proposed the notion that the new generation of school pupils should become a 'treasury' of their own language. Behind such statements was, presumably, the desire to encourage what seemed to be a politically useful awareness of national heritage and identity. Indeed, this was not without controversy: John Cheke's championing of the importance of pronunciation in teaching and learning Greek, for example, was unpopular with powerful figures such as the conservative Bishop Gardiner, chancellor of the university in the 1540s, perhaps because of its religious implications. According to the treatises of Erasmus and Vives, students were also encouraged to learn to write quickly and accurately, keeping their own exercise books, which they should organise according to personal taste, selecting passages from well-known writers for later use and criticism in their own scholarly arguments.[31]

One individual, Robert Record, is generally considered to have made a very important contribution to disseminating new educational practices, particularly in the field of mathematics. But whereas Record has become a significant figure in the history of educational reform, William Buckley has not.[32] This is despite Buckley's involvement with practising the 'new' teaching methods: according to Robert Mulcaster, a well-known mathematician and educationalist of the next generation who was taught by Buckley, this schoolmaster was an inspirational teacher. In the beginning of one of his own mathematical books, Mulcaster tells of Buckley's generous distribution to his pupils of Euclid's mathematical tracts, copied in his own hand. It may be one of these that Buckley bequeaths, as 'one of my Euclids', to King's college library.[33]

Nelson Burnett, 'Bucer, Discipline & Moral Reform', *The Sixteenth Century Journal*, 22/3 (1991): 439–56, p. 443, 454.

[29] Simon, *Education and Society*, pp. 114–119, 120–121.

[30] See O'Day, *Education and Society*, p. 166, on the important contribution of Roger Ascham's *The Scholemaster* on this subject.

[31] Simon, *Education and Society*, pp. 109–8.

[32] O'Day, *Education and Society,* pp. 167–8, for a discussion of the professionalisation of teaching, often associated with individuals like Record and Mulcaster.

[33] For Mulcaster's comments on Buckley see BL MS Add 5815; and NA PROB 11/35/88v for Buckley's bequests to King's College Cambridge. See also Peter Dear, *Revolutionizing the Sciences: European Knowledge and Its Ambitions, 1500–1700* (London, Palgrave, 2001), pp. 78–9; Dear proposes that during the second half of the sixteenth century, mathematicians, especially in England, had begun to make strong claims for their discipline that revolved around its practical dimensions rather than focusing on the more philosophical justifications preferred by increasing numbers of bookish mathematicians. In 1570, for example, there appeared a new translation into English of Euclid's *Elements*,

William Buckley as a Writer of Textbooks

William Buckley's schoolbooks and other didactic tracts were written and printed between 1546 and 1635. Once again there are some uncertainties about authorship. He probably wrote an untitled introductory arithmetical tract, which survives in manuscript form in the British Library;[34] and a treatise called *Arithmetica Memorativa*, which used rhyming hexameters to help students remember the laws of mathematics.[35] Buckley also wrote a treatise on the use of the astronomical and horological instrument called a 'ring dial'.[36] This work was originally dedicated to the Princess Elizabeth, future queen, in 1546 and in his dedication of the book to her, Buckley records that he actually made her a ring dial at her request. Reputedly the scientific instrument was presented to the princess, together with the instruction manual, in 1546.[37] Both the introduction to arithmetic and the ring dial tract survive in manuscript form in the British Library. The hand used for these manuscripts, whilst varying in size and spacing, appears to be the same and I tentatively suggest this to be the hand of William Buckley.[38] While these books probably had quite different intended audiences, their styles of prose and the nature of their commitment to the use of example show some common themes of educational practice that are similar to those ascribed to John Cheke. So it seems appropriate to propose these books, written or edited by Master Buckley, to be significant evidence for one individual teacher's perspective on this sixteenth- century movement of educational reform.[39]

The untitled 'introduction to arithmetic' is a small volume containing 18 pages. Written on paper in an even, clear, and elegant hand, it was unfortunately rebound in the eighteenth century, although fortunately this does not appear to have reduced

---

bearing a preface written by John Dee of Mortlake. Buckley's bequest to King's College also includes Ptolomy's *De Geographia* and Pliny's *Natural History*; on the renewed interest in Ptolomy's work, see Dear, *Revolutionizing*, p. 13.

[34]   BL MS Royal 12 A XXII. The authorship of this volume has been ascribed to William Buckley, although this may require further clarification, although see below on the question of its relation to the work of Robert Record.

[35]   BL RB.23.A.47 (2); this edition dates from 1617.

[36]   BL MS Royal 12 A XXV.

[37]   Thompson Cooper, 'Buckley, William (1518/19–1571)', rev. Anita McConnell, in *ODNB*, http://www.oxforddnb.com/view/article/3869.

[38]   Further evidence for this speculation is provided by the engraving on one of Buckley's quadrants, for which see later in this Chapter.

[39]   All these works are written in Latin, albeit generally simple prose, see O'Day, *Education and Society*, p. 64, on the attitude that the learning of Latin grammar was the most important aspect of education. On this subject see also Kenneth Charlton, *Education in Renaissance England* (London, Routledge and Kegan Paul, 1968).

its size. The tract, which is written in Latin, begins with an introduction outlining the ethos of the book: it is about the art of arithmetic, and concerned to define an appropriate method to teach mathematics in a practical way. The book operates from the principle that all arithmetic relies on the simple sequence of 1, 2, 3, 4, 5, 6, 7, 8, 9, 10 and calculations of these numbers in the customary manner.[40] Having set out this principle, there is then a brief outline of the contents of the book, which is in five chapters: Chapter 1, 'Numeration', Chapter 2, 'Addition', Chapter 3, 'Subtraction', Chapter 4 'Multiplication' and Chapter 5, 'Division'. Any cursory comparison between Buckley's chapter headings, and those adopted by the famous educational treatise attributed to Robert Record is startling – Record's headings are the same as Buckley's. Record's book was written, famously, in English (in c. 1543), but it is extremely similar to William Buckley's which survives in a copy dating from about 1546. Perhaps Buckley translated a version of Record's treatise into Latin; or perhaps Record translated an earlier copy of Buckley's treatise into English.

As the introduction gives way to the first chapter, Master Buckley cites Euclid's, *De Arte Geometria* to remind his pupils that numbers, whilst being called by one name, are in fact made from many units. He continues with a discussion of the way to arrange tens, hundreds, and thousands on the page, providing a simple tabular example.[41] The chapter continues with instructions about how to pronounce the numbers when reading them from the page: that is, to begin with the left digit.[42] There follow two tabular illustrations: in the first he uses a conventional date to illustrate the way numerical values are attributed to the different positions, the diagram uses the date '1546' as an example, showing that the six is the 'first position' (*primus locus*), the four the 'second position' (*secundus locus*), the five the 'third position' (*tertius locus*) and the one the 'fourth position' (*quartus locus*).[43] In the second more generalised diagram, Buckley gives the unit position and the names of the numerical places (that is, from 10s, 100s 1000s, up to 10s of millions and ending with a hundred million).[44] This ends the first chapter or 'lesson'.

The second chapter continues in the same explicatory vein, explaining that 'adding' is when two or more numbers are added to make a new number. The book then gives advice on the correct way to write an addition sum, the one number being written perpendicularly above the second number to which it is to be added.[45] The book continues by explaining with an instructional tone that 'if you would like' to add the numbers in one sum, as is made visible in the example, then a line is drawn under these two and the units are added, 10s to 10s, 100s to 100s

---

[40]   BL MS Royal 12 A XXII, fol. 1r.
[41]   BL MS Royal 12 A XXII, fols 1v–2r.
[42]   BL MS Royal 12 A XXII, fol. 3r.
[43]   BL MS Royal 12 A XXII, fol. 3r.
[44]   BL MS Royal 12 A XXII, fol. 3v.
[45]   BL MA Royal 12 A XXII, fols 4v–5v.

and so on. Below this, three examples are drawn, each showing the answer, accompanied with an instruction that the answer may be put below the line. The text continues, each time providing several examples, showing that the same principle applies for greater numbers and covering how to carry numbers into the next column with examples that show how and where to write and cancel carried numbers to prevent confusion with the additions. The lesson on addition ends with a paragraph pointing out the practical relevance of this skill when using money, describing again the way that monetary units are written with the smallest at the right and the greatest at the left; they are read from left to right.[46] Finally, there is a number-square table, which shows all the possibilities of addition between 1 and 20 [see FIG. 7.1].[47] The following chapters continue in much the same style frequently using a combination of written instruction about the purpose, numerical examples, written emphasis on the proper way to write the sums and diagrammatical number tables.[48]

	1	2	3	4	5	6	7	8	9	10
1	2	3	4	5	6	7	8	9	10	11
2	3	4	5	6	7	8	9	10	11	12
3	4	5	6	7	8	9	10	11	12	13
4	5	6	7	8	9	10	11	12	13	14
5	6	7	8	9	10	11	12	13	14	15
6	7	8	9	10	11	12	13	14	15	16
7	8	9	10	11	12	13	14	15	16	17
8	9	10	11	12	13	14	15	16	17	18
9	10	11	12	13	14	15	16	17	18	19
10	11	12	13	14	15	16	17	18	19	20

Figure 7.1 Arithmetic Diagram

Clearly, these first two chapters of this textbook provide a set of basic introductory lessons in arithmetic. The book does not reach the complexity of calculation doubtless used by Buckley for his astrological investigations. The intention here is pedagogical and indicates his skills in teaching. The emphasis on learning by example, practical application and the importance of writing are all instructive. Whether he invented them or translated them, Buckley's books therefore represent this schoolmaster's perspective on the styles of teaching recommended by well-known educational reformers of this time such as John Cheke.

---

[46]   BL MS Royal 12 A XXII, fol. 6r.
[47]   BL MS Royal 12 A XXII, fol. 6v.
[48]   Dear, *Revolutionizing,* p. 47, notes the stress made by Euclid on demonstration.

This mathematical textbook, albeit in Latin, is not a dry tract, complying merely with a set of reforming rubrics about how to teach. I would venture to suggest that there is a warmth and enthusiasm in this text, which goes beyond the arithmetic. Take the opening to the final chapter, which naturally in the progressive scheme covers the most difficult of the skills, division: it begins with a lengthy introduction to this chapter in which the tutorial voice narrates the pleasure that 'we' have now come to this most senior part of arithmetic. The tutor hopes that his explanations so far have given his pupils the necessary knowledge to understand this most difficult aspect of the art. He praises and affirms their efforts by comparing the study of mathematics to the labours of Hercules, suggesting that it is only by careful practise of the required mathematical skills that its difficulty may be conquered. This schoolmaster's appreciation of the difficulties experienced by the pupil, affirmation of effort, and sense of common goal, may be evidence of this educational reformer's personal methods of teaching.

Buckley's *De Anulus Horari* (*Of Ring Dials*) is a manuscript of very similar proportions to his Euclidian mathematical textbook.[49] It too was rebound in the eighteenth century and, like the mathematical textbook, it fortunately does not appear to have been clipped too heavily. The book is written in an elegant hand like the other, although the line spacing is slightly more cramped. This palaeographical difference may reflect the different subjects of these literatures and the difference in intended audience. The text is devoted to explaining the design and workings of one particular ring dial. Such dials existed in a variety of levels of complexity, being basically a ring with a hole or holes drilled into it, through which the sun's rays pass. The time may be ascertained by checking the engraved hour scales on the inside of the ring to see where the sun's rays land.[50] The ring dial that William Buckley describes is relatively complex as it is designed for calculating the zodiacal calendar as well as the time according to hours, days, and months.

This text begins with a dedication to the Princess Elizabeth in which Buckley extols the importance of astronomical and horological knowledge.[51] *De Anulis Horarii* is a manual with about twenty sections not quite long enough to be called chapters. It progresses from the basics of ring dial use to the more complex possibilities of the instrument. It begins with a chapter entitled '*Temporis Divisio*' ('Divisions of Time') which gives the basic units of year, month, day, hour, minute; and how to work out the lengths of these time divisions.[52] This immediately provides a complex picture of the difference between naturally and artificially based calculations, which are defined by the astronomical principle being used in the calculation. A natural day is the space of twenty-four hours in which the whole heavens make one circulation such that the stars within the

---

[49]   BL MS Royal A XXV.
[50]   See Turner, *Elizabethan Instrument Makers*, pp. 143–5.
[51]   BL MS Royal A XXV, fols 2r–v.
[52]   BL MS Royal A XXV, fols 3r–4r.

heavens make a complete revolution. An artificial day is the time in which the sun remains above our horizon giving light. The unequal circulation of the equinoxes means that sometimes more or sometimes fewer hours are 'starred' or in other words that the artificial day varies in length.[53]

The second section is entitled 'Description of the Parts of the Ring [dial]'. This is a complicated description of the design of the instrument: the ring dial consists of two rings, one convex and one concave. In the outside part, convex, there are three lines making two spaces in which all the zodiac signs are written with their characteristic symbols. This begins with Aries and divides each space into six parts. The angles for each sign are written in the same ring.[54] It would indeed be easier to understand the instructions if the object itself accompanied the text, but sadly this small ring dial is probably lost.

The third section concerns how to know what sign the sun occupies for a certain month. Here, Buckley uses an example – written in the first person – to illustrate the method, which translates as follows:

> Example: I wish to know in which sign the sun moves in December, wherefore, first in the circle [ring?] of the months is the letter D which signifies December and above there is found the character Capricorn, in which the sun moves, through that month.[55]

The rhyming mathematical treatise called *Arithmetica Memorativa* appears to have had sustained popularity well into the seventeenth-century.[56] This treatise appears to follow a very similar structure to the other arithmetic textbook (the one which is very like Robert Record's, but in Latin), the main difference being that *Arithmetica Memorativa* is written in rhyming verse. This rhyming treatise is confidently attributed to William Buckley in its seventeenth century editions. Assuming that he did write this, the rhyming form of this textbook throws some further light on Buckley's attitude to teaching mathematics. Maybe the fact that it rhymes suggests that he wanted learning maths to be fun. It certainly seems to suggest that he knew how important memory and memorising are for learning and applying the rules of mathematics. Perhaps the fact that it rhymes and is in Latin indicates that he enjoyed using mathematics lessons as a vehicle for his pupils to also learn Latin. Perhaps this was his perspective on the other mathematical treatise, suggesting that he might have viewed the translation of Robert Record's English text into Latin as a means of enhancing the educational experience of learning mathematics.

The 1617 edition of *Arithmetica Memorativa* also provides another perspective on the biography of Master William Buckley because it includes two panegyrics commenting on his learning and also his skills as a teacher. The preface, addressed in a customary way to the 'benevolent reader' for example, is relentlessly

---

53   BL MS Royal A XXV, fol. 4r.
54   BL MS Royal A XXV, fols 4r–5v.
55   BL MS Royal A XXV, fol. 5v.
56   See BL RB.23.A.47 (2); this edition dates from 1617.

superlative about his achievements, pointing out that although he is dead, his mathematics lives on. At the end of this introduction there is also a short 'biography' which details some key points in Buckley's career – that he came from the Lichfield area, was educated at King's College Cambridge where he received academic acclaim, and was involved with the talented young King Edward VI.[57] The epitaph, in a more poetic mode, celebrates the place of Buckley who was always interested in the mysteries of the skies, in the heavens.[58]

The mathematical tract and the ring dial have similarities in tone and a similar didactic quality, even though they are dealing with quite different subjects, and were probably originally intended for quite different audiences. They were probably also produced at much the same date. The edition of *Arithmetica Memorativa* in the British Library, which was printed over fifty years after Buckley's death, also has similar qualities as a teaching text despite its differences in form. It seems clear that William Buckley was a man of considerable intellect who had gained, by the time he wrote these books, a very wide range of learning. The books he names in his will alone indicate that this was a man proficient in Greek and Latin and well read in the liberal arts of natural history, geography, philosophy, mathematics and astronomy (in this case I think it is appropriate to assume he had read the texts he mentions). His objects of scientific study suggest further depths to the nature of his intellectual inquiries. The arithmetic textbooks and *De Anulus Horarii*, however, are simple, basic, instructional manuals. They teach by example, emphasise the importance of practice, and in the case of the arithmetic text, encourage the development of written skills and stress the importance of writing down this knowledge in an acceptable form. All these practices were encouraged by the famous writers Vives and Erasmus and practitioners such as John Cheke. They are, therefore, precisely the kinds of texts one might expect a learned schoolmaster and educational reformer of this time to write. There is, it seems, no awkward dislocation between William Buckley the gifted intellectual and William Buckley the author of beginners' guides and textbooks.

William Buckley as Poet

William Buckley also wrote commemorative poems, which were printed in collated collections in the late sixteenth and early seventeenth centuries. The subjects of these books are, on first appearances, quite different. One book commemorates the lives and deaths of two brothers, Dukes of Suffolk, who died as children from the sweating sickness that hit London in 1550–51.[59] The other book

---

[57]   BL RB.23.A.47 (2), fol. 1v.

[58]   BL RB.23.A.47 (2), fol. 7v.

[59]   Diarmaid MacCulloch, *Tudor Church Militant: Edward VI and the Protestant Reformation*, (London, Penguin Press, 2001), pp. 128–9.

commemorates the life and death of Martin Bucer, an influential religious reformer who originated in Strasbourg but lived the latter part of his life in Cambridge.[60] Such epitaph-based poetry became a popular vogue during Buckley's lifetime, partly perhaps because it was reminiscent of the elegiac forms used by the poets of classical times.[61] Indeed, the collections in which Buckley's verses are found, first printed in 1551, may have been some of the earliest of their kind to reach print in England, giving them their own claim to historical importance.[62] While his hexametrical *Arithmetica Memorativa* suggests that Buckley was not unversed in the arts of poetry, these commemorative works seem to be more obviously 'literary' compilations, which have been ascribed their own genre amongst the literatures. In William Buckley, it seems, we have a truly interdisciplinary 'Renaissance man' who wrote both historically interesting literature and historically interesting science.

The titles of the two books are: *The Lives and Deaths of Two Brothers, Suffolks, Henry and Charles Brandon* .... [*Vitae et Obitus Duorum Fratrum Suffolciensium, Henrici & Caroli Brandoni* ....] and, *Of the Death of the Most Learned and Most Holy Doctor of Theology Martin Bucer* .... [*De Obitus Doctissimi et Sanctissimi Theologii Doctoris Martini Buceri* ....].[63] They are small printed volumes produced in London, containing 56–60 pages, printed on both sides. The Bucer volume was collated by Sir John Cheke and printed by the 'protestant publisher and chronicler' Richard Grafton; the Suffolk volume was printed by another printer with Protestant interests, Thomas Wilson.[64] The books have strong similarities in organisation and content, which are reflected in the frontispieces. First the title is given at length, in both volumes, praising the subject/s in the superlative and ending by informing the reader that there follow two 'epistles' which explain the nature of the subjects' greatness. Both front pages then have an explanation of the second section of the book, which contains epitaphs and epigrams written in Greek and Latin by scholars from the universities of Cambridge and Oxford. Each book actually contains more than two prose entries concerned with primarily the life and then the death of the subject/s. The verse section of each book consists of poems, acrostics and homilies of varying lengths and meters written by between twenty and thirty named individuals, some of whom have contributed several separate entries.

---

[60]   On Bucer's life and works, see Constantin Hopf, *Martin Bucer and the English Reformation* (Oxford, Basil Blackwell, 1946).

[61]   James W. Binns, *Intellectual Culture in Elizabethan and Jacobean England: The Latin Writings of the Age* (Leeds, Francis Cairns, 1990), p. 459, n. 62, and 460, n. 66.

[62]   Binns, *Intellectual Culture*, p. 459 ff.

[63]   *Vitae et Obitus Duorum Fratrum Suffolciensium, Henrici & Caroli Brandoni* ... (London, Thomas Wilson, 1551); *De Obitu Doctissimi et Sanctissimi Theologii Doctoris Martini Buceri* ...(London, Richard Grafton, 1551).

[64]   For references to Grafton's Protestantism and printing activities, see MacCulloch, *Tudor Church Militant*, p. 23.

The title page and content of the Dukes of Suffolk volume insists on the splendid example of nobility and virtue that these Dukes, the Brandon brothers, represented. They were companions and fellow pupils of the young King Edward VI. It is often suggested that the young king was a dedicated scholar with particular potential.[65] The Suffolk brothers, too, have been given this reputation, which may indeed have arisen from the verses that commemorate them. Many of the verses refer to the boys in terms of 'hope' – of their parents, of the nation, of nature. They were 'lights' to those who knew them, 'clever', 'virtuous', 'illustrious', and 'noble'. In his own poems, Buckley's fervent praise of the two young scholar – dukes constructs two young geniuses that all nature praised and yet, dying so young, could not attain the full honour that fortune had bestowed upon them.[66]

It may be precisely because of the process of myth-making that surrounds notions of 'the Renaissance' and the new learning associated with this that these young men of the sixteenth century (the future rulers and leaders) are described as brilliant. After all, for those such as William Buckley who subscribed to the ideal of the Renaissance as a transformation of intellectual and social sophistication, it was necessary to believe that the new learning available was actually being learned. Where better for this to be happening than at the King's court? Indeed, perhaps the myth was actually being constructed as a form of reformist propaganda by those who contributed to this anthology.[67]

Certainly, the known contributors to this volume, Sir John Cheke, Walter Haddon, Thomas Hatcher, appear to have been involved with the educational reforms at Cambridge; at least three contributors – Cheke, Temple and Hatcher – were also close associates of William Buckley as they (or their close relatives) were named in his will, the surviving copy of which, interestingly, was made just one day after the deaths of the two young Dukes. Maybe Buckley's was also a propagandist representation, but whether that is the case or not, this schoolmaster's superlatives may also actually represent the sense of excitement that he and his circle experienced at this time of change and also therefore the sense of desolation he felt at the loss of his gifted pupils.

The book commemorating Bucer mainly focuses on two aspects of this theologian's life and work: firstly, his virtuous and scholarly life, which is compared to the life of Christ. These elements are praised by the young Charles and Henry Brandon, Dukes of Suffolk, whose own commemorative compositions are included in the volume.[68] Secondly, some poems focus on aspects of Bucer's relationship with his country of birth, Germany, and his country of death, England.

---

[65]   See Jennifer Loach, *Edward VI*, posthumously edited by George Bernard and Penry Williams (New Haven and London, Yale University Press, 1999); MacCulloch, *Tudor Church Militant*, p. 31.

[66]   *Vitae Duorum Fratrum*, fol. A 5v.

[67]   On the Hobsbawmian 'invention of tradition' by Edward VI himself, see MacCulloch, *Tudor Church Militant*, pp. 30–31.

[68]   *De Obitu Buceri*, fols I, 2r–v.

Martin Bucer (1491–1551) was born in Alsace. He came into contact with Luther in the Heidelberg disputation of 1518. After a brief spell as a parish clergyman, he moved to Strasbourg where he was in contact with the intellectual community there, working towards theological and educational reform with known reformers such as John Sturm and Paul Fagius.[69] Bucer was involved with international negotiations concerning the future of the church, preaching, 'a richly social doctrine of the church'.[70] Patrick Collinson says of Bucer, '[H]is theology was "typically urban", even "bourgeois", itself a social product and distinguished from Lutheranism by the affinity it enjoyed with the civic notion of *publica utilitas* and by the strong measure of civic humanism which it had absorbed'.[71]

Bucer's works include texts condemning idolatry, tracts about the Eucharistic Controversy between Luther and his opponents, and Latin commentaries on the psalms and other biblical books.[72] Some of these were translated into English in the 1530s, although these volumes were banned for some years because of Bucer's connections with Luther and Calvin.[73] Strasbourg was an important centre and safe haven for reformers from all over Europe. While he lived there, Bucer built contacts with England: he met English emissaries to Germany who were sent after the English Crown's split with Rome in the 1530s; and he had a long-running and frequently printed argument with the influential Bishop Gardner of Winchester (adversary of John Cheke). Bucer finally moved to England in 1549, when his non-absolutist commitments brought him into disagreement with powerful figures in Europe such as Emperor Charles V.[74]

The exiled theologian lived in Cambridge, having a position there as Doctor of Divinity. He spent a considerable amount of time at the royal court, in Greenwich and London, as well as with other friends such as the Duchess of Suffolk, the mother of the two dukes. He produced his final work, *De Regno Christi*, which

---

[69]   For a narrative of Bucer's life see Hopf, *Martin Bucer*; also, James M. Kittelson, 'Martini Buceri Opera Omnia', Book Review, *The Sixteenth Century Journal* 20/4 (1989), pp. 691–2.

[70]   Patrick Collinson, 'The Reformer and the Archbishop: Martin Bucer and an English Bucerian', in *idem, Godly People: Essays on English Protestantism and Puritanism.* (London: The Hambledon Press, 1983), p. 21.

[71]   Collinson, *Godly People,* p. 22; see also Martin Greschat on how Bucer's doctrine and ecumenical mission focused on cooperation between church and society, in Wright (ed.), *Martin Bucer.*

[72]   See Kittelson, 'Martini Buceri Opera Omnia'pp. 691–2, for a review of the nature and content of Martin Bucer's works and the plans to edit his complete works. See Diarmaid MacCulloch, *The Later Reformation in England 1547–1603,* British History in Perspective (Basingstoke, Macmillan, 1990), for an outline of the Eucharistic Controversy, p. 13; on Bucer's instrumental involvement in the production of the new Book of Common Prayer, printed in 1552, see p. 17.

[73]   Willem van Spijker, 'Bucer's Influence on Calvin: Church and Community', in Wright (ed.), *Martin Bucer,* p. 32.

[74]   MacCulloch, *Later Reformation,* pp. 13–15.

Collinson describes as, '[t]he great book[...], containing amongst much else Bucer's mature reflections on the church's polity and ministry'.[75] It was presented to the young King Edward VI as a New Year's gift, just about a year before Bucer died.[76]

William Buckley's commemorative poem in honour of Martin Bucer is a short six-line elegy. Like a poem by his associate, William Temple, it draws attention to issues of national identity and national pride.[77] The tone of Buckley's poem is that Germany was lucky to be the birthplace of this most esteemed citizen of the world. However, England is more fortunate because, due to his death, English poets are able to honour Bucer now that he is a citizen of the heavens.[78] This is echoed by William Temple's poem, which takes the form of a conversation between England and Germany. Germany begins by asking England why it is sad, England explains that Bucer is dead and Germany then bewails the expulsion of its countryman.[79]

Such issues of political and national identity and pride are also raised in the commemoration of the Dukes of Suffolk, as in the poem written by Thomas Wilson.[80] The sentiment of Wilson's poem, as well as being very moving, is a clear comment on the condition of England: an England which has been reduced in greatness by the terrible combination of internal strife and contagious disease; an England whose condition is causing the deaths of the bright young hopes of the next generation.

In the two commemorative books, recurring themes focus on the condition of England: its pride, and its connection through Martin Bucer with Germany, as well as England's internal strife and its future hopes. This certainly sounds like it has the potential for political propaganda. But such propaganda surely needs an audience wider than the intellectual élite of Cambridge and Oxford: codicological evidence suggests that the Suffolk book probably existed in a previous form as at least two separate collections.[81] These may have been cheaply produced as

---

[75]   Collinson, *Godly People*, p. 25; see also Wright, 'Introduction', in *Martin Bucer*, p. 1, who calls *De Regno Christi*, 'the most comprehensive blueprint for a Christian society produced anywhere in the sixteenth-century Reformation'.

[76]   Collinson, *Godly People*, p. 25. See also Bernard M. Reardon, *Religious Thought in the Reformation* (London and New York, Longman, 1981), pp. 147–159, for the suggestion that *De Regno Christi* was very specifically directed towards Edward VI and the reformation of the English godly community, and pp. 263–4.

[77]   *De Obitu Buceri,* fols L 4 r– M 4r, and M 4v.

[78]   *De Obitu Buceri*, fol. M 4v.

[79]   *De Obitu Buceri*, fols L 4r–M 4r; see also Burnett, 'Bucer, Discipline & Moral Reform', p. 455.

[80]   *Vitae Duorum Fratrum,* fol. D 2r.

[81]   In this version of *Vitae Duorum Fratrum,* the folios are paginated by quires A, B, C, and so on. The first section of the book, mainly prose, is labelled A–E, after which the second section, mainly epigrams, is labelled beginning again at A through to K. It seems unlikely that the two books were joined together at the subsequent rebinding as the title page

pamphlets as were other reactions to these deaths.[82] Such texts, like the many others circulated at this time, might have reached many readers. But aside from popular appeal and a wide circulation, is it too bold a speculation to suggest that in William Buckley's poems we have access to ones man's version of the mixed emotions experienced at this time of reformation? His contributions would seem to indicate feelings and experiences that encompassed intellectual excitement, loss, bitter disappointment, and national pride.

Neither of these poetic works is mentioned in the will of William Buckley, perhaps suggesting that he viewed the verses as something to be kept separate or perhaps not appropriate for his bequests. Or perhaps he never actually owned copies of these books himself. However, the way the will is structured suggests that Buckley did not consider the different areas of his learning and expertise as separate. The different types of books are given in conjunction with maps (charts of Greece and England) and other instruments of science, such as the brass sphere, the instrument with wheels, the little astrolabe, and the great quadrant that he gives to Master John Cheke.

William Buckley as Maker of Scientific Instruments

There survives in the British Museum, in London, a brass quadrant which is finely engraved and unusually large, and which is said to have been made for Edward VI, in 1551[see FIG 7.2].[83] It is brass and about 270mm in radius.[84] Astronomical quadrants such as this were used mainly for determining the altitude of a celestial body such as the sun or a bright star above the horizon.[85] This particular quadrant is ascribed to Thomas Gemini, the Flemish instrument maker who settled in London.[86] Gemini was an associate of John Cheke, amongst others, in a group that also involved William Buckley. The initial letters JC, WB and TG, which are engraved into the quadrant, appear to agree with this proposed provenance.

Gerard L'E Turner's descriptive catalogue of Elizabethan scientific instruments suggests that Cheke, Buckley, and Gemini were also 'associated in an astrolabe made for Edward VI in 1552 and now in the Royal Belgian Observatory,

---

at the start of the volume notes that the epitaphs are 'adduntur' and the epigrams are 'assignatur'. The quires of both sections contain 4 folios.

[82]　　See Hopf, *Martin Bucer*, p. 29.

[83]　　This is London British Museum, Horary Quadrant, 8–21.1.

[84]　　EPACT Electronic Catalogue, 'Scientific Instruments of Medieval and Renaissance Europe', http://www.mhs.ox.ac.uk/epact/ ; see also, *A Catalogue of European Scientific Instruments in the Department of Medieval and Later Antiquities of the British Museum*, compiled by F.A.B. Ward (London, British Library, 1981), pp. 56–7, where the lengths of its sides are measured as 268mm and 271mm.

[85]　　See, 'Medieval and Renaissance Mathematical Arts and Sciences', EPACT, http://www.mhs.ox.ac.uk/epact/essay.asp.

[86] Turner, *Elizabethan Instrument Makers*, pp. 16–17, and 97.

Brussels'.[87] It is possible that this astrolabe, apparently made for the king, may also be one of those mentioned in William Buckley's will, although it is equally likely that this group of scholars and practitioners was associated in making a number of such instruments, including the ones bequeathed by Buckley, some of which have not survived.

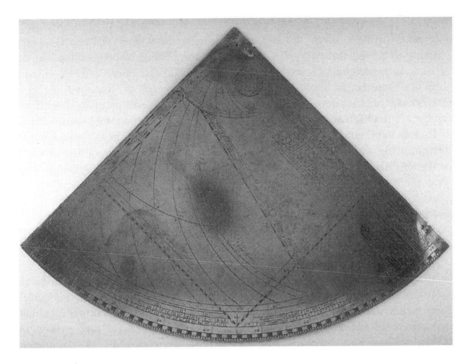

Figure 7.2 Brass Quadrant, attributed to Thomas Gemini, dated 1551

Until now, and in the absence of the evidence provided by William Buckley's will, this unusually large brass quadrant has been listed as belonging to King Edward VI.[88] But, Buckley's bequest of a quadrant to his associate suggests that the British Museum's quadrant, or at least one very like it, was in fact in Buckley's own possession until he bequeathed it to Cheke, as follows:

> Item, to Mag Cheke my greate quadrant of brass with a saphea [scipha] upon the backside [89]

87 *Catalogue of European Scientific Instruments*, p. 57.
88 *Catalogue of European Scientific Instruments*, p. 56.
89 NA PROB 11/35/88v. The term 'saphea', used to describe Buckley's quadrant is a slight mystery. There is a type of boat called a 'sciph', which may have some linguistic connection to a 'ship' engraved onto one of the other scientific instruments bequeathed by

The quadrant in the British Museum is described as a particularly complex instrument of its sort as it has many more tables for telling the time than most others surviving from this date.[90] It is engraved all over with a variety of finely worked lines, tables, and also some verbal inscriptions. In the more technical language of the catalogue, these engravings consist of 'hour-scales' and 'hour lines' numbered in Arabic, 'zodiac scales', 'date scales', a small ring of 'planetary symbols', 'a lunar cycle', 'a scale for calculating the sines and cosines of angles' and so on.[91] Above where the letters WB are engraved there are two tables of years, at nineteen-year intervals, between 1539 and 1868, which are called 'cycles of the sun and moon'.

With the aim of recovering something of the experience of 'Renaissance' for a Renaissance man such as William Buckley, it is worth imagining the excitement for Cheke, Buckley, and Gemini as they worked together, pooling their expertise and skills, to produce these innovative, scientific, and beautifully crafted instruments.[92] As William Buckley and his fellow scholars and craftsmen constructed this great quadrant and the other scientific instruments, perhaps they imagined themselves on the threshold of a new dawn of science. A time, the date calculating tables would suggest, of such revolutionary changes that their instruments would last for some 300 years (to 1868). Or, perhaps this was part of their own invention of the future, a myth of a future dawn of scientific discovery. Perhaps such ambitions might account for the unusually large size of what Buckley describes as his 'greate quadrant'.

There are also poetic verbal inscriptions, or 'mottos' on the quadrant in the British Museum, with quotes from the Book of Solomon about the nature of time, such as '*Omni negotio tempus est et op[]tu[]tas Salom*' which translates as 'For every activity there is an appropriate time, Solomon'.[93] The letter and numbers in all the engravings are elegant, neat and refined; the catalogues use the phrase 'florid line-work' to describe the tendency to decorate the start and end of the words or phrases engraved into the brass. Certain particular letters are also more ornate; in particular the lower case 't' which is taller than usual being the height of the letter 'l', and has a long line across it, which spreads over the rest of the word. On comparing the two handwritten tracts ascribed to William Buckley (the ring dial manual and the mathematical treatise), it is just possible that the handwriting

---

Buckley. However, there was no boat engraved onto the British Museum quadrant – only a 'sinical quadrant', which might also possibly be what is meant by 'sapha'.

[90]   I should like to thank Dr. Silke Ackermann of the British Museum for her help on the occasion that I examined the horary quadrant.

[91]   *Catalogue of European Scientific Instruments*, p. 56.

[92]   Jan Golinski, *Making Natural Knowledge: Constructivism and the History of Science* (Cambridge, CUP, 1998), p. 60.

[93]   Turner, *Elizabethan Instrument Makers*, p. 98; and on the interests in Solomon in the court of Edward VI, see MacCulloch, *Tudor Church Militant*, pp. 15, and 105–56.

in these texts was the same hand as the engraving on the quadrant. Was it William Buckley's design that the engraver traced onto the brass of the quadrant? One of the other quotes on this quadrant also portrays interests in teaching which are not dissimilar to those shown by William Buckley in his didactic tracts on arithmetic and the ring dial. The second motto reads, '*Illud Metiri quadrans tamen iste docebit. Et quota sit fias certior hora fecit*' or 'Yet this quadrant will teach how to measure it [time] and makes you become more certain of what hour it is'.[94]

The Discovery of a Renaissance Man

There are a number of parallel strands in this chapter, all of which arise from the chance find of a new piece of evidence about the life of one individual in the mid-sixteenth century. Buckley's will document is the central element in this particular micro-study which results in the reconstruction of elements of an individual life. Without the will document, it would not have been possible to bring these strands of evidence together. In writing this chapter, and in tracing the different strands of William Buckley's innovations and creations through the various evidences that survive, it has always been my intention to allow this individual to insist on a re-reading of the cultural phenomena of his time. This is not to claim that William Buckley was a-typical; he was indeed a true 'Renaissance man'. Rather, this reconstruction of a life differs from the grander narratives of this period because it provides a new emphasis on the contemporary perception and experiences of the tensions and excitements of this time. In a grander narrative, the intricacies and implications of the perspectives of individuals like Buckley and his associates have generally become lost.

My way of including William Buckley's views has been to focus on him and the interesting range of material and textual evidences that survive for his life and work. This is the William Buckley who was very committed to teaching mathematics and to explaining science. It is also the man who contributed to a new fashion of poetry; and a man committed to the new age of learning and its social and religious reform. And this is also the scientist and 'mechanician' involved with the production and design of new scientific technology.

In so many ways, Buckley's life fits neatly into the usual themes for a grand narrative of what is sometimes called the 'early English Renaissance'. But the small-scale detail of his life, including his emotions and ambitions, fit less comfortably into such a narrative. In what remains of this man's life, there is a silver goblet which represents the *gratitude* displayed to his uncle as his educational benefactor; and evidence of his attempts to also in turn be a benefactor to his own nephew, with a substantial bequest of the books and instruments necessary for a good education. There are hints of personal dislocations of status between William's family and his friends. Buckley's textbooks show him to be a

---

[94]   Turner, *Elizabethan Instrument Makers*, p. 98.

generous and patient educator unafraid of the laborious production of elementary maths and science, while his other writings suggest an *emotional* poet distraught at the loss of his genius pupils. The material remains of his life suggest a careful designer of beautiful brass instruments and perhaps an *excited* scholar hoping for a new age of discovery. These, of course, are not such acceptable sentiments for writing a narrative of the sixteenth century, but they do indicate the innovation, creativity, and experiences of one 'Renaissance man' who died, at a young age, in 1552.

Chapter 9

Conclusion

The contents and nature of this book defy a conclusion. Nevertheless, in this short chapter I hope to draw together some of the strands discussed in the six life-chapters in order to make a few suggestions about the implications of this study, and the scope for further investigations, without sealing it by a neat statement of closure.

Evidence for Six Lives

The book as a whole uses various types of evidence in the reconstruction of the six lives; indeed, most individual chapters discuss several sorts of sources. This is guided in the first instance by the fragments of evidence which survive: Gilbert Banaster's and William Cornysh's chapters, for example, investigate literature (poetry and/or prose), music, and an administrative document (the last will and testament); William Buckley's chapter adds to this list a scientific instrument and some teaching texts; and Katherine Styles's chapter focuses on her last will and testament and those of her family network. Elizabeth Philip's chapter begins from records and accounts of the royal household as does the reconstruction of The Anonymous Witness which also focuses on a printed pamphlet.

Interdisciplinarity

Because this book ranges across various types of source (poetry, music, prose, science, objects, administrative documents) it will probably be labelled 'interdisciplinary'. By 'interdisciplinarity' I mean here the practice by which one individual investigator uses types of evidence which cross between various of our artificially defined 'disciplines' and sub-disciplines, such as 'Literature', 'History', 'History of Science', 'Music' and so on. I do not mean the sort of 'multidisciplinarity' which involves individuals of different artificially defined disciplines working together. I personally feel that 'disciplinarity' is also something of a nonsense especially for the reconstruction of lives. It is particularly nonsensical when it comes to the investigation of life-experiences at any time in history because, to state the obvious, lives cross disciplinary boundaries. This is the case now and was the case in the early English Renaissance, although the boundaries (or the ways they are crossed), are slightly different. But this crossing is perhaps a particularly poignant theme at a time which not only precedes the nineteenth-century categorisation of scholarly disciplines, but also at a time (the 'Renaissance') when there was a concerted advocacy of polyvalent investigations of music, science, mathematics, literature, classics and so on. But being interdisciplinary in method and outlook is also challenging as there is, naturally, a wide range of approaches and critical literatures to span.

I set up certain key issues for my approach in the Critical Introduction, Chapter 2 – to which I would refer the reader who is beginning at the back of the book. In each of the six life-chapters, I have sought to maintain a light touch on the bibliographic and historiographical baggage associated with the sources discussed therein. My intention has been to explore how the bringing together of the interdisciplinary range of surviving evidences for each life might enhance an understanding of each individual's experiences of the early English Renaissance, and in so doing to build a picture (albeit partial) of Renaissance experiences more generally. The chapters should not, however, be considered complete or definitive statements on the identity and perceptions of any individual, nor are they intended to be. In some chapters this is particularly obvious as there are, clearly, some pieces of evidence not covered here, and a lot of material that might be investigated in more detail: further work on Gilbert Banaster, for example, might involve greater investigation of the contents of the contemporary manuscripts containing his version of the 'Sismond' story. Alongside this, it would be useful to analyse the later English versions of this Boccaccio story. These were produced (and printed) in the first and second halves of the sixteenth century. The different motivations and nature of these later stories would add another perspective on the aims and intentions of Banaster in his translations. The questions surrounding William Cornysh's identity in relation to the older person of the same name, and the compositions that each composed, also require more examination. Some of the productions of William Buckley such as his *Arithmetica Memorativa* and his mathematical treatise would benefit from detailed scrutiny, particularly with reference to the products of contemporaries such as Robert Record. In the case of Katherine Styles, the sentiments, views and family concerns revealed in her last will and testament would benefit from the comparative analysis of other such documents made at the same date. Some such work has been pursued, but there is so much detail in each individual will, that to take a 'slice' of all the documents available in The National Archive for the date that Katherine's will was produced, 1530, would be a fascinating and revealing project. An unfolding realisation in the writing of this book has been the extent of the possibilities for investigation elicited by these six lives, despite the fact that such a relatively small corpus of disparate evidence survives.

Fragments

A key principle in the research and writing for this book has been to examine lives for which there remains relatively little evidence. In other words, these are people who were not so politically, socially, or culturally famous during their lifetimes that the dossiers of their papers were carefully and systematically preserved. And they are not people who received the sort of posthumous recognition which caused their papers to be collected together soon after their death. Nevertheless, I would like to stress that these six people were significantly involved in the making of history, and that their connections with the Tudor royal households of Henry VII to Edward VI placed them in a particularly privileged position of creative influence, and gave them special access to experiences of the early English Renaissance in England. Clearly, there is much more available evidence for some of the individuals than for others. This pattern corresponds with the extent to which the people are already known through various biographical sources (Banaster, Cornysh, and Buckley who all have entries in the *DNB* and *ODNB*, for example, each have greater amounts and varieties of evidence than the other three subjects).

I discussed my use of fragmentary evidences in the Critical Introduction, Chapter 2. Here, I emphasised the ways that the disparate nature of the fragments which remain of individual lives helps to resist the production of seamless grand narratives of a historical period. I proposed, therefore, that individual lives should not be taken as *simply* representative of a specific period in history. Nevertheless, I do wish to advocate a method which sees the lives and life experiences – and, very importantly, the fluctuations and inconsistencies of a single life – as very significant for understanding the historical period in which that life was lived.

Experience?

I am not satisfied that I have adequately reconstructed Renaissance 'experiences' in this book, although I shall hastily add that I hope this book has gone further in this process than many studies of the period, partly because of its focus on the non-famous, and also because of the attempt not to impose simplified or presentist categories of description onto these lives. The example of William Buckley is useful here. As I have suggested in his chapter, the categories and nature of the evidence which survives for his life seem, on the surface, to make him a quintessential 'Renaissance man'. However, it is those elements of emotion and ambition (commitment, excitement, distraction, gratitude and so on) evinced from an examination of the small-scale details of this man's life (through his works and documents) which take this exploration a little closer to an understanding of Renaissance experiences.

The Cumulative Effect

A main purpose of the book has been to produce a cumulative exploration of Renaissance experiences. In other words, while I have evaluated the evidence for each individual separately in the six chapters, I have also sought to enable the reader to build a picture of Renaissance experiences which is greater than the sum of the book's parts. I have deliberately not explicitly labelled many areas of obvious comparison between the six individuals during the course of the chapters, hoping that the reader will make his or her own connections. But I will rehearse here some of the 'conclusions' which the six life-chapters cumulatively appear to invoke, and give a few select examples as illustrations.

Experiences of Transition

Firstly, there is a pervading sense of the fluid boundary existing between attitudes towards the old apparently 'Medieval' forms and the new forms which are conventionally associated with a Renaissance society. Some issues of the blurred boundaries between these traditionally defined chronological periods are discussed in the Critical Introduction with reference to definitions of 'Renaissance'.[1] Personal experiences of this transition are particularly available through the evidence for religious sensibilities. Katherine Styles, for example, expresses a classic transitional sense of piety by seeming to adhere both to the traditional practices of Medieval Catholic devotion and commemoration whilst introducing a vocabulary which seems to allude to Protestant sensibilities. As I have said in her chapter, there is nothing specifically unusual about this mixture of views and sentiments in a last will and testament of the early 1530s. But seen against the various styles of composition produced by Gilbert Banaster and William Cornysh, there appears to be a broader pattern of fluidity emerging.

Both Banaster and Cornysh composed settings for devotional poems which fit neatly into the Medieval affective tradition of Catholic piety, whilst they were also involved with experiments in new styles of musical representation and other new or different forms of cultural product (in translation, pageant design, and so on). Perhaps Banaster's connection with affective traditions whilst composing in the 1470s is less surprising than Cornysh's, composing in the 1510s. However, it is interesting to note that each of the settings of devotional poetry ascribed to these two would usually be categorised as being of precisely the same sort of affective ilk (and indeed both poems may well date back to the religious lyrical tradition of the thirteenth century). Of course, each composer's experience of producing the setting for his particular devotional poem was very different. Outside of the effects of the fifty-year separation, this difference of experience is also because they each compared their own setting of devotional poetry with the specific set of their own other compositions. If audiences' understandings of these compositions are also taken into consideration, then the range of individual experiences of these compositions is, of course, multiplied.

I have proposed that the works of Banaster and Cornysh must be considered as essentially different in terms of the experience each had of producing them. However, despite the fifty-year gap, the collective outputs of both Banaster and Cornysh each appear to exemplify the generalised set of transitions in representation, attitude, and style that were being experienced in this period of

---

[1]   See Chapter 2, this volume.

change. It seems, therefore, that the effect of examining particular individuals' compositions and works emphasises the extent of the different experiences of producing apparently similar cultural products. And this poses a question about the ways the term 'transition' should be understood – not, presumably, as a unified experience.

I have suggested that Banaster may have actually been manipulating the disjunctures between new and old forms of representation to convey certain political messages, as in the case of *O Maria et Elizabeth*. I am sure, similarly, that Katherine Styles was not unaware that her testament employed different traditions of vocabulary and sentiment, and that this transitional expression of her religious identity may well have been highly self-conscious. One lesson to learn from these uses of various styles of expression is that the modern tendency to separate categories of 'Medieval' from 'Renaissance' or 'Medieval' from 'Early Modern' (or 'Medieval Catholic' from 'post-Reformation Protestant') is defied by the experiences of the individuals living across that period. There is no period of history that is not experiencing transition, but for those periods of time (such as the period covered in this book), which are traditionally associated with major transitions (however artificial) it is particularly important to maintain a sense of the small-scale experiences of these immense changes by those living through them.

Structures of Identity

A second theme which emerges from the cumulative findings of the six chapters is the multiplicity of structures through which identity was expressed, structured, imagined, and understood by these six people. Clearly, the nature of the surviving fragments of evidence governs the levels and modes of these expressions. The three people with the more varied collection of fragments (Banaster, Cornysh, and Buckley) seem to demonstrate this to a greater extent. For example, aspects of Buckley's identity show him to be an innovator and a reformer both as a scholar and as a teacher: his scholarly identity as a humanist overlaps with, but is not entirely the same as, his role as a schoolmaster and also as a writer of poetic epitaphs. Buckley's involvement with scientific discovery also indicates his interest in experimentation and innovation. There are also distinctively innovative elements of Cornysh's identity, particularly perhaps through his connections with royal revels. Cornysh's involvements with pageantry and performance raise particular issues of public and private identity because, as I show in Chapter 5, his expert knowledge of the drama – gained through his public role as Master of the Chapel for the royal household – seems to have sensitised him personally to issues of performance, as indicated by the special testamentary requests he makes for his commemoration.

It is clear that there is a specific range of possibilities for these individuals by virtue of their position in society, connected (albeit sometimes peripherally) with the Tudor royal households. Alongside the three people with the higher profiles (Banaster, Cornysh, Buckley), this is also the case for those individuals with relatively less evidence remaining (The Anonymous Witness, Katherine Styles, and Elizabeth Philip). Through her involvement with the production of costumes for fantastic representations of contemporary politics in pageants and revels, Elizabeth Philip had privileged access to ideas about identity both in terms of present and ancient myths of English identity and also other national identities. She also had special knowledge concerning the production of symbolic representation, as she was required to produce costumes to represent different factions for fantastical battle scenes using colour coding and specific fashions of dress. By virtue of the pamphlet, The Anonymous Witness is granted the privilege of imaginatively entering the ceremonial and ritual associated with the royal wedding, and enabled therefore to keep this experience in his (or her) imaginative store for future personal ceremonies. It seems that the pamphlet also specifically identifies its readers as members of the civic community of London whose cooperation was required for the smooth running of the marriage ceremonies. Whether or not the Anonymous Witness was a member of this community, he (or she) is therefore given imaginative access to this civic identity by virtue of the details provided by the pamphlet.

The Writing Process
A third issue, which is of a different order from the previous two, concerns the process of writing involved in producing these reconstructions of lives. Certainly, on writing the six chapters, there has been a cumulative (or perhaps a better word is 'consistent') sense of the difficult relationships between the evidences which survive and the interpretation of these in terms of individual identity, biography, and experience. The sorts of evidences which survive are not entirely easy to understand, partly because of the distance of several centuries which separates the period of their production (roughly 1450–1550), from the present day. It is actually very important to maintain a sense that there is a great perceptual distance between now and then. In other words, the motives, attitudes and senses of style which informed the cultural products of the early English Renaissance are very different from today and it would be a mistake to collapse this separation into some generalised notion of human experience. For this reason, I have found it important and necessary to engage in some passages of detailed description and explanation concerning the nature and meanings of specific sources. There is a definite tension, however, between this necessary process of description and elucidation and the apparently less complicated quest after more person-centred issues of individual experience, emotion, and sensibility.

Throughout the chapters it has been a central aim to treat these complicated evidences in a way which does not seek to make them seem concordant (each within itself, or in comparison to each other) for the sake of proposing a simple interpretation of the relation of each to its producer. In order to do this, a little detailed examination of the specific piece of evidence is necessary as a precursor to making suggestions about those more person-centred issues. So I hope that a cumulative effect for the reader is of there being a great amount of evidence for the cultural productions (and so the attitudes, perceptions, experiences, motivations) of

Renaissance individuals such as these, all of which evidence defies simple and definite interpretations.

This is an issue which marks a separation between the types of subjects covered in the chapters of this book and the contents and plot lines of a related form of historical reconstruction, the historical novel. In my digression into this form of literature in the Critical Introduction, Chapter 2, I explored several examples of the use of 'Mills and Boon'-style plot lines which, I suggest, are used to draw the reader into the novel. These elements may in part account for the popularity of this genre. I do not think it is only the fact that the surviving evidence for the six individuals does not provide information about these elements of their lives that makes such salacious, sexy, and erotic elements of plot inappropriate to this book. There is a more general issue which concerns the type of fictional intrusion and invention required to narrate such personal intimacies of individual feelings, wants, and desires (and the speaking of these). I would hope that this book adds one more element to the argument which denies that a true reconstruction of the past is possible. However, there is a definite line to draw between the fictions appropriate to the reconstruction of the lives in this book and the fictions of intimacy (and dialogue) sometimes found in the historical novel. Although it is interesting, in this context, that some reassurances and claims to historical accuracy, or truth, seem to be important to the authors of historical novels as part of the process of legitimating the story.

In my discussion of using fragmentary evidences in the Critical Introduction, I proposed their resistance to the production of any seamless narrative and the ways that this necessitates some abrupt transitions in writing about them and the individual lives of those who produced them. This is partly because there is only limited survival of the cultural productions for each of the six people explored here. The surviving evidences, therefore, do not make a neat story of each individual's life – they do not provide the evidence for a traditional biography (from childhood to death). And so one cumulative effect of the book should not be to build a number of apparently whole life stories.

The various cultural products of the six Renaissance men and women are not in general the sorts of 'life-writings' which have become increasingly recognised over the last twenty years as a more democratic alternative to biographical and autobiographical writing.[2] The evidences do, however, provide the material for writing about lives and the approach taken in this book has a connection with the interpretative trend that has seen the growing interest in life-writing. Work on life-writing goes hand in hand with more reflexive approaches to the interpretation of evidence – that is, approaches which acknowledge that there is no single version of what a piece of evidence represents (just as there is no single interpretation of a life). I hope that, cumulatively, the reader gains an impression of the various overlaying fictions which contribute to the interpretation of Renaissance individuals' experiences of life.

---

[2]   On 'life-writing', see Chapter 2, this volume.

Index

academic discourse 14
academics, attitudes of 15
Accounts, Revel and Wardrobe 2
Aers, David 11
anecdotes 12
Anglo, Sydney 80, 81, 82, 96, 97, 102, 109
Annales School 19
annotations 59, 86, 93
    whimsical rhyme 94
annotator 61
Anonymous Witness, The 153, 157, 158
antiphon 51
apprentice 63
Archbishop of Canterbury 87, 90
Armitage-Smith, Sydney 23
astronomy 137
Atkinson, Elizabeth 66
attitudes
    fifteenth-century 2
    personal and public 115
    postmodern 29
audience 106
author 39
Author's note 29
authorship 35, 109

Banaster, Gilbert 2, 21, 113, 114, 153, 154,
    156, 157
    attitudes to style 53
    biographical accounts 41
    compositional styles 53
    devotional works 61
    'gentilman' 31
    last will and testament 30–32
    literary works 32–43
    Miracle Poem and Interlude 41
    musical compositions 44–61
    My Feerfull Dreme 45, 47–51, 52, 60

O Maria et Elizabeth 51–55, 56
    'Sismond and Guistard' 2
Barron, Caroline 63
Becket, St Thomas 41
Bennet, H.S. 20
Billingsgate, London 125
biography 4, 13, 14, 158
Bishop Gardiner 137
Bishop of Lincoln 83
Boccaccio, Giovanni 2, 36, 154
    Decameron 33
    'Ghismonda and Ghisconda' 33
books 32, 125, 135, 138
    devotional 122
    as a gift 122
boundaries,
    appropriate 12
    disciplinary 153
boundary 3
Bowdice, Geram 72
Bowers, Roger 103–4, 107, 110, 113
British Museum 3
Bucer, Martin 144, 145–8
Buckley, Geoffrey 134
Buckley, William 3, 7, 30, 153, 154, 155
    Arithmetica Memorativa 138–41, 142,
      143
    book bequests 135
    De Anulus Horari 141
    family and friends 152
    last will and testament 131–6, 148
    Master 138
    'mechanician' 133
    poetry 143–8
    Schoolmaster 130, 133
    scientific instrument maker 148–51
    social connections of 134–6
    textbooks written by 138–43, 152

Burkhardt, Jacob 10
Buttry, William 72
calendar, zodiacal 141–2
Cambridge 130, 136, 144, 147
   Jesus College 123
   King's College 133, 135, 137, 143

canon 5
canonical authors 18
Canterbury Cathedral 43, 57
Carew, Nicholas 71
carols, clerical and popular 49
categories, contemporary perception 12
   of description 155
   life-writing 15
   Medieval, Early Modern 157
Catholic 121
   imagery 60
   piety 156
Catholicism 115
Caxton, William 82
ceremonies 94
Chambers, E.K. 109
change 3
   radical 39
changing world 41
Chaucer, Geoffrey 2, 5, 16, 18, 22, 109
   Book of the Duchess 25
   Canterbury Tales 33
      'The Franklin's Tale' 39
   Consolation of Philosophy 81
   Legend of Good Women 34, 38
   imitation of 37
Cheeseman, Master John 120, 122, 127
Cheke, Sir John 133, 134, 136, 137, 138, 140,
   144, 145, 146, 148
Chevalier, Tracey 22
children 72
choirbook 44, 45, 46
Christ Church Priory, Canterbury 43
Chute, Marchette *Geoffrey Chaucer of
   England* 23
Claver, Alice 66
Colbarne, William 79

Coley, William 134
Collinson, Patrick 147
commemoration 118
commemorative performance 107
compositions 1
consumption 6, 126
context, 2, 4, 5, 9, 15, 29, 34, 39, 43, 105
   cultural 8, 11, 58, 86
   devotional 53
   European 5
   and lives 8
   manuscript 37, 38
   particularity 10
   performative 115
   personal 113
   of production 55
   of reception 55
   social 33
   Tudor 29
   visual 90
contextualising 10
Cooke, Anne 120
Cooke, Emma 120
Cooke, Jane 120
Cooke, Katherine 121
Cooke, Thomas 120
Cooke, William 119, 124, 126
Corbrond, William 44
Cornysh, William 21, 45, 67, 68, 82, 153,
   154, 156
   alias Nysshewhete 108
   commemoration 106
   composer 96, 110
   death wishes of 116
   flamboyance 99
   genius 103
   innovator 102–3
   last will and testament 104–6
   legends of 107
   Master of the King's Chapel 96, 107
   pageant designer 98–104
   poetry of 108–113
   revel-maker 102
   Treatise 108

uncertainty of identity 97
Woefully Arrayed 113–115
costumes 67, 75
    decorative 100
    fashionable 1
creativity 1, 6 (n. 6), 12 (n. 33), 30 n.1, 96,
        105 (n. 35), 115, 118 (n. 2), 132 (n.
        6), 152
Crofte, Sir Richard 83
crying 39–40
cultural artefacts 57
cultural context 8, 11, 29, 55, 58, 86
cultural expression 105
cultural forms, old and new 54
cultural history 11, 20
cultural innovation 6, 30
cultural interests 30
cultural productions 29, 115, 128, 156
culture contact 76

Dale, Marion 63
Davies, Lady Eleanor 8
Deptford 124
description 158
    categories of 155
devotional poetry 156
Digges, Leonard 6
disciplinary boundaries 153
discoveries 2
disguisings 98
documents, legal and administrative 89, 117
Dowe, Dennis 121
dowry 126
drama 10
Draper, William Esquier 120, 121
Duchess Blanche 22
Duchess of Suffolk 147
Dudley, John (Lord Lisle) 135
Dukes of Suffolk (Henry and Charles
        Brandon, d. 1551) 144, 145, 147
Dyce, Alexander 110

early English Renaissance 10, 30, 84, 128,
    129, 151, 153

Early Modern 3, 7, 11, 157
Early Modernists 10, 11
educational provision 136
educational reform 130, 136, 138
Edward IV 66, 123
Edward V 123
Edward VI 133, 143, 149
Ellis, Steve *Chaucer at Large* 18
emblems 76
emotion 158
Emperor Charles V 146
Empson, Sir Richard 108
England 6, 124, 147
    fifteenth-century 2
    silk work in 63
English literatures 16, 19
English nation 76
English polyphonic style 113
English Renaissance (see Renaissance) 10,
    79, 130, 155, 158
English Tudor Dynasty 63
English writers 5
epitaph 10
ethnography 20
Eton Choirbook 55, 56
Eton College 133
Euclid 137
    De Arte Geometria 139
evidence 2, 3, 9, 104, 147, 158, 159
    archival 29
    discovery 151
    documents 129
    fragmentary 11, 130, 153, 155, 159
    manuscript 108
    textual 20
experience 6, 50, 131, 151, 155, 158
    complexities and intricacies 18
    contemporary 151
    female 11
    human 158
    of performing 73
    reader's 85, 86
    Renaissance 154
    significant 84

experiences 29, 129, 152
  of life 159
  of transition 156–7

family networks 117
fashions 10, 88
  new 84
fiction 159
fifteenth-century 41
  music 45
Folwer, [?] 44
Fowler, Alastair 8
fragments 29, 153, 154, 157
  of evidence 11, 130, 153, 155, 159
Free, John 123
Frye, Walter 44
funeral account 79

Gemini, Thomas 133, 148
genius, cult of 16
Germany 147
Gibson, Richard 69, 71
Gilbert, William 7
Gold of Venice 64
Grafton, Richard 144
grand narrative 4, 151
grander narratives 131
Greenblatt, Stephen *Renaissance Self-
  Fashioning* 7, 8, 12, 13, 17, 19
Greenwich 100, 105, 108, 116, 124, 130, 133,
  147
  Rood Chapel 105, 115
Gregory, Philippa 21, 22, 24, 26, 27, 28, 29
Gressam, Richard 72
Gunthorpe, Doctor John (Dean of Wells) 121,
  123
Gyllforth, Harry 67

Haddon, Walter 145
Harrison, Frank 45, 104
Hatcher, Doctor John 134
Hatcher, Thomas 145
Hawte, Sir William 44
heirloom 73, 117, 118

Henry VII 6, 108, 123
Henry VIII 2, 6, 56, 62, 63, 70, 96, 98, 99
Herald 79, 82, 83
Hewster, Jerome 127
Hilton, William 72
historical discourse 12
historical novel 4, 24, 159
historical specificity 8
historiography 4, 10
history from below 19
History of Reading 85
history, making of 155
Hoccleve, Thomas 5
Holmes, Richard 14, 15, 21, 29
Hoptons, Margarete 120
horological instrument 138
Hosyer, William 72
household (see royal household)
household goods 125
Howard, J.E. 8
humanism 5, 130
  civic 146
  social 136
humanist poetry 10
Humphrey, Duke of Gloucester 6
Hunter, John 121
ideals, traditional 30
ideas, Renaissance 5, 6
identity 17, 19, 83, 117, 158
  ancient 76
  civic 158
  national 75, 77
  personal 94
ideology 3, 129
individual lives 11
individuals, perspectives of 151
  Renaissance 21, 159
inheritance, *post mortem* 117
innovation 5, 6, 30, 96, 103, 115, 116, 151,
  152, 157
  cultural 6, 105, 130
  and tradition 105
inscriptions 150
interpretation 158

Italian fashion 75
Italian sensibilities 37
Jardine, Lisa 9
jewellery 125
John of Gaunt 22
Jolly, Margaretta 15
journey, imaginative 92
Katherine of Aragon 23, 99
Kempe, Margery 8, 62
    The Book of Margery Kempe 17
kin network 126
Kipling, Gordon 103
knowledge 84
    extensive 106
    special 77

lace 65
last will and testament 3, 30, 107, 117–118,
    128, 131, 151, 154
    formulaic 117, 118
    identity in 117
learning, new 136
legitimation 56
Lewisham (West Greenwich) 124
life-writing 4, 13
Lindley, Phillip 6
literacy 85, 130
literary works 30
literature 3
lives, 13–28
    contextualising 8–10
    experiences 159
    individual 5, 6, 7, 11
    lost to history 118
    reconstruction of 2, 98, 158
    stories of 159
    women's 11
London 66, 80, 92, 126, 147, 158
    aldermen 91
    citizens 91, 84
    civic community of 93
    descriptions 82
    entry into 89
    Great Chronicle 98, 108

mayor 91
National Archives 118
silkwomen 63
topography 82

Manuscript, Additional 5465 (Fayrfax
    Manuscript) 44, 45
    Cambridge Magdalene College Pepys
        1236 44–45, 46, 57
    Eton College 178 44
marriage service 89–91
Mary Rose 71
Master of the Revels 74
Master of the Wardrobe 73
material goods 126
Medieval 3, 7, 157
    Catholic orthodoxy 116
    Catholicism121
Medievalists 10
memory 78
mentalité 19
micro-study 151
Middle Ages 11
Middlesex 124
Moffet, Thomas *The Silkewormes and their*
    Flies 65
Monmouth, Geoffrey of 80
moral, dilemmas 41
    meaning 112
    position 39
More, Thomas 23, 109
Morland, Sir John 121
motet 51
Mulcaster, Richard 137
music 1, 3, 50
    fifteenth-century 45
musical composition 10
musical metaphors 109, 110
musical settings 53
myths, of English Tudor Dynasty 63
    Tudor 3, 76

narrative 11, 12, 151
    grand 4, 151

grander 131
national identity 75, 77
Nesbet, John 44
networks 117
   of kin 126
New Historicism 7, 9, 12
notation, Medieval 50
novels, biographical 14
   historical 4, 24, 159

Owdale, Sir William 83
Owen, Doctor 135
Oxford 144, 147

pageant 72, 76, 79, 97, 158
   ancestry 79
   ancient tradition 79
   Arcturus 81
   'Castle' 101
   cosmology 79
   cosmopolitan 75
   'disguisings' 98
   final 108
   'Four Cardinal Virtues' 81
   Garden de Experance (1516) 100, 101
   'Golden Arbour' (1511) 99
   Gregory the Great 81
   national identity 79
   New Testament 81
   Pleiades 81
   spectators 108
   speeches 101
   symbolic battles 102
   'Troylus and Pandor' 100, 101
pageantry 1, 10, 96, 157
   'Burgundian style' 103
pamphlet 85, 91, 92, 93, 153, 158
   reading 84, 86
   Remembraunce for the Traduction 84–94
Parys, John de 72
Paston, Margery 62
Penshurst Place (Kent) 135
performance 82, 104, 110, 112, 157
   commemorative 107

personal perceptions 105
performers 72
Philip, Elizabeth 2, 128, 153, 158
   knowledge 77
   life experiences 73–7
   in royal household accounts 70–2
piety 10
   affective 51, 60, 61
pilgrimage 124
poem, printed layout of 50
poetic style 10
poetry 1, 3, 130
political alliance 78
political propaganda 52
politics 158
polyphony 50, 54, 115
popular culture 19, 21
postmodern attitudes 29
post-Reformation 157
Power, Eileen 20
Prince Arthur 56, 82, 83, 86, 93, 98, 99, 102–3
Princess Elizabeth 141
Princess Katherine 82, 87, 88, 92, 93, 102–3
print culture 130
procession 90
propaganda 56, 57
property 31
Protestant 121
   interests 144
Protestantism 130, 136, 157
public festivities 78

reader 87, 156, 159
   anonymous 84–88
   expectations 86
   Renaissance 85
   unknown 86
readers 92
readership, expected 92
reading 84
   experience 85
   practice 84, 85–88
   and women 122

reception 55
reconstruction 11, 153
    imaginative 85
    of lives 158
Record, Robert 137
Reformation 6, 60
religion 1, 10, 52
religious books 86
Renaissance 3, 5, 7, 10, 83, 115, 154, 157
    definitions of 4
    English 10, 79, 130, 155, 158
    experiences 154, 155
    ideas 5, 6, 16
    individuals 159
    innovation 103
    literary 5
    'Renaissance man' 135, 152, 155
    reader 85
    society 156
    Tudor 1
representation 110
    forms 79
    new fashions 84
Revel Accounts 64, 70
Revels 67–70
    Epiphany (1511) 68
    Epiphany (1515) 73
    June (1520) 69
    Master of the 74
    New Hall Essex (1519) 69, 73
    recycled 69
    Richmond (November 1510) 70
    Tudor 96
Reynolde, Anne 120
Reynolde, Margery 120
Richard III 66, 123
Richmond 124
    Palace 83
Ridge, Richard 121
ring dial 138
River Thames 62, 88, 91
Roet, Katherine de 22, 24
Rome 23
Royal Belgian Observatory 149

royal household 1, 2, 3, 6, 21, 22, 24, 30, 41,
        53, 62–8, 70–75, 77, 78, 79, 83, 84,
        89, 92, 98, 99, 123, 153, 155, 157
    humble members of 72
    Tudor 155

St Katherine 79, 80
St Paul's Cathedral 87, 89, 90, 93
St Ursula 79, 80
schooling 138
science 3
scientific, discovery 6
    instruments 1, 3, 148
    re-birth 10, 130
Seneske, George 71
sensibility 158
sentiments, acceptable 152
Seton, Anya 22, 24, 26, 27, 28
Seymour, Jane 23
Shakespeare, William 16
Sidney, Philip 135
Sidney (Sydney), Master Henry 135
silk, thread 64
    corses, 64
    fringes 64
    laces 64
    ribbons 64
    tassels 64
    trading 64
    work 2, 63
silkwomen, in London 63
silver ware 31, 125
Skelton, John *Pithy and Pleasant* 109
Skerme (Skern), Edward 119, 127
social connections 134
social networks 117
social position 94
social status 129
Southampton 88
Southwark 80
Spanish work 75
spectator 84
Stafford, William 23
Stepney (marsh) 124, 125

Stevens, John 114
Stevenson, Hugh 121
Stone, John 43
stories 159
story-line 100
Stow, John 109
Styles, Katherine 153, 154, 156, 157
    gifts 125
    identity 128
    last will and testament of 117, 118, 119–
        121, 128
    marriages 126
    possessions of 125
    social networks 117
    wealth and status 124–5
Styles, Sir John (Knight) 119, 120, 121, 124
    will 127
Styles, Richard 127
Sutton, Anne 63
Swinford, Hugh 24

Tanner, Thomas 42
Taylor, E.G.R. 21
textual narrative 100
textual production 58
Thomas Duke of Norfolk 121, 126
Tiverton, Devon 125, 128
    Saint Peter's Church 128
tradition 30
    and innovation 105
traditional ideals 30
transition 6, 121, 157, 159
    experiences of 156–7
translation 154
Tuder, John 44
Tudor dynasty 56, 78
Tudor, myths of identity 76–77
    myths 3

revels 96
royal court 63, 106
    (see royal household)
royal lineage 55
Turner, Gerard L'E. 7, 133, 149
Tyrell, Master John 93

Ustwaite (Ustwayte), Robert 123, 124, 127

Verona, Guarino de 123
vocabulary, administrative 92

Wallace, Charles W 35, 41
Waller, Marguerite 9
Walsingham, Our Lady of 124
Wardrobe, royal 62, 67
Warnieke, Retha M 23
Warren, Christina 72
Warton, Thomas 41
Water, Edward 127
Water, Jane 127
Watt, Diane *Secretaries of God* 8, 11, 17
Wendy, Master 135
Wentworth, Harry 69
Westminster Palace 90
Whitwhange, Elizabeth 121
Williamson, Magnus 52
Wilson, Thomas 144, 147
witness 84
women 2, 11
woodcut image 87, 88
Woodsend, Sir Edmund (parson)134
Woodward, Florentine 71
Woolf, Virginia 21
Worcester, William of 123
Wright, Herbert 34, 36
writing process 20 158–9
Wyatt, Thomas 23